CHAUCER'S LANGUAGE

Related titles from Palgrave Macmillan:

Allen, V. (ed.) *Chaucer* (New Casebook)

Andrew, M. *The Palgrave Literary Dictionary of Chaucer*

Ashton, G. *Chaucer: The Canterbury Tales*

George, J-A. *A Reader's Guide to the Essential Criticism of Chaucer –
   The General Prologue to the Cantebury Tales*

Pope, R. *How to Study Chaucer* (2nd edn)

Chaucer's
Language

Simon Horobin

First published 2007 by
PALGRAVE MACMILLAN
Houndmills, Basingstoke, Hampshire RG21 6XS and
175 Fifth Avenue, New York, N.Y. 10010
Companies and representatives throughout the world

PALGRAVE MACMILLAN is the global academic imprint of the Palgrave
Macmillan division of St. Martin's Press, LLC and of Palgrave Macmillan Ltd.
Macmillan® is a registered trademark in the United States, United Kingdom
and other countries. Palgrave is a registered trademark in the European
Union and other countries.

ISBN-13: 978–1–4039–9355–7 hardback
ISBN-10: 1–4039–9355–6 hardback
ISBN-13: 978–1–4039–9356–4 paperback
ISBN-10: 1–4039–9356–4 paperback

This book is printed on paper suitable for recycling and made from fully
managed and sustained forest sources.

A catalogue record for this book is available from the British Library.

A catalog record for this book is available from the Library of Congress.

10 9 8 7 6 5 4 3 2 1
16 15 14 13 12 11 10 09 08 07

Printed in China

For Jennifer

Contents

Preface

This book is a guide to the language of Chaucer, intended to be used by students studying Chaucer who have little or no experience of Middle English (ME). As such it does not presume any knowledge of ME and technical linguistic terminology is introduced with appropriate explanation and defined in a separate glossary at the back of the book. When discussing pronunciation, I have employed phonemic symbols for those students with some background in linguistic study, as well as giving representations based on present-day English spellings for those students unfamiliar with such symbols. Quotations from Chaucer's works are taken from Benson 1988.

In addition to its focus on Chaucer's language, this book also aims to situate this particular variety within ME more generally and so will be of use to students whose principal interest is in the linguistic study of ME. As an example of the London dialect of the fourteenth century, Chaucer's language is a particularly important reference point for the student of ME, and for study of the subsequent development of the standard English that descended from this variety. A particular theme of this book is variation, a concept central to modern approaches to language study, such as sociolinguistics, and how Chaucer exploited the variety available to him in his writing. It is only by fully understanding the nature of ME and the diversity of its dialects, especially that of London, that we can fully appreciate Chaucer's skill and the subtlety of his writing.

I am very grateful to my colleagues and my students in the Department of English Language at Glasgow, with many of whom I have had helpful discussions concerning various issues covered in this book. This book has also benefited from suggestions made by anonymous readers for the press and the commissioning editor, Kate Wallis, to whom thanks are also due. I am also grateful to my family for their support and encouragement during the writing of this book, particularly my wife Jennifer to whom this book is dedicated.

SIMON HOROBIN

Abbreviations

BD	*Book of the Duchess*
El	Ellesmere manuscript
EModE	Early Modern English
HF	*House of Fame*
Hg	Hengwrt manuscript
IPA	International Phonetic Alphabet
LGW	*Legend of Good Women*
ME	Middle English
MED	*Middle English Dictionary*
MS	Manuscript
OE	Old English
OED	*Oxford English Dictionary*
OF	Old French
ON	Old Norse
PDE	present-day English
PF	*Parliament of Fowls*
RR	*Romaunt of the Rose*
TC	*Troilus and Criseyde*

1 Why study Chaucer's language?

All living languages are subject to change. Linguistic change may happen in various different ways for a variety of different reasons, affecting the pronunciation, grammar or vocabulary of a language. We are often made aware of such changes by the media who lament the corruption and decay of the English language as reflected in such changes as the spread of estuary English, the spelling of text and email messages, and the inclusion of slang terms in dictionaries. Yet all these changes are simply reflections of the fact that languages are in a continual process of flux, adapting to reflect changes taking place in the society within which they are used. So, for instance, the revolution in information technology has led to the coining of new words such as *download* and *email* which have become adopted into English and are thus included in new editions of dictionaries. If we take a broader historical perspective, then we can see that over the past 500 years the English language has undergone numerous changes that have radically altered its structure, making it increasingly difficult for us to read texts written in English of earlier periods. Chaucer was aware of the inevitability of language change and its effects, and he considers these in the proem to Book 2 of *Troilus and Criseyde*:

Ye knowe <u>ek</u> that in forme of speche is chaunge	also
Withinne a thousand yeer, and wordes <u>tho</u>	then
That hadden pris, now wonder <u>nyce</u> and straunge	absurd
Us thinketh hem, and yet thei spake <u>hem</u> so,	them
	(2.22–5)

Linguistic change means that to read Chaucer today we need a good understanding of his language and how it differs from our own. This is most evident in the case of vocabulary, as many of the words used by Chaucer have since fallen out of use and become obsolete. An example of this is the word *ek* found in the above quotation, where it means 'also'. This is a common word in Chaucer and therefore its meaning needs to be learned, just as today we learn common French words to help us to read texts written in that language. In fact the number of such words is comparatively small and many of the words used by Chaucer are still recognizable to us. So, for instance, in the above extract, the majority of the words are familiar enough that someone with no knowledge of Chaucer's language could probably make some sense of what is being said.

However, while the familiarity of Chaucer's words can be helpful, it can also cause problems. The availability of Chaucer's work in translations into modern English, or modernized versions, encourages the view that Chaucer's work is more similar to present-day English (PDE) than is really the case. The similarity of Chaucer's language to our own is also frequently emphasized by writers on the history of English, often as support for the view that Chaucer was responsible for creating the English literary language that we use today. For instance, in his recent book *The Adventure of English*, Melvyn Bragg describes how, in Chaucer's work, 'English speakers talk directly to us, through skilful stories told by a group of pilgrims' (2003, 69). The suggestion is that Chaucer's characters speak in a language that can be easily understood by a modern reader, thereby ignoring the linguistic divide that separates us from Chaucer's language. This view of Chaucer as a modern writer is further encouraged by current trends in Chaucer criticism that tend to emphasize the similarity between Chaucer's works and modern literature, rather than its difference. This has the effect of de-emphasizing the linguistic differences between Chaucer's language and our own, which may cause problems when it comes to reading his works. While Chaucer's works are indeed relevant to a modern audience, their language differs from that of PDE in a number of ways, and it is important that we are aware of such differences when reading Chaucer to prevent us misunderstanding his meaning.

The most obvious way in which Chaucer's language may appear similar to our own is in the survival of many of his words into PDE. But here we must be careful as a word may have kept the same appearance but have changed its meaning. This becomes apparent if we consider the phrase 'nyce and straunge' in the above passage. On the surface this phrase does not appear to cause many problems as it is easily recognized as the equivalent of 'nice and strange'. But what does that mean? Can words be described as being 'nice and strange'? So while the apparent familiarity of these words might trick us into thinking that there is no difficulty, we must remember that words that look like PDE words may have had different meanings in Middle English (ME). So, even though the word *nyce* looks familiar, we must check in a dictionary to see how it was used in ME. The *Riverside Chaucer* gives two main senses for this word as follows: (1) foolish; (2) scrupulous. The first thing to notice about this definition is that neither of these meanings is the same as the main meaning in PDE of 'agreeable, pleasant, satisfactory'. So whenever we encounter the word *nyce* in Chaucer's works we must be careful not to give it our PDE meaning.

Armed with the *Riverside Chaucer*'s definition, we can now return to our passage and see which of these two senses is the more appropriate in this context. Clearly the intended sense here is 'foolish', although we might prefer to gloss this particular example as 'ridiculous' or 'absurd'. So by looking the word up in the glossary, we are able to determine the correct meaning of this word in this particular context. However, there are other examples of the word *nyce* that may cause us further problems. For instance, later in Book 2 of *Troilus and Criseyde*, Pandarus makes the following appeal to his niece Criseyde:

> 'Wel,' quod Pandare, 'as I have told yow <u>thrie</u>,   thrice
> Lat be youre nyce shame and youre <u>folie</u>,   folly
> And spek with hym in esyng of his herte;
> Lat nycete nat do yow bothe smerte.'
>
> (2.1285–8)

In this example neither of the definitions given by the *Riverside Chaucer* seems particularly appropriate. 'Foolish shame' might seem the most fitting translation, although this would make the following noun *folie* 'folly' seem redundant. In this case we need a more comprehensive definition, as provided by the *Middle English Dictionary* (*MED*). Instead of the two senses offered by the *Riverside Chaucer*, there are four major senses listed for this word in the *MED*; these can be summarized as follows: (1) foolish, frivolous, absurd; (2) sluggish, weak, timid; (3) fastidious, fussy, dainty; (4) extravagant, self-indulgent. Given this greater range of meanings, it becomes apparent that sense 2, not given in the *Riverside* glossary, is the most appropriate meaning for the example given above. Pandarus is instructing Criseyde to put aside her timid shame rather than her foolish shame, which would imply a much more judgmental and dismissive attitude.

This example has shown us that we need to be wary of words that may seem familiar to us because their meanings have often changed. We also found that we should not rely entirely on the single-word glosses provided by editors, but turn to a more comprehensive dictionary, such as the *MED*, for a detailed definition of a word. The greater range of definitions provided by the *MED* means that we have to work harder to determine the correct meaning for a particular use of a word, forcing us to analyse the context more closely. This might seem like an unnecessary amount of extra effort, but it is extremely important if we are to appreciate fully Chaucer's writing.

There are many other words like *nyce* which have survived into PDE with similar spellings but with different meanings. Another good example is the word *buxom*, as in the following rhetorical question in the Merchant's Tale: 'For who kan be so buxom as a wyf?' (E 1287). It would be easy to view this as a reference to a woman's physical appearance, reading *buxom* according to its present-day meaning 'plump' or 'busty', but this meaning is not recorded before the sixteenth century; the ME meaning of the word is concerned with moral behaviour and means 'obedient' or 'submissive'. Such distinctions are clearly important as they radically alter our perception of attitudes to women in the Middle Ages. While physical appearance, and especially youth, is clearly important to the lecherous old bachelor in the Merchant's Tale, he is primarily looking for obedience and subservience in his future bride.

Another word that survives into PDE with a different meaning is *sely,* which is PDE *silly*, meaning 'foolish'. However, in ME the word can mean 'holy', as in the description of the saintly heroine in the Man of Law's Tale as 'this sely innocent, Custance' (B1 682). It can also have the meaning 'simple' or 'innocent', as in the Host's reference to 'sely men' who are at the mercy of the deceit and trickery of women. There is clearly a link between the meaning 'simple or 'innocent' and the PDE meaning 'foolish' and it is easy to see how the modern meaning has developed from the ME one. In fact, there are instances in Chaucer where the word seems to be used in a similar way to that of PDE *silly*. For example, in the Reeve's

Tale the two students who are tricked by the miller are described as being 'sely clerkes'. We could read this sympathetically as 'innocent' but the tone seems more critical, while the ridiculous image of the students charging round the fens trying to catch their runaway horse makes the sense 'foolish' seem more appropriate.

In the case of *silly,* it is apparent that in some instances the PDE meaning is appropriate, while in others, senses found only in ME are correct. This situation forces us to be particularly alert to the subtle shifts in meaning and connotation that can only be gauged from a close reading of the immediate context. Another good example of this is the ME word *corage,* which can be used with the PDE sense 'courage' as well as 'spirit' or 'temperament'. But in ME it can also refer to 'sexual desire', as in the reference to Walter fulfilling his *corage* in the Clerk's Tale (E 907). It is important to be aware of this range of meanings so as not to attribute the wrong meaning to a particular instance, such as the 'ful devout corage' with which Chaucer and his fellow travellers set out on the Canterbury pilgrimage (A 22). In most cases the correct meaning can be determined by a careful analysis of the context, although in some instances it is not so simple. For example, in the Merchant's Tale we are told that, in his old age, January had 'a greet corage' to get married. The intended meaning here is probably 'inclination', although the fact that he wants a young and beautiful wife makes the sense 'sexual desire' seem equally appropriate. This example shows how a good knowledge of Chaucer's vocabulary helps us to appreciate the range of meanings available to Chaucer, and the ambiguities and subtle distinctions in connotation that he was able to exploit. If we are unaware of such distinctions, we are likely to miss many of the nuances and ironies that are central to a true appreciation of Chaucer's work.

A sound understanding of the full range of meanings associated with Chaucer's vocabulary is particularly important when dealing with certain key terms. For instance, the adjective *gentil* and the related noun *gentilesse* occur frequently throughout Chaucer's works, representing a complex network of moral and social qualities. It is therefore important that we have a good understanding of the range of applications of these terms, especially as the word *gentle* has changed its meaning significantly since the Middle Ages. In PDE, the word signifies 'soft', 'mild' or 'tender', but these meanings are not found in Chaucer's usage. For Chaucer the word signified rank or status, indicating that someone belonged to a noble family. By association with this meaning, it is also used to describe qualities generally associated with the well-born, such as 'courteous', 'noble' and 'generous'. A good example of this usage is found in Chaucer's description of the knight in the General Prologue, whom he calls a 'verray, parfit gentil knyght' (A 72). Given the long list of military battles and conquests Chaucer has just described, it would be odd to label the knight 'soft' or 'tender'; here the word signifies both his rank and the noble qualities associated with it. The use of this word to signify degree and rank has not survived into PDE, except in the term *gentleman*, although the original meaning of this term is no longer recognized. We might contrast this development with that of the adjective *lowely*, which is used to describe the knight's son, the Squire (A 99). In PDE this word tends to signify low status, whereas here it signifies humility and modesty.

Another key term in Chaucer's writing is the adjective *fre*, as in the Franklin's concluding question to the issues raised by his tale: 'Which was the mooste fre?' (F 1622). To begin to answer this question we need a detailed definition of the word *fre*. The *MED* gives the following main senses for this word: (1) free in rank or condition, having the social status of a noble or a freeman, not a slave or serf; (2) noble in character; gracious, well-mannered; (3) generous. Despite the obvious differences between these three senses, they overlap in complex and subtle ways. For instance, someone who is of noble birth is likely to act in a noble way, and generosity may well be part of this behaviour. People of noble birth may do ignoble acts, while it is also possible that someone who is of a low social status may act nobly in spite of their rank. This distinction is also complicated by those who belong to neither the noble nor the peasant classes, as well as those who are born peasants but who achieve noble status through the acquisition of wealth and social status. All these interlocking issues are raised by the Franklin's Tale, so that it is apparent that the Franklin is invoking each of these senses of the word when posing his final question.

Another aspect of a word's meaning and use that we need to be aware of when reading Chaucer is its connotation. Connotation is much harder to define, and it is an aspect of a word which cannot be determined simply by looking in a glossary or a dictionary. As speakers of English, we are aware of a complex network of associations for individual words that cannot be gleaned from a dictionary entry, but require an understanding of the cultural setting within which a word is used. For instance, the words *truth* and *veracity* have similar meanings, although their connotations are quite different, with *veracity* appearing only in formal contexts. Similarly *lie* and *fib* have similar meanings, but *fib* is limited exclusively to colloquial usage. Such distinctions existed in ME as well, although it is much harder for us to reconstruct the connotations words had for native speakers of ME.

One way of determining the connotations associated with a particular word is to examine all instances of its use, taking note of a range of contextual factors, such as whether it appears in a piece of high style description in the Knight's Tale, or in direct speech uttered by a person of low social standing in one of the fabliaux. This type of analysis helps us to understand why Chaucer should use a particular word instead of another with a similar meaning. For instance, there are many words in ME with the core meaning of 'noble', raising the question of why Chaucer should select a particular one in a certain context. If we examine the distribution of some of the words meaning 'noble' used by Chaucer, we find a number of restrictions which help to isolate factors conditioning their use. For instance, the words *hende*, *joly* and *gent* are only ever used to describe characters whose nobility is decidedly dubious, suggesting that, for Chaucer, these words belonged to a lower register than others such as *digne*, *free*, *gentil*, *noble*, *riche*, *worthy*, which are frequently used to describe genuinely noble characters.

A related problem concerns words which are borrowed from French. Students tend to make the assumption that all words of French origin were of high status, and that any passage making use of French vocabulary was intended to be high style. While it is broadly true that French words were stylistically marked, it is certainly not the case that all French words belonged to a higher register. To determine which French words were elevated and which were less marked is a complex process and requires more than a simple check of a word's etymology in a dictionary. As well as knowing its etymology, we also need to be aware of its history in ME and its use, both in Chaucer and in other ME works. This is because a French word that was borrowed early on in the ME period, sometime in the twelfth or thirteenth centuries, is likely to have been assimilated into the English language by the time Chaucer used it in the late fourteenth century. A similar situation is found in PDE, where we are more aware of the French origins of words like *milieu, apropos, chaise-longue,* which still retain their French pronunciations, than of words like *problem, place, uncle,* which have become fully assimilated so that we think of them as English words.

So a true understanding of the status of Chaucer's vocabulary demands a sensitivity to the connotations of the individual words that goes beyond the simple fact of their etymologies. This is particularly important when reading Chaucer, as one of Chaucer's achievements as a poet was to exploit the connotations of words by using them in original and unusual contexts.

So far I have focused entirely on vocabulary, as this is the level of language that is likely to cause most problems of interpretation for students with no knowledge of ME. But there are also differences between the grammar of ME and PDE that it is important to be aware of when reading Chaucer. For example, students are often confused by the frequent switching between the present and past tenses in Chaucer's work, as in the following extract:

The moone, whan it was nyght, ful brighte shoon,	
And Absolon his <u>gyterne</u> hath ytake;	cittern
<u>For paramours</u> he thoghte for to wake.	because of love
And forth he gooth, jolif and amorous,	
Til he cam to the carpenteres hous	
A litel after cokkes hadde <u>ycrowe</u>,	crowed
	(A 3352–7)

This is a piece of narration in the past, although the verb *gooth* is in the present tense. Many students fail to recognize such switches into the present tense and so translate the passage as if it was consistently in the past. But, having identified this switching between tenses, they remain uncertain as to why Chaucer should do this. In PDE, switching between the past and present tense is not generally found in written English, although it is common in speech, as in an example like, 'A chap went into a bar and says to the barman ...'. It is easy to assume that the same rules apply in ME, and that switching between tenses in writing is evidence of colloquial usage. This seems a logical explanation of the above example, especially given the frequent use of colloquial language in the Miller's Tale. However, this explanation does not account for the switching between present and past tenses in passages written in high style, such as the following example taken from the Knight's Tale:

> The sesoun <u>priketh</u> every gentil herte,　　　　　　　　　incites
> And maketh it out of his slep to sterte,
> And seith 'Arys, and do thyn <u>observaunce</u>.'　　　　　　　duty
> This maked Emelye have remembraunce
> To doon honour to May, and for to ryse.

(A 1043–47)

So how do we explain these frequent shifts between the present and past tenses? One reason for the shift from the present to the past tense is to indicate a move from continuous to completed action, as in the above example from the Knight's Tale. The switch from the past tense to the present, as in the example from the Miller's Tale, serves to quicken the pace of the narrative, giving it greater immediacy as well as highlighting the beginning of a new stage in the story's development. The present tense may also be used within a piece of past narration to mark a statement that has a significance which goes beyond the limits of the story. So the comments on the joys of marriage in the introduction to the Merchant's Tale are in the present tense, and read like a set of pronouncements made by a character within the tale, although they are not in fact in direct speech:

> And certeinly, as <u>sooth</u> as God is kyng,　　　　　　　　true
> To take a wyf it is a glorious thyng,
> And <u>namely</u> whan a man is oold and <u>hoor</u>;　　particularly; grey
> Thanne is a wyf the fruyt of his tresor.

(E 1267–70)

Another possible explanation for the switching of tenses concerns metre. For example, the choice between *maketh* and *made* affects the metre, so that Chaucer may decide to employ the present tense when he needs a form with two syllables, or the past tense when one syllable is required. Whatever the reason for such switching, it is clear that we cannot judge such passages by modern standards, but need a good understanding of Chaucer's own practices in order to be able to appreciate all the stylistic implications of such details.

Applying modern notions of correct grammar to Chaucer's text can cause us many other problems, prompting us to misjudge constructions that are deemed incorrect according to the rules of standard English. A good example of this is the double negative which we meet frequently in Chaucer, but which is frowned upon in standard English. In PDE the double negative is considered a non-standard feature, found in certain dialects such as Cockney, spoken in the East End of London, and is therefore socially stigmatized. As a result, when we encounter such constructions in Chaucer, it is tempting to regard them as incorrect, or to assume that they are intended to reflect badly on a particular narrator or character. However, such notions of correct and incorrect usage, and the stigmatization of the double negative, are eighteenth-century developments, and it would be anachronistic to apply them to Chaucer's work. In ME double, or even triple and quadruple negatives were used to add emphasis to the negation, so that Chaucer's famous description of the knight was intended to stress the purity of his speech rather than call it into question:

He nevere yet no <u>vileynye</u> ne sayde	rudeness
In al his lyf unto no <u>maner wight</u>.	sort of person
	(A 70–1)

Not only can we not apply the grammatical rules of standard English when reading Chaucer, but we must also put aside the preconceptions that we have concerning the importance of correctness and consistency when using language. This is because Chaucer wrote before the English language had become standardized, so that there was much greater variation in the use of language, which in turn allowed Chaucer considerable flexibility. Because we are taught that there are correct and incorrect ways to use language, we are often intolerant of variation. As a result, students are often confused and frustrated by the range of variant spelling forms that they frequently encounter in Chaucer, and there is a tendency to see this as poetic licence, especially where variant spellings appear in rhyme. However, such variation was commonplace and perfectly acceptable in ME, and we must not impose our modern preference for consistency upon a period when the language permitted much greater variation.

This book also includes a chapter which provides guidelines as to how Chaucer's language was pronounced. I often encourage students to spend time learning how to pronounce Chaucer correctly, as this can be a useful guide to recognizing particular words and their meanings. As well as helping with understanding the text, being able to pronounce Chaucer's works is an important way of appreciating his work. This is because it is likely that Chaucer's works were composed for oral performance, and his first audience was probably composed of listeners rather than readers. By reading the text aloud, we gain important insights into how this method of presentation affected the way the text was composed and circulated, as well as coming closer to the way medieval readers first experienced Chaucer's poetry.

One way of coping with the difficulties presented by Chaucer's language is to turn to a translation into PDE, although by doing this you will miss out on many of the subtleties and nuances of Chaucer's work that cannot be conveyed in a PDE representation. The difficulties involved in providing a faithful translation of Chaucer's work are further compounded by an attempt to preserve the metre and rhyme of the original, so that many of the choices of specific words may be governed by practical concerns as much as semantic ones. For example, in the opening line of the Miller's Tale, John the carpenter is described by Chaucer as a *gnof*, a word which means 'churl' and thus has connotations of low social status (A 3188). In the verse translation by Nevill Coghill, this word is rendered as 'old codger', no doubt in order to facilitate a rhyme with 'lodger' in the following line. The clerk Nicholas is then introduced as 'Nicholas the Gallant', an epithet which does not do justice to the ironic and satiric connotations that are implied in Chaucer's use of the adjective *hende* to describe Nicholas.

We noted above the complex range of interlocking associations represented by the word *fre*, and their significance for our understanding of the Franklin's final question: 'Which was the mooste fre, as thynketh yow?' (F 1622). In the Coghill translation, the complexity of this question is considerably reduced, by the rendering of the Franklin's question as 'Which seemed the finest gentleman to you?' Similarly, we might consider the translation of another complex term such as *trouthe*. This word has a range of meanings in ME, encompassing concepts such as 'fidelity', 'loyalty', 'honour', 'honesty', 'moral soundness', 'faith' as well as the PDE meanings 'correspondence to reality' and 'speaking without deceit'. We need to be aware of this wide range of potential meanings when encountering Chaucer's use of the word, as in the description of the knight in the General Prologue who loved 'Trouthe and honour, fredom and curteisie'. In the Coghill translation, the word *trouthe* is rendered as 'truth', a translation which considerably narrows the range of available meanings. A similar range of concepts is encompassed by the term *curteisie*, which is defined by the *MED* as 'the complex of courtly ideals', and includes 'chivalry, kindness, nobleness, generosity and refinement of manners'. Only the last of these is associated with the PDE equivalent term *courtesy*, which is the word selected by Coghill in his translation of this line.

So, by relying on a translation, a reader of Chaucer is likely to miss much of the density of Chaucer's vocabulary and the subtle shifts of nuances and connotations, as well as the many ironies that are evident when reading the original. To read Chaucer exclusively in translation is like going to see a Shakespeare play in translation – much of what makes it Shakespeare would be missing. In fact, the production of Shakespeare's plays has recently moved in the opposite direction, with the reconstructed Globe Theatre now staging plays with the original Shakespearean pronunciation. If we want to read Chaucer, and be alive to the nuances and subtleties of his work, then we also need to read Chaucer in the original, equipped with a good understanding of his language.

2 Writing in English

Chaucer wrote in English. That may seem like a completely obvious statement to us today: what other language would an English writer choose to write in? But it was not such an obvious choice for Chaucer when he embarked on his writing career.

During the fourteenth century, aristocratic court culture was predominantly French, and much of the literature that was read by this group was in French. The dialect of French used in England was the Anglo-Norman variety, which derived from the northern French dialect brought over by William the Conqueror, following the Battle of Hastings in 1066. Anglo-Norman was primarily a language of bureaucracy, and was the language used by Chaucer for much of his administrative work. One document which survives from Chaucer's time at the Wool Quay is a memorandum in Anglo-Norman appointing a deputy to help Chaucer with his work. In the two centuries following the Norman conquest, the French language occupied an important role in England. It was the first language of the nobility and the court, and was used in numerous official and administrative arenas, such as the law, the guilds and the royal and civic administration. The central French dialect was also used in England, and this more prestigious variety was the language of the king and his court, and of courtly literature, both on the Continent and in England. Chaucer was well read in the work of French poets like Machaut and Deschamps. Jean Froissart, who wrote a chronicle of the Hundred Years War, was the secretary to Philippa of Hainault who married Edward III. Chaucer was also connected with this household through his wife, Philippa, who was the daughter of Sir Paon de Roet, a knight in the retinue of Philippa of Hainault. It is possible that Chaucer began his career by writing French verse, and some surviving poems, attributed enigmatically to 'Ch' in their manuscript, may be his work (Wimsatt 1982). Chaucer was certainly fluent in French, and one of the first works he wrote was a translation of the hugely influential Old French poem the *Roman de la Rose*.

This allegorical love poem was composed by two writers, Guillaume de Lorris and Jean de Meun, in the thirteenth century. Chaucer drew heavily on it in many of his works, and some of his best-known characters, such as the Wife of Bath and the Pardoner, have models in the *Roman de la Rose*.

Chaucer might also have chosen to write in Latin, an authoritative language used by the great classical writers, as well as the primary language of the universities and the Church throughout the Middle Ages. Classical Latin texts, such as *De Consolatione Philosophiae* by Boethius, were among Chaucer's favourite reading. Like the *Roman*, Boethius' work was widely read in the Middle Ages, and Chaucer plundered it for many of his most celebrated philosophical passages, as well as translating the entire text into Middle English: a work now known as his *Boece*. Latin was not just the language of the great classical writers, but was also used by the scholastic writers of the twelfth and thirteenth centuries, whose works were also influential for Chaucer. Latin was the principal language of study and debate at medieval universities, as well as the language used by the religious and monastic orders. Latin was not simply the language of the texts under discussion, but also the language in which the discussions were carried out, and was spoken fluently by medieval students. An example of this use of Latin is found in Chaucer's Franklin's Tale, where the two students of Orleans in France greet each other in Latin (F 1174). One hugely popular work written in Latin in this period is Pope Innocent III's *De Contemptu Mundi*, which survives in an incredible 600 manuscripts. This too provided important source material for Chaucer's writings, such as the Man of Law's Prologue, and Chaucer tells us that he translated the text into English, although there is no surviving manuscript of Chaucer's translation.

Latin was, however, primarily an ecclesiastical, learned and administrative tongue rather than a spoken language, and had no living native speakers. Its use in medieval administration meant that it became highly formulaic, as is true of most official documents. The increasing complexity of this administration, and the greater demands it placed upon the language used to record it, meant that new terms needed to be coined to keep pace with these changes. As Latin was a dead language, these new terms were borrowed from Anglo-Norman rather than from Classical Latin. As a result, much Latin of this period is in fact a mixture of Latin and Anglo-Norman words and phrases given Latin endings, arranged according to Anglo-Norman word order. These borrowed Anglo-Norman terms frequently have no French equivalent, showing that they do not derive from the Continent, but are home-grown French terms. In some cases these words are given Latin endings, while in others they are simply placed unaltered within a Latin text. This kind of writing, where two or more languages are employed, is known as 'macaronic', and the majority of documents composed in England in the late fourteenth century may be described as macaronic. This mixed, or Vulgar, Latin was probably used as a kind of lingua franca, a mixed language used by speakers who have no common language, by merchants, pilgrims and other travellers in medieval Europe as a means of communication between speakers of different languages. A good example of this is found in Chaucer's Man of Law's Tale, where Custance, the daughter of a Roman Emperor, finds herself shipwrecked off the coast of Northumberland. She is discovered by a local constable whom she addresses in a 'maner Latyn corrupt', a mixed Latin which was apparently understood by the English-speaking constable.

So Chaucer could have chosen to write in French, the language of the court and aristocratic culture. He could have chosen to write in Latin, a language with the authority of centuries of tradition, the language of the great classical writers and medieval scholasticism and the Church. In fact, a contemporary of Chaucer's, John Gower, chose to use all three languages for his three poems: the *Vox Clamantis*, *Mirour de l'omme* and *Confessio Amantis* in Latin, Anglo-Norman and English respectively. But Chaucer chose to write in English. It is important to emphasize that the decision to write literature in English was not an entirely new one. Despite the monopoly of French culture in the early ME period, literature in English did continue to be written. For example, the various Anglo-Saxon chronicles which were begun in the reign of King Alfred were discontinued, or continued in Latin. But one important exception is the Peterborough Chronicle, which continued to be copied in English until 1154. English is also employed in a documentary capacity in a Proclamation issued by Henry III in 1258, although this document survives in both English and French copies.

Literature composed in the vernacular during this period includes an alliterative chronicle by a West Midland priest, Laʒamon, known as the *Brut*, which includes much Arthurian material in English for the first time. There is a debate poem, *The Owl and the Nightingale*, the famous religious and secular lyrics known as the Harley Lyrics and the devotional prose treatise called *Ancrene Wisse*. While these works are relatively sophisticated, and often appear in manuscripts alongside Anglo-Norman works, they are few in number and address a specialized and local audience. For example, the *Ancrene Wisse* is a spiritual guide written for three noble sisters who had decided to become anchorites. The text shows similarities with another group of devotional texts addressed to women, such as *Hali Meiðhad*, *Sawles Warde* and a group of female saints' lives. The use of English in these texts seems to be a reflection of their intended female audience, who would not have been able to read Latin.

As well as being few in number, English texts of the early ME period survive in small numbers of manuscripts: there are two copies of the *The Owl and the Nightingale* and the *Brut*, while many of the Harley Lyrics are unique to that collection. The *Ancrene Wisse* did achieve a wider reputation and now survives in a total of seven copies, although it is interesting to note that several of these are much later than its date of composition and others are translations into French and Latin. It is also significant that many of the manuscripts in which these vernacular works survive were copied by scribes working in private households in the provinces, and there is little evidence from this period of professional, commercial book production in London. The main exception to this is the Auchinleck manuscript, a large anthology of vernacular romances copied in London by a group of scribes around 1340. But even this impressive collection seems to be a personal collection put together privately, rather than the sole survivor of a large-scale industry satisfying a demand for collections of romances in English. The majority of the professional literary manuscripts produced in London during this period contains texts written in French rather than English.

While the early ME period was dominated by francophone culture, the early thirteenth century began to witness a shift in England towards the use of English rather than French. The loss of Normandy to the French crown in 1204 marks a beginning in the separation of English and French culture and, following this, many nobles with lands in both countries gave up their French estates in favour of those in England. Successive generations of the nobility were progressively less competent in French, which became a language that was taught rather than acquired as a native tongue.

This change is marked by the appearance of French grammar books and word lists, and the hiring of French tutors in the thirteenth century. The Barons' Wars of the thirteenth century also encouraged nationalistic attitudes, as both Henry III and his opponents attempted to exploit notions of Englishness for their own propaganda. Henry's opponents, who were especially critical of the way he favoured his French subjects, attempted to portray Henry as responsible for filling the country with foreigners who were unable to speak English. Henry's critics, writers like the chronicler Matthew Paris, used Latin or French to express their disdain for his policies, and it is interesting that none appears to have felt that an expression of nationalism and nationhood should be made in English.

In contrast, Henry III does appear to have drawn upon the potential for nationalistic propaganda provided by the English language, choosing to issue his Proclamation of 1258 in both French and English. This is the first royal document in English since the conquest and, as such, reveals a deliberate attempt to use English to encourage a unity with his people. In it Henry explicitly addresses all his subjects, the 'learned and the lewed', emphasizing that this is a document for all his people, not just those who can read French. While scholars are united in seeing this use of English as a strategic attempt to employ the language to foster a sense of national identity, there is disagreement about the wider implications of the Proclamation. Thorlac Turville-Petre (1996) views this as pointing forward to later manipulations of linguistic identity for political ends, such as Edward I's accusation that potential invaders from France were intending to exterminate the English language. Tim William Machan (2003), however, rejects the traditional view that the use of English in the Proclamation was a nationalistic appeal, arguing that it represents a rhetorical strategy by Henry III to manipulate the hostility to foreigners fostered by his baronial opponents.

Similar nationalistic concerns are apparent during the Hundred Years War, which served to fuel anti-French feeling during a lengthy period of hostility between the two countries, lasting from 1337 to 1453. This anti-French feeling was exploited by the English king, Henry V, whose letters from his French campaigns requesting increased financial support were written in English, perhaps a deliberate act of propaganda appealing to national pride. French did remain in use in England during the fourteenth century, although increasingly it became a second language spoken alongside English.

During this period the Norman French dialect began to lose status to the central French dialect spoken in Paris, and became a technical written language associated with the law and administration. Its position as a spoken language was also undermined by the frequent portrayal of its pronunciation as provincial. For instance, the chronicler Walter Map spoke scornfully of insular French as 'Marlborough French', while Chaucer's Prioress speaks French 'after the scole of Stratford atte Bowe', in the manner of the London suburbs rather than the royal court. However, despite its dire public image, Anglo-Norman continued to function as a legal and documentary language throughout the ME period.

Changing social conditions during this period also had an effect on the status of the English language. The latter half of the fourteenth century saw major social changes, following the successive outbreaks of the Black Death, which reduced the population by approximately a third. This caused a major labour shortage, leading inevitably to the inflation of labourers' wages and their subsequent rise in the social system. During this period the feudal system began to break up, and the traditional social structure constructed upon the model of the three estates, peasants, clergy and knights, was replaced by a much more fluid system based upon economic ties rather than ones reliant on service and loyalty. A middle class emerged who were literate and wealthy, and who aspired to the literary and social pursuits previously enjoyed only by the nobility. This group consisted of monolingual English speakers, creating a demand for literature in English that was of sufficient status to stand alongside the great literary achievements of the French and Italian vernaculars. The fourteenth century also witnessed the reintroduction of English in the education system, marked by the decision of the grammar master John of Cornwall to use English in 1349. French continued as the language of the law and parliament throughout much of the ME period, with parliamentary debates being recorded in French until 1386.

During the fourteenth century a number of writers state that they have chosen to write in English so that their work can be read by those who do not understand French. In 1300, the author of a vast work of biblical history known as the *Cursor Mundi* claimed to use English out of a dedication to the language, the nation and the people, many of whom were unable to read French. The author argues that French is a suitable medium in France but of little use to the English who are unable to understand it. Another northern religious work, *Speculum Vitae*, written around 1350, adopts English out of a desire to communicate to the widest possible audience. The poet states that everyone born in England understands English, while French and Latin are more specialized skills associated with the court and the universities. Such comments are not restricted to religious works; we find a similar attitude in an ME romance, *Arthur and Merlin*, where the poet says that while gentlemen speak French, every Englishman can understand English. He even goes on to claim that he has seen many noblemen who cannot speak French, hinting at the changing status of English as it came to be adopted by the nobility. While these comments make clear the authors' desire to communicate to the widest possible audience, they also make a link between the language and the nation suggestive of patriotic and nationalistic sentiments. It has been argued that the use of English by these and other writers during this period was partly driven by nationalistic concerns, and the desire to identify the English language with the nation and its people.

Similar arguments have been made concerning Chaucer's use of English, most recently by Terry Jones, who argues that Chaucer's works were part of a deliberate attempt to promote Richard II, lord of an illustrious nation with a language and a literature to rival other European cultures (Jones 2003). One problem with this view is that there are few references in Chaucer's works, or in the records of his life, that associate his works with royal patronage, nor do any presentation manuscripts of his works survive. Another objection is that there are no comments in his works that read as deliberate promotion of the vernacular, nor any attempt to link language and nation. The only comment that could be read as part of a programme of the promotion of English appears in the prologue to his *Treatise on the Astrolabe*, where Chaucer writes: 'God save the king, that is lord of this langage'. Taken on its own, this comment seems to make the connection between the king and the English language that supports the case for Chaucer's use of English being politically motivated. But we need to see this comment in context. It occurs in the prologue to a translation of a Latin treatise on the construction and use of an astrolabe, which he wrote for his son Lewis. As Lewis is just 10 years old, and so not yet sufficiently skilled in Latin, Chaucer tells him he is translating the text into 'light' English for his benefit. He goes on to stress that English is just as good at doing the job of communicating as Latin, or any other language. The Greeks read texts in Greek, the Jews in Hebrew and Arabs in Arabic and, despite their linguistic differences, their content remained the same. These comments stress the importance of English as a means of communication which can be understood by a greater range of readers than classical languages, in a similar way to the comments quoted above.

The primary motivation behind the translation of this text into English is communicative: so that a young boy whose Latin is still a bit shaky can read the text. While the same argument does not apply to Chaucer's decision to use English for his poetic works, many of these works were also closely based upon Italian and French sources. While a work like *Troilus and Criseyde* is not a translation like the *Boece* or the *Romaunt*, there are many parts of the work where Chaucer is translating very closely from an Italian work by Boccaccio. Perhaps we should view such acts of translation and reworking as deliberate acts of literary and linguistic appropriation, attempts to add status to the English vernacular and rival those of France and Italy? But Chaucer's works do not reveal any desire to promote an English national identity, and his close reliance on works composed in French and Italian seems more likely to reflect a wish to provide a vernacular literary culture for England that would be worthy to stand alongside the more advanced vernacular cultures found in Europe, especially those of Italy and France. Rather than deliberately promoting a national identity to compete with other European identities, Chaucer seems more concerned with emphasizing the place of English culture within a European, or international context.

Chaucer's European outlook is further indicated by the lack of any appeal to national consciousness or pride in his works. Only a small proportion of his works are set in England, and most of these satirize the petty concerns and immorality of the peasant classes, emphasizing their distance from the world of the aristocracy and wealthy merchant classes that constituted Chaucer's primary audience. The only tales to have an English setting are the fabliaux tales of the Miller, Reeve, Cook, Friar and Summoner; the world of the peasant widow in the Nun's Priest's Tale; the disreputable underworld represented by the Canon's Yeoman's Tale, and part of the Man of Law's Tale. It is particularly notable that the only tales with London settings are the fragmentary Cook's Tale and the Canon's Yeoman's Tale, where London is depicted as a place where robbers and thieves lurk in blind alleys and where apprentices spend their time drinking, gambling and visiting brothels. In the Nun's Priest's Tale, there is a reference to the brutal massacre of the Flemish weavers, a group of immigrants who were attacked by the London mob as part of the Peasants' Revolt of 1381. None of these portrayals of England and his native city suggest that Chaucer was concerned with promoting English nationalism, making it difficult to attribute his use of English to such an objective.

While there is no clear evidence linking Chaucer's decision to use English with a royal campaign to promote the use of the vernacular, scholars have argued that Chaucer's works were deliberately promoted after his death by Henry V as a means of legitimizing the Lancastrian claim to the throne (Fisher 1992). Chaucer's use of the vernacular as a vehicle for his verse, based on prestigious French, Italian and Latin literary models, as well as his connections with the previous Ricardian court, made him an ideal symbol for the unification of the country under the new Lancastrian administration. The fifteenth century witnessed an increased use of English, especially as the language of royal proclamations and administrative documentation such as that produced in the Chancery, Signet and Privy Seal offices.

During this period the London guilds began to adopt English for their record keeping, and the decision of the Brewers' Guild to switch to English in 1422 is recorded in their Abstract Book as follows:

> Whereas our mother-tongue, to wit the English tongue, hath in modern days begun to be honourably enlarged and adorned, for that our most excellent lord, King Henry V, hath in his letters missive and divers affairs touching his own person, more willingly chosen to declare the secrets of his will, and for the better understanding of his people, hath with a diligent mind procured the common idiom (setting aside others) to be commended by the exercise of writing: and there are many of our craft of Brewers who have the knowledge of writing and reading in the said English idiom, but in others, to wit, the Latin and French, before these times used, they do not in any wise understand. (Chambers and Daunt 1931, 139)

The Brewers' explanation of their decision to adopt English for their records makes an overt link with the king's use of the vernacular for his own letters, suggesting that the Brewers' decision was a nationalistic response to Henry's act of linguistic propaganda. But it is also apparent that the Brewers saw Henry's act as primarily concerned with communication: 'for the better understanding of his people', and that they saw their own use of English as similarly motivated: 'there are many of our craft of Brewers who have the knowledge of writing and reading in the said English idiom, but in others, to wit, the Latin and French, before these times used, they do not in any wise understand' (Chambers and Daunt 1931, 139). We certainly need to be wary of imputing too much political and nationalistic motivation upon a single document, where other explanations are also possible. This is further implied by the fact that the record of this decision in the Brewers' record book is in Latin, and, while subsequent records are mostly in English, there are occasional lapses back into French and Latin.

The fifteenth century also witnessed much clearer instances of royal patronage of English translations of major works than found in the fourteenth century, such as Henry V's request that John Lydgate produce an English version of the story of Troy. In Lydgate's account of the commission, he states that the king wished for a version of this noble story in English, to rival the versions already available in French and Latin:

Bycause he wolde that to <u>hyghe</u> and lowe	high
The noble story openly wer <u>knowe</u>	known
In oure tonge, aboute in every age,	
And ywriten as wel in oure langage	
As in latyn and in frensche it is;	
That of the story the trouthe we nat mys	
No more than doth eche other nacioun:	
This was the <u>fyn</u> of his entencioun.	aim

(Lydgate, Troy Book, prologue 111–18)

If we return from this brief foray into the fifteenth century back to the fourteenth, we can see how different Chaucer's remarks regarding his use of English in the *Astrolabe* are from Lydgate's comments above. Both poets are engaged in a process of translation, although Chaucer is translating a specialized astronomical treatise for an audience unable to read Latin, while Lydgate is producing an English version of one of the most important and influential classical stories at the request of the king himself.

Several of Chaucer's works were translations into English, and a contemporary French poet, Eustace Deschamps, referred to him as 'le grant translateur'. But this kind of literary activity seems more likely to derive from a desire to communicate these seminal and highly popular works to a larger audience, not literate in French or Latin, rather than from a wish to promote the status of the English language. Chaucer's extensive use of these works in his own compositions also indicates the potential usefulness of a complete English translation to Chaucer himself. Chaucer's poem *Troilus and Criseyde* is derived extensively from an Italian source by Boccaccio, *Il Filostrato*. Chaucer's poem is so close to the Italian version in places that scholars have suggested that he began his work on the *Troilus* by producing a translation of the poem, and subsequently reworking and adding to it to produce his own distinctive work (Windeatt 1984).

The status of the vernacular in the 1380s was radically affected by the views of the theologian John Wycliffe, whose campaign of religious reform advocated the availability to laymen and women, illiterate in Latin, of the scriptures in English (Aston 1987). Wycliffe and his followers, known as the Lollards, embarked on a major programme of translation of the Bible and biblical commentaries into English. As well as translating biblical texts into English, Wycliffe issued tracts explaining his controversial theological views on topics such as the nature of the eucharist, in English as well as Latin, so that they could be read by both clergy and laypeople. Wycliffe's views were condemned as heretical at the Blackfriars Council in 1382 and, following this, and the subsequent outlawing of biblical translation and theological discussion in the vernacular by Archbishop Arundel in 1409, many vernacular texts of this period came under scrutiny. As a result, many of the orthodox responses to Lollard attacks were written in Latin, although an English translation of the Latin *Meditationes Vitae Christi*, known as the *Blessed Life of Jesus Christ*, by a Carthusian monk called Nicholas Love was authorized by Archbishop Arundel for general release. Chaucer's awareness of Lollard ideals has been traced in his portrait of the parson in the General Prologue to the *Canterbury Tales*, whose opposition to swearing is greeted with the accusatory 'I smelle a Lollere in the wynd' in the Man of Law's Endlink (B1 1173). This endlink does not appear in all the extant manuscripts, which has led some scholars to suggest that it may have been cancelled by Chaucer, perhaps an indication that Chaucer wanted to deliberately distance his use of English from Wycliffe's.

The widespread adoption of English in the latter part of the four-teenth century had a great levelling effect, in removing a major distinction between the French-speaking nobility and the monolin-gual lower classes. In order to signal their social superiority over other Englishmen, the nobility adopted the practice of using French-derived words in preference to native equivalents. Polysyllabic Romance words belonged to a higher social register than monosyl-labic English equivalents; a distinction that remains today. How often do you find yourself reaching for a thesaurus when writing an essay in order to find a synonym that is longer and sounds more impressive? The use of French and Latin phrases to sound more learned or polite is satirized by Chaucer in characters like the Pardoner, who confesses to switching into Latin for a few words in order to 'saffron' his sermons (C 344–5). The Friar of the Summoner's Tale also uses Latin and French phrases, such as 'Deus hic!', 'je vous dy sanz doute', as part of his strategy to extort money from his parishioners. The Summoner switches into Latin when he has had too much to drink, although he only knows a few words and parrots them without understanding their meaning.

So, while Chaucer clearly drew upon the stylistic and sociolin-guistic distinctions found in English, he was not responsible for creating them. This is an important point, as another claim often made of Chaucer's decision to use English is that he introduced large numbers of new words into English and thereby somehow 'created' the English literary language. This view is a myth that has built up over generations of scholarship, although it is partly based upon analyses of the evidence of the *Oxford English Dictionary (OED)*. Scholars noted that many of the words that are borrowed from French or Latin during the ME period are first recorded in Chaucer's works. However, many ME texts were not read by the editors of the *OED*, so that since its publication many earlier or contemporary occurrences of such words have been identified. The *Middle English Dictionary (MED)*, based upon a much fuller analysis of the ME record, shows that many of the words which the *OED* records as appearing first in Chaucer's works are in fact found earlier in other ME texts. For instance, that very modern-sounding word *administra-tion* was first used by Chaucer, according to the *OED*, although the

MED shows that it was in fact used by another ME writer much earlier. Even the process of borrowing words from French and Latin adopted by Chaucer was not original, and had been used by earlier writers to a similar extent, so that Chaucer's practice was traditional rather than new and innovatory.

We should also remember that many of Chaucer's works drew upon, or were translations of, works in Latin, Italian and French, so it is perhaps not surprising that words from these languages enter the English language for the first time in his writings. Before Chaucer, the range of writing in English was very limited, so that English words simply did not exist to express the concepts found in specialized texts such as scientific and philosophical treatises. It has recently been argued that the view of Chaucer as single-handedly establishing English as a literary language was invented by his followers, poets such as Thomas Hoccleve and John Lydgate, as a means of authorizing their own vernacular writings (Cannon 1998). By reusing many of the words coined by Chaucer, these writers helped to ensure that these words became established features of literary English.

So, if the English language was already making a comeback before Chaucer, and if he did not introduce large numbers of new words, then what exactly did Chaucer do for the English language? Why is he often described as the 'father of English poetry'? One important aspect of Chaucer's significance for the history of English concerns the rhetorical concept of *proprietas*, or stylistic propriety. This concept is similar to the modern linguistic notion of 'register', in which a particular kind of language is appropriate to a specific linguistic mode. Although we may not know the term for it, we are all aware of the notion of register in the way we modify our usage when talking to friends or in an interview, or when writing a formal letter or using email. Chaucer gave a richness and density of expression to the English language by writing in a range of linguistic registers, from the dazzling high style of the 17-line opening sentence of the *Canterbury Tales*, to the earthy bickering of the Miller and the Reeve. One of the delights of reading Chaucer is his mastery of this vast stylistic range, and the ways in which he exploits and captures the resonances of contemporary speech. Think of Alison's giggle in the Miller's Tale following the successful tricking of the love-sick Absolon: '"Teehee!" quod she, and clapte the wyndow to', and Absolon's pathetic response: 'Fy! Allas! What have I do?'

As well as exploiting register variation for comedy, Chaucer is the first writer in English to employ dialect variation. In the Reeve's Tale he portrays the two students as northerners and gives them northern accents, and they use words only found in the north of England. There is much debate about the significance of the use of dialect in this tale, but one obvious effect is to add to the comedy. These observations point to an important reason why I think Chaucer chose to write in English rather than French or Latin, which has nothing to do with nationalism, politics, heresy or class consciousness. English was a living language with a large and diverse population of speakers, and as a consequence was full of variety, nuance and associations not found in dead languages. Think of the speed with which words come in and out of fashion today, particularly slang terms used at school. Words like *dude*, *groovy*, *wicked* were all fashionable terms once but now sound dated. Chaucer exploited these subtle shifts in usage, and the variation that was available in a language that was dynamic and in a process of continual change. By writing for a range of characters, in a range of voices, as well as writing scientific, moral, philosophical and penitential prose tracts, Chaucer showed that the English language was capable of a range of functions not witnessed since before the Norman Conquest. Earlier I noted that English was used before Chaucer, but only in restricted domains such as religious writings. Chaucer demonstrated how the English language could be used for all types of writing, particularly for secular literature.

Further reading

The status of the English language in the early ME period, and its relationship to national identity is discussed by Turville-Petre (1996). Machan (2003) provides an interesting response to Turville-Petre, and supplies an assessment of the role of English in the Middle Ages informed by modern sociolinguistic theory. The trilingual nature of fourteenth-century England is described by Rothwell (1994), while specialized studies considering multilingualism and macaronic writing can be found in Trotter (2000). Chaucer's decision to write in English is considered in illuminating studies by Pearsall (1999) and Salter (1980).

3   What was Middle English?

The Middle English (ME) period is dated to the period between 1100 and 1500, although these two dates are more scholarly convenience than linguistic accuracy. It is important to emphasize at the outset that the changes that distinguish ME from its ancestor, Old English (OE), did not occur overnight, but are the culmination of a series of gradual changes which took place over a period of time.

The date of 1100 is often used as a starting point for the ME period because of the significance of the Battle of Hastings of 1066, and the subsequent Norman Conquest for the status and future development of the English language. Before the conquest, the English language, known as Old English, or Anglo-Saxon, had developed a standard form which was employed throughout the kingdom for a variety of functions, including administrative, legal, ecclesiastical and literary writing. Following the conquest, English was replaced in all these areas by French, more specifically the Norman dialect of French used by the Norman invaders, and by Latin. English did continue to be used, but it became a largely spoken language, rather than a written one. Written records in English do survive from this period, but they are few and were designed for a local rather than a national audience, as described in the previous chapter.

Middle English dialects

As a result of this shift in the status of English, there was no longer a standard variety of the language that could be used and understood by all, and speakers and writers of English used their own local dialects. An awareness of these differences is apparent from scattered references by various authors to their own dialects, or to problems encountered in understanding other dialects. For example, a monk of Canterbury called Dan Michel, described his work *Ayenbite of Inwyt* (1340) as written in the 'Engliss of Kent', while a fifteenth-century friar called Osbern Bokenham tells us that he wrote in 'Suffolk speche'. Such references are few and sporadic and do not imply any sense of apology for writing in dialect. The author of the biblical history *Cursor Mundi*, written in a northern dialect in the fourteenth century, describes how his work is a translation of an original composed in southern English into 'our langage o northrin lede', our northern language, for those who cannot read any other type of English. The crucial emphasis here is on communication; the translation is being carried out to enable a different local audience to have access to the text. Neither Dan Michel nor Osbern Bokenham makes any apology for his regional dialect, and the fact that both authors seem to have written for a predominantly local audience suggests that they had no need for a variety that could be understood more widely. Thus where Dante in Italy searched among the 'cacophony of the many varieties of Italian speech' for a 'respectable and illustrious vernacular' that could be used by all writers (Botterill 1996, Book I), English writers appear to have been content to use their native dialect without fear of being stigmatized.

In the Old English period, the dialect of the southwest, known as Late West Saxon, functioned as a standard language, and, as a consequence, much of the surviving OE written record is copied in this dialect, despite being written down in various locations across the country. In the Middle English period, there was no such standard language and writers used their local dialect. There were four main dialect areas in the Middle English period: southern, West Midland, East Midland and northern, although of course these broad categories comprised considerable internal variation. In the Early Middle English period many works were composed in the West Midlands dialect, while, in the later period, the East Midlands area was particularly productive. Much less survives in the southern and northern dialects, although in the fourteenth century a number of texts were composed in the northern dialect, particularly in the Yorkshire area. The history of the dialect of the city of London is a special case, as its dialect was subject to the influence of the dialects of other parts of the country, as a result of immigration into the capital. The basis of the London dialect is a southern variety, although this gradually shifted to a Midlands-based dialect following interaction with speakers from East Anglia and the central and northern Midlands throughout the fourteenth and fifteenth centuries.

As there was no standard language in this period, a Middle English writer used his native dialect as his medium for composition. This meant that the audience for a particular work was often local, restricted to those who were also familiar with the peculiarities of this dialect. For instance, an anonymous contemporary of Chaucer's composed several works, including *Sir Gawain and the Green Knight*, in his native northwestern dialect which would have caused some problems of comprehension for a southern audience. Here is an extract from this poem which shows some of the important differences between Chaucer's language and that of a contemporary writing in a different dialect:

Now wyl I of <u>hor</u> servise say yow no more,	their
For <u>uch</u> <u>wy3e</u> may wel wit no wont þat þer were;	each; person
Anoþer noyse ful newe <u>ne3ed</u> <u>bilive</u>,	approached; quickly
þat þe <u>lude</u> my3t haf leve <u>liflode</u> to cach,	knight; food
For <u>uneþe</u> watz þe noyce not a whyle sesed	hardly
And þe fyrst cource in þe court kyndely served	
þer <u>hales</u> in at þe halle dor an <u>aghlich</u> mayster,	comes; terrible
On þe <u>most</u> on þe <u>molde</u> on mesure hyghe;	greatest; earth
Fro þe <u>swyre</u> to þe <u>swange</u> so sware and so þik,	neck; waist
And his <u>lyndes</u> and his lymes so longe and so grete,	loins
Half <u>etayn</u> <u>in erde</u> I <u>hope</u> þat he were,	giant; on earth; think
Bot mon most I <u>algate</u> <u>mynn</u> hym to bene,	at any rate; declare
And þat þe <u>myriest</u> in his <u>muckel</u> þat my3t ride;	merriest; size
For of bak and of brest al were his bodi sturne,	
Both his <u>wombe</u> and his wast were worthily <u>smale</u>,	stomach; slender
And alle his fetures <u>fol3ande</u> in forme þat he hade	in like manner
Ful <u>clene</u>.	elegant

(*Gawain*, lines 130–46 cited from Tolkien and Gordon 1967)

The most obvious difference between this extract and Chaucer's work concerns its metrical form, as *Gawain* is written in an alliterative metre rather than in rhyme. However, here we will focus more on the differences in dialect that distinguish the work of the *Gawain* poet from his London contemporary.

One obvious difference concerns the use of the letters <þ> and <3>, which are not found in modern editions of Chaucer's works, although they do frequently appear in original manuscripts. This is therefore a rather artificial difference, because if we modernized all instances of <þ> and <3> by replacing them with their modern equivalents, the above passage would look more like a modern edition of Chaucer. However, certain differences are not a result of editorial preference. For example, the pronoun *hor* 'their' in the first line represents a northwestern form, distinct from Chaucer's own preferred forms *hir* or *her*. There are differences in verb endings, such as the use of the <-es> ending for the third person present indicative in *hales*, where Chaucer would use the southern <-eth> ending, and in the present participle ending <-ande>, in *folȝande*, where Chaucer would have <-ing>.

It is not always easy to recognize which features belong to which dialect, as certain features which are northern in ME have since become adopted in our PDE standard language. The <-es> ending found in *Gawain* is a good example of this, as we now use this ending rather than Chaucer's <-eth>, although it is the southern form of the present participle which is the standard form rather than the northern one. As well as these grammatical features, we also find variation in spelling between Chaucer and *Gawain* which probably testify to pronunciation differences. For example, the word 'each' is spelled *uch* in the above extract, where this is always *ech* in Chaucer. Similarly, *Gawain* uses *mon* where Chaucer has *man*, again probably reflecting a difference in pronunciation.

The difference that poses the greatest problems for students concerns vocabulary, as *Gawain* contains words restricted to northern dialects not found in Chaucer's southern variety. Often these words are derived from Old Norse (ON), as in the example of *mynn* in the above extract, a verb meaning 'declare', found only in texts written in the north in Middle English. As well as containing words not used by Chaucer, the vocabulary of *Gawain* differs from Chaucer in using the same words with different meanings. This is exemplified above in the verb *hope*, which is here used to mean 'think' rather than 'desire' as in Chaucer. There are other words used in *Gawain* which are not found in Chaucer, but whose histories suggest that they were considered to be archaic, poetic words, generally restricted to alliterative verse. These include words like *molde*, *lude* and *muckel* in the above extract, whose poetic provenance is shown by their appearance in alliterative stock phrases: 'most on þe molde' and 'myriest in his muckel'. It is apparent that the dialect of *Gawain* differs in many key ways from that of Chaucer, so that Chaucer's southern audience would probably have had some difficulty reading it.

Such problems were often avoided by the common practice of 'translating' between dialects. When a scribe carried out a copy of a particular text, he frequently translated the dialect of that text into another one, either his own or that of the person for whom he was producing the copy (Benskin and Laing 1981). This practice meant that texts could be made accessible to a range of readers from all over the country, not just those whose dialect was similar to that of the author. Dialect translation was therefore a practical solution to the problem of dialect variation, and the widespread use of this process indicates that no one dialect was considered to be superior to another. A writer simply wrote in his local dialect and then left it to scribes to make his work accessible to their clients.

A good example of this is the northern writer Richard Rolle, whose didactic religious works were read by a large and diverse readership, and so had to be translated into other dialects to be understood by his southern audience. This is openly acknowledged in an East Anglian copy of his prose treatise known as *The Form of Living*, which the scribe says he translated out of the northern tongue into a southern one, so that it might be better understood by men of that country. John Gower, Chaucer's fellow Londoner and contemporary writer, used a dialect which reveals his provincial origins, comprising features of the Kentish and Suffolk dialects, and Gower made no attempt to adopt the London dialect used by Chaucer (Smith 2004).

Chaucer's own works were also translated into other dialects by scribes copying manuscripts for provincial clients, and there are surviving manuscripts of Chaucer's works copied in dialects representing a wide range of counties: southwestern, West Midland, northern, East Anglian, Kentish and Scots (Horobin 2003). As an example of the way Chaucer's works could be translated into these other, non-metropolitan dialects, here is a short section taken from the opening of the Wife of Bath's Prologue from a manuscript translated into the northwestern dialect, similar to that of *Gawain*:

Experiment þouhe none auctorite
Where in þis werlde is riht ynouhe for me
To speke of woo þat is in mariage
For lordeinges sen I twelue ȝere was of Age
þonked be god þat eterne alyue
Hosbondes att þe cherche dor I haue hadde five

If I so oft myht haue wedded be
Bot al were worþi men in her degre
Bot me was tolde certein nouȝt longe a gon es
þat seþen criste ne went neuer bot ones
To weddeinge in þe Cane of Galile
That be þilke ensample tauht he me
þat I ne scholde wedded bue bot ones

(British Library Lansdowne MS 851)

This extract shows a number of differences in dialect from Chaucer's own. There are spelling differences, some of which appear not to reflect differences in pronunciation, such as *scholde* rather than *sholde* and *þouhe* instead of *though*, and others which were probably pronounced differently, like *seþen* for *sith*, *es* for *is*, *bue* for *be* and *þonked* for *thanked*.

This example shows how Chaucer's language could be translated into a regional dialect for local readers, without any need to preserve features of the author's own dialect. The manuscript from which the above extract is taken is a deluxe and expensively illuminated copy of the *Canterbury Tales*, one of only a few copies to include a portrait of the author, further helping to dismiss any preconceptions we may have that provincial dialect is indicative of a lack of cultural status. This is further indicated by the lack of evidence in this period of the stigmatization of different dialects that is common in modern attitudes to dialect variation. Many speakers of English today consider certain dialects to be inferior to their own and there are many dialectal stereotypes, and it is tempting to assume that these same attitudes applied in the Middle Ages.

However, there is little evidence of similar kinds of attitudes in the Middle Ages. John Trevisa, a writer of southern origins, writing in 1387, noted the difficulties southerners have understanding northerners, whose language he describes as 'so scharp, slyttyng [piercing], and frotyng [harsh], and unschape [formless], þat we Souþeron men may þat longage unneþe [hardly] undurstonde'. While these comments reveal Trevisa's southern prejudices, they do not appear to be typical of contemporary attitudes to the northern dialect. Trevisa goes on to claim that the best dialect to use is the Midlands one, as this shows the greatest similarity to the others because of its central position in the country, suggesting that Trevisa's concerns are more with communication than with prestige. Given that what we know of Trevisa's life indicates that he was of Cornish origin and spent much of his life in the Midlands, it may be that his comments represent little more than personal preferences.

Chaucer draws on dialect differences on just one occasion in his works, in the Reeve's Prologue and Tale. In the General Prologue, we are told that the Reeve is from Bawdeswell in Norfolk, and in the prologue to his tale he uses a handful of features characteristic of this dialect, such as the first person singular pronoun *Ik*. The tale concerns two Cambridge students who are of northern origins and whose dialogue contains a number of characteristically northern dialect features. It is important to recognize that this imitation of northern dialect is not entirely consistent, but rather it is limited to a number of salient features that give a flavour of the dialect. Here is an extract of a speech by one of the students, John, addressed to the miller Symkyn:

'Symond,' quod John, 'by God, nede has na <u>peer</u>.	equal
<u>Hym boes</u> serve hymself that has na <u>swayn</u>,	he must; servant
Or elles he is a fool, as clerkes sayn.	
Oure manciple, I <u>hope</u> he wil be deed,	think
Swa <u>werkes</u> ay the <u>wanges</u> in his heed;	ache; teeth
And <u>forthy</u> is I come, and <u>eek</u> Alayn,	therefore; also
To grynde oure corn and carie it <u>ham</u> agayn;	home
I pray yow spede us <u>heythen</u> that ye may.'	hence
	(A 4026–33)

This short extract contains a number of the dialect features used by Chaucer to signal the differences between the southern and northern varieties. Firstly, we see the use of the long *a* sound in words like *na*, *swa*, *ham,* where the southern dialect would have *no*, *so*, *home*. The construction 'I is', rather than 'I am', is a feature of northern grammar in this period, and the use of the <-es> ending of the singular and plural forms of the present tense are also northern features. There are also a number of words of ON derivation, like *swayn*, meaning 'servant', and *heythen*, meaning 'hence'. Another northern dialect word is the verb *werkes*, meaning 'aches', a usage which survives into the modern northern dialect. The use of the verb *hope* to mean 'think' rather than 'wish' in this context, that is, 'I think our Manciple will die', rather than

'I wish him dead', is another northernism which produces a rather subtle joke. As you may have already noted, several of these features correspond with those we identified earlier in the dialect of the *Gawain* poet.

The question remains as to why Chaucer should trouble himself with representing the northern dialect of two characters in one of his tales. Some scholars have suggested that it is an early instance of the stigmatization of the northern dialect by a southerner, similar to Trevisa's comments quoted above. But, as there was no standard variety of English during this period, this explanation does not seem particularly compelling. Just because today's society tends to see accents as social markers does not mean that this was true in the Middle Ages. In a society where there was no single prestigious variety, it is difficult to imagine how different varieties could lack prestige. To put it simply: without a standard variety you cannot have non-standard varieties. We should also remember that the northerners in the Reeve's Tale are Cambridge undergraduates, while the southerner is a miller, so the link between dialect and social class makes little sense in the world of the tale. Ultimately the students get their revenge upon the cheating Miller, so it is difficult to imagine that Chaucer's use of the northern dialect was to patronize them. I suspect the main reason for the use of northern dialect was comic and has little to do with class distinctions. It is remarkable that this tale is the only time that Chaucer chooses to represent a dialect different from his own, despite the variety of regional backgrounds represented by his pilgrim characters. The Wife of Bath and the Dartmouth Shipman do not speak with West Country accents, nor does the Oxford carpenter in the Miller's Tale. The Summoner's Tale is set in the 'mersshy contree' of Holderness in Yorkshire, but here there is no attempt to give the locals regional accents.

Standardization

In the previous section we saw that ME comprised a number of different dialects, and that there is no evidence that one dialect was considered to be socially superior to another. In the spoken language this tolerance of dialect variation continued throughout the ME period, and it is only in the sixteenth century that we begin to see the stigmatization of certain dialects, and the emergence of notions of 'correct' speech. The spoken dialect that was selected as the basis of the standard accent in this period was that of London, on account of its social and economic importance. As we have seen, the London dialect was also that used by Chaucer, although it is important to stress that this was a natural decision for a Londoner and not an indication of its greater social prominence. It is true that the later prominence of the London dialect benefited Chaucer in maximizing his audience, although the standard language that emerged is not identical to that used by Chaucer. While Chaucer's use of English contributed to the authority attached to the vernacular, it is unlikely that his use of the London dialect played any part in ensuring its success as the basis of the standard language.

While there is no evidence of a standard spoken variety of ME, there is some evidence indicating the emergence of a standard written language. Throughout much of the ME period, spelling was much more varied than in PDE, as a result of its lack of status and its local functions. However, by the end of the ME period, the vernacular began to be used for communication on a wider scale and this kind of variation became inefficient. As a result there was an increased need for a standardized written variety of Middle English that could be understood over a wide geographical area. In an important discussion of the development of London English during the fourteenth and fifteenth centuries, Samuels (1963) distinguished four 'types' of written standard which he labelled types I–IV. Type I, also known as the Central Midlands Standard, is found in a number of texts associated with John Wycliffe and the Lollard movement. This language is found in a large number of manuscripts of religious texts and Bible translations produced by the Lollards, copied and circulated widely throughout the country. This type of language is based upon the dialects of the central Midlands counties, and characteristic forms include *sich* 'such', *mych*, 'much', *ony* 'any', *silf* 'self', *stide* 'stead', *ȝouun* 'given', *siȝ* 'saw'.

Samuels' Type II is found in a group of manuscripts copied in London in the mid to late fourteenth century. This group includes the Auchinleck manuscript which was produced in London around 1340 by a number of scribes, some of whom were Londoners and others native West Midlanders. Characteristic Type II features include forms which are common to the Norfolk and Suffolk dialects, and are thought to derive from immigration into the capital from those counties. Examples of such forms are *þai*, *hij* 'they', *þeiȝ* 'though', *werld* 'world', *þat ilch(e), ilch(e)* 'that very'.

Type III is the language of London in the late fourteenth and early fifteenth centuries, recorded in, for example, the earliest Chaucer manuscripts: the Hengwrt and Ellesmere manuscripts of the *Canterbury Tales* and Corpus Christi College, Cambridge MS 61 of *Troilus and Criseyde*. Other Type III documents are early civic documents such as the London guild returns and the Petition of the Mercers' Company, and the holograph manuscripts of the poet Thomas Hoccleve. Characteristic features of this language are forms common to the central Midlands dialects, including *they* 'they', *hir(e)* 'their', *though* 'though', *yaf* 'gave', *nat* 'not', *swich* 'such'.

Type III was subsequently replaced in the early fifteenth century by Type IV, also termed by Samuels "Chancery Standard", which is found in government documents produced in the capital from about 1430. Type IV also shows the influence of forms found in the central Midlands dialects, although these have been further supplemented by forms originally restricted to the north Midlands, for example *theyre* 'their', *thorough* 'through', *such(e)* 'such', *gaf* 'gave', *not* 'not'. So, while Chaucer's dialect played an important role in the standardization of written English, it was not ultimately the ancestor of the standard language.

It is important to realize that these types are not equivalent to our PDE standard written language. PDE standard written English is a fixed standard in that it consists of a fixed set of rules from which deviation is not permitted. These standardized types of written language are focused standards, in that they comprise a number of salient features, not all of which will be employed in every instance. So while PDE standard written English does not permit variation, in that only one spelling of a particular word is correct, these standardized types do allow a certain amount of variation.

A good way of demonstrating this tolerance of variation is by comparing several texts copied in Type III London English. Let us begin by comparing the opening 28 lines of the Wife of Bath's Prologue in two of the earliest extant manuscripts of the *Canterbury Tales*, known as the Hengwrt (Hg) and Ellesmere (El) manuscripts. These manuscripts were both written by the same scribe, yet there are a number of differences in their spelling which show that the scribe did not have a single preferred spelling for each word:

The Hengwrt manuscript:

Experience thogh noon <u>Auctoritee</u>	authority
Were in this world is right <u>ynogh</u> for me	enough
To speke of wo that is in marriage	
For lordynges, <u>sith</u> þat I twelf yeer was of age	since
5 Thonked be god, that is eterne on lyue	
Housbondes atte chirche dore I haue had fyue	
If I so ofte myghte han wedded be	
And alle were worthy men in hir degree	
But me was told certeyn, noght longe agon is	
10 That sith þat Crist ne wente neuere but <u>onys</u>	once
To weddyng in the <u>Cane</u> of Galilee	town of Cana
That by the same <u>ensample</u> taughte he me	example
That I ne sholde wedded be but ones	
<u>Herke</u> eek, lo, which a sharp word for the nones	listen
15 Bisyde a welle, Ihesus, god and man	
Spak in <u>repreeue</u> of the Samaritan	reproof
Thow hast <u>yhad</u> fyue housbondes quod he	had
And that ilke man which that now hath thee	
Is nat thyn housbonde, thus he seyde certeyn	
20 What that he mente ther by I kan nat seyn	
But þat I <u>axe</u> why þat the fifthe man	ask
Was noon housbonde to the Samaritan	
How manye myghte she han in mariage	
Yet herde I neuere tellen in myn age	
25 Vp on this nombre <u>diffynycioun</u>	limitation
Men may dyuyne and <u>glosen</u> vp & doun	interpret
But wel I <u>woot</u> <u>expres</u> with outen lye	know; clearly
God <u>bad</u> vs for to <u>wexe</u> and multiplye	commanded;
	increase

The Ellesmere manuscript

Experience though noon Auctoritee
Were in this world were right ynogh to me
To speke of wo that is in mariage
For lordynges, sith I . xij . yeer was of Age
5   Ythonked be god, that is eterne on lyue
Housbondes at chirche dore I haue had fyue
For I so ofte haue ywedded bee

And alle were worthy men in hir degree
But me was toold certeyn, nat longe agoon is
10 That sith that Crist ne wente neuere but onis
To weddyng in the Cane of Galilee
By the same ensample thoughte me
That I ne sholde wedded be but ones
Herkne eek, which a sharp word for the nones
15 Biside a welle Ihesus god and man
Spak in repreeue of the Samaritan
Thou hast yhad fyue housbondes quod he
And that man the which ?at hath now thee
Is noght thyn housbonde, thus seyde he certeyn
20 What that he mente ther by, I kan nat seyn
But þat I axe why that the fifthe man
Was noon housbonde to the samaritan
How manye myghte she haue in mariage
Yet herde I neuere tellen in myn age
25 Vp on this nombre diffiniciounv
Men may deuyne and glosen vp and doun
But wel I woot expres with oute lye
God bad vs for to wexe and multiplye

The opening lines of these extracts show variation in the spelling
of the word 'though': Hg has *thogh* while El has *though*. Another
difference is found in lines 5 and 7 where the Hengwrt manuscript
has spellings of two past participles without the <y-> prefix, where
Ellesmere has the more archaic-looking *ythonked* and *ywedded*. In
line 9 these manuscripts have different spellings of the word 'not':
Hg has *noght* and El has *nat*. However, if we look at line 19, we see
that here the forms of 'not' are reversed: Hg has *nat* and El has
noght. This indicates that this scribe did not simply use different
spellings for 'not' when copying these two manuscripts. Both the
spellings *nat* and *noght* are found in both manuscripts, although not
in the same positions or proportions. As well as these differences,
there is also variation at the level of individual letters: such as the use
of <i> and <y>, or <th> and <þ>.

While there are clearly differences between these two texts, the
fact that they are both copies of the same text means that they imply
a greater uniformity in the scribe's spelling practice than was really
the case. This becomes clearer when we compare these examples
with two other documents copied by this same scribe, neither of

which contains Chaucer's works. The first is the Petition of the Mercers' Company, copied in 1386, and recently identified as the work of this same scribe (Mooney 2006). The document was written in London and uses several spelling forms characteristic of Type III, but also differs in a number of ways from the usage of the Hengwrt and Ellesmere manuscripts. Some of these differences can be seen in the following sentence from the petition:

> For we knowe wel as for by moche the more partye of vs, and, as we hope, for alle, alle suche wronges han ben vnwytyng to vs or elles outer-lich ayeins owre wille. (Chambers and Daunt 1931, 37)

In just this single sentence we find several variants from the spelling choices shown in the scribe's work on the Hengwrt and Ellesmere manuscripts. For instance, here he uses *suche* rather than *swiche*, *moche* rather than *muche* and *ayeins* rather than *agayns*. In the first two cases, the spellings *suche* and *moche*, the scribe uses forms that are never found in either Hg or El, while the form *ayeins* is found less commonly in Hg and never in El. Elsewhere in the Mercers' Petition, we find the scribe using *whether*, rather than his preferred form in Hg and El *wheither*, *nought* rather than *nat/noght*, and *thourgh* rather than *thurgh*.

A further example of this scribe copying a non-Chaucerian text is a manuscript of Langland's *Piers Plowman* also in his hand. Here is a short extract from this text, showing the scribe's spelling practices in this manuscript:

She blesseþ þise Bisshopes, <u>þeiʒ</u> þei be lewed;	though
<u>Prouendreþ</u> <u>persones</u> and preestes maynteneþ	provides for; parsons
To haue <u>lemmans</u> and <u>lotebies</u> alle hire lif daies	lovers; concubines
And bryngeþ forþ <u>barnes</u> ayein forbode lawes.	children
Ther she is wel wiþ þe kyng, wo is þe <u>Reaume</u>-	realm
For she is fauourable to fals and <u>defouleþ</u> truþe ofte.	injures
By Iesus! wiþ hire <u>Ieweles</u> youre Iustices she <u>shendeþ</u>	jewels; corrupts
And <u>liþ</u> ayein þe lawe and <u>letteþ</u> hym þe gate,	lies; obstructs
That feiþ may noʒt haue his <u>forþ</u>, hire floryns go so þikke.	course
She ledeþ þe lawe as hire <u>list</u> and louedaies makeþ,	pleases
And <u>doþ</u> men <u>lese</u> þoruʒ hire loue þat lawe myʒte wynne-	makes; lose
The <u>maze</u> for a mene man, þouʒ he <u>mote</u> hire euere!	confusion; litigate

(*Piers Plowman*, III.149–60, Trinity College Cambridge MS B.15.17)

While the spelling of this extract is broadly similar to that of Hg and El, there are some differences. Several differences relate to the greater use of <þ> and <ȝ> in this manuscript; for instance, the scribe uses *noȝt* rather than *noght*, *þouȝ* rather than *though* and <þ> appears in a number of other places where it is not found in Hg or El, for example *þikke* 'thick', *þei* 'they'. As well as *þouȝ* 'though', the scribe also uses the form *þeiȝ* in the first line of the extract, the equivalent of the Hg spelling *theigh*, a form not found at all in El. The scribe's spelling *ayein* 'against' is similar to that recorded in the Mercers' Petition (see above) but only found sporadically in Hg and not at all in El. The spelling *þoruȝ* is not found in any of the scribe's other manuscripts, adding another variant spelling alongside those found in Hg, El and the Petition: *thurgh* and *thourgh*.

The purpose of this discussion has been to consider a single scribe's spelling habits to highlight how much variation was tolerated in London English of the late fourteenth and early fifteenth centuries. So, while London English of this period shows a greater amount of uniformity than earlier stages in Middle English, we must be careful not to view it as completely uniform or standardized.

Characteristics of Middle English

In the rest of this chapter we will look briefly at how the factors outlined above affected the English language more generally during this period, and chart the most salient features which distinguish Middle English from its ancestor, Old English, and from the Early Modern English period that followed it.

Vocabulary

The most obvious way in which French influenced the later history of English is the large influx of French vocabulary into English during the ME period. Borrowing of words from French during the ME period can be divided into two main stages. During the first stage, borrowed words are of Norman French origin and often relate to areas of most importance to the Norman conquerors. These include words relating to the law and government, such as *justice*, *chancellor*, *prison*, *noble*. Another area which saw the importing of large numbers of French words was the church; during this period we see the first use of words such as *mercy*, *pity*, *preach*, *clergy* and many other words of this kind. In the second stage of borrowing we see the introduction of words from the central French dialect that are not restricted to any specific field. Although, as French speakers remained the aristocratic class during this period, it is not surprising that these words generally relate to refined and elevated areas of English culture, including the arts, learning, fashion and food.

It is not only French words which enter the English language during the Middle English period. A number of words of Old Norse origin make their first appearance in the written record during this period. This might strike us as rather odd, given that the Viking invasions and settlements date as far back as the eighth century. But while ON words were evidently in use in England during the OE period, they seem to have been restricted to the spoken language. Following the demise of the OE standard language, these words were adopted into written English, and many make their first appearance in ME. These include words like *ugly*, *egg*, *window*. It is notable that words borrowed from ON are generally common, everyday terms which are not marked as belonging to a particular domain or register. In fact ON influence even extends to the English pronoun system, with the ON plural pronouns giving us our present-day paradigm: *they*, *their*, *them*, which made their first appearance in English during the ME period.

Grammar

While vocabulary might be the most obvious area in which French influence on English may be seen, the impact was felt at all linguistic levels. In certain cases the changes were the result of a process that had begun in the Old English period, and which was accelerated by the conquest. This is perhaps most evident in the shift in English from a largely synthetic structure to a predominantly analytical one. A synthetic language is one where relationships between words are indicated by special endings, called 'inflexions', where an analytical language relies more on word order. In OE inflexions were added to nouns to indicate number (singular or plural) and case (nominative, accusative, genitive and dative). Adjectives and determiners also had endings that were added to make them agree with the noun they were describing, in number, case and gender (masculine, feminine or neuter). If you have studied a language like French or German, you will be aware of these concepts. Compare, for instance, *le grand chien* and *les grands chiens*, where an -s is added to the adjective to indicate agreement with the plural noun. By the end of the Old English period, these inflexions were becoming less distinct in the spoken language and began to be reduced to the sound schwa, a sound similar to the vowel on the end of *china*, spelled <-e> or <-en>.

In the Middle English period this process of change continued so that all such inflexions were lost, apart from the -s plural ending on nouns, and the -e ending on adjectives. The -e adjective ending was used throughout the ME period as a way of indicating that an adjective was plural, or that it was definite, that is, following a determiner such as a definite article or demonstrative. This means that in ME there was a distinction between *the olde man*, *olde men* and *old man*, where the adjective has no ending as it is indefinite. Plural forms of nouns continued to be marked by the addition of the -s inflexion, which became the most common plural ending, although the -en derived from OE weak nouns continued to be used, as it still is today in words like *children* and *oxen*.

These changes meant that inflexions were no longer available to indicate the relationships between words, and this led to the establishment of a more fixed word order. Where the order of subject, verb and object was comparatively flexible in Old English, Middle English is more consistent in the use of the subject-verb-object word order that we are familiar with today. The main difference between ME and PDE word order is found when the head of the sentence is an adverbial, such as *when* or *then*, which causes the subject and the verb to be inverted, giving the word order adverbial-verb-subject-object.

The pronoun system continued in a similar form to that of OE, although a number of important changes occurred. Middle English retains both singular and plural forms of the second person pronoun: *thou* and *ye*, as in OE. However, contact with French altered the pragmatic function of these pronouns, introducing a new distinction based on formality. As a result, the singular *thou* pronoun was selected to express informality or intimacy, and the plural *ye* form was reserved for formal usage, a similar distinction to that of modern French *tu* and *vous*. The OE third person nominative singular feminine pronoun *heo* was replaced by a new form *she*, while the third person equivalent *hit* was gradually replaced by *it*. In the genitive, the neuter pronoun retained the same form as the masculine pronoun *his*, which was only replaced by *its* in the Early Modern English period. As mentioned above, the ME period also saw the replacement of the OE third person plural pronouns with the ON equivalents, *they*, *their* and *them*, although these are found earliest in areas of densest Norse settlement, and were adopted later in the more conservative southern and western dialects.

The ME period also witnessed a number of changes in the inflexional system of verbs, caused by the weakening of unstressed syllables. The OE present tense inflexions are reduced to -(e)st, -eth, -(e)n, with some forms having no inflexion. The third person singular present indicative ending -eth was gradually replaced by the -(e)s ending, although in the southern and western dialects, the -eth ending survived throughout most of this period. The present participle inflexion varied according to dialect, with the -yng/-ing ending found in PDE emerging in the southern dialects of ME. The reduction in the inflexional system led to a blurring of the distinction between indicative and subjunctive moods, leading to an increased reliance on the modal auxiliaries. These verbs, including *shall* and *will*, were grammaticalized and were used to indicate time, tense and mood as in PDE. In OE the verb *will* implied volition and desire, so that the phrase 'I will help you' means that I wish to help you, rather than I am going to do so. Similarly, in OE the verb *can* meant knowing how to, rather than being able to, do something. In ME these changes are in a process of transition, so that writers were able to draw upon both kinds of usage.

Spelling

During the Middle English period, the OE letters <æ>, <ð> and the runic letter <p> disappeared, and were replaced by the equivalents <a/e>, <th> and <w>. The runic letter <þ> survived throughout much of the ME period, alongside the equivalent <th>, only disappearing with the arrival of printing in the fifteenth century. In early printed books <þ> was often represented with a <y>, which led to the emergence of an unhistorical form *ye*, preserved in PDE in phrases like 'ye olde tea shoppe'.

Chaucer's dialect

Chaucer was born into a merchant family in London in the 1340s and received his education working as a page in the household of the Countess of Ulster. He made a number of trips overseas in the service of the king, visiting France, Spain and Italy; visits which may have given him access to the work of influential poets such as Dante, Boccaccio and Petrarch. His later career included several important royal appointments, including stints as controller of the customs office and clerk of the King's works. None of the five hundred or so surviving documents referring to Chaucer makes reference to his poetry, which appears to have been composed outside working hours. Despite his lengthy career working for the royal administration, there is little evidence of royal patronage for his poetry, and only the *Book of the Duchess*, a consolation for John of Gaunt on the death of his wife, can be linked with a specific member of the royalty. Chaucer's primary audience was made up of members of the king's household in the wider sense, encompassing the so-called Chamber knights, as well as civil servants, clerks and minor officials.

Following Chaucer's death in 1400, numerous manuscripts containing his works were produced, many of them by scribes working in London, although during the fifteenth century Chaucer's works circulated throughout England and were read by a socially and geographically diverse audience. The extent of the demand for copies of Chaucer's works can be gauged from the large number of surviving manuscripts. There are, for instance, over eighty manuscripts preserving complete or fragmentary copies of the *Canterbury Tales*, more than any other ME secular poem.

As a Londoner, Chaucer naturally wrote using the London dialect, and we should not see this choice as evidence for the superior status of this dialect during this period. The best way of demonstrating the features which characterize this variety of ME is to examine a sample extract. Below are the opening lines of the General Prologue to the *Canterbury Tales*, which exemplify many of the characteristic features of ME described above:

Whan that Aprill with his <u>shoures</u> <u>soote</u>	showers; sweet
The <u>droghte</u> of March hath <u>perced</u> to the roote,	drought; pierced
And bathed every veyne in <u>swich licour</u>	such liquid
Of which <u>vertu</u> engendred is the <u>flour</u>;	power; flower
Whan <u>Zephirus</u> eek with his sweete breeth	the west wind
Inspired hath in every <u>holt</u> and heeth	wood
The tendre <u>croppes</u>, and the yonge sonne	shoots
Hath in the <u>Ram</u> his half cours <u>yronne</u>,	the sign of Aries; run
And smale <u>foweles</u> maken melodye,	birds
That slepen al the nyght with open <u>ye</u>	eye
(So <u>priketh</u> hem nature in hir <u>corages</u>),	incites; hearts
Thanne <u>longen</u> folk to goon on pilgrimages,	desire
And <u>palmeres</u> for to seken <u>straunge</u> <u>strondes</u>,	pilgrims; foreign shores
To <u>ferne halwes</u>, <u>kowthe</u> in sondry londes;	distant shrines; known
And <u>specially</u> from every shires ende	particularly
Of Engelond to Caunterbury they <u>wende</u>,	travel
The hooly blisful martir for to <u>seke</u>,	seek
That hem hath <u>holpen</u> whan that they were <u>seeke</u>.	helped; sick
	(A 1–18)

The first feature to note in the above extract is the high proportion of French-derived vocabulary, including words like *licour*, *engendred*, *melodye*, *corages*, *straunge*. The prominence of the French vocabulary in this passage adds to the stylistic ornamentation of these opening lines, as is particularly true of technical words like *licour* and *engendred*. Despite the unfamiliarity in the appearance of this text, many of these words are remarkably similar to their PDE equivalents: compare *droghte* and *drought*; *shoures* and *showers*; *hooly* and *holy*; *flour* and *flower*; *londes* and *lands*; *Thanne* and *then*; *seeke* and *sick*. These correspondences show how many similarities there are between ME and PDE. In fact it is surprising how few of the words found in this passage have not survived into PDE. These include *ferne*, meaning 'remote'; *holt*, meaning 'wood'; *strondes* meaning 'shores'; *wende* meaning 'travel'. Two such words are technical religious words: *palmeres* meaning 'pilgrims' and *hallows* meaning 'saints', or 'shrines'; preserved in All Hallows Day, or All Saints Day. Other words do survive but their meanings have changed, as in the case of *foweles*, which means 'birds' in ME, but survives into PDE with the narrower meaning of 'domestic cocks or hens'. Another example is *corage*, which here refers to the heart, a sense which has not survived in the PDE equivalent *courage*. The word *straunge* survives as PDE *strange*, although the meaning here is 'foreign' rather than 'unusual'.

The inflexional system of ME can be seen in the use of the -e ending on the end of *yonge* in 'the yonge sonne', where the adjective follows the definite article. The -e ending is also found in 'smale foweles' where it indicates agreement with the plural noun. In verb forms we can see the -th ending of the third person singular present indicative in *hath* and *priketh*. There are examples of both the -e and -n endings of the present plural indicative in *wende* and *slepen*. Forms of the past participle display several variants, including forms without the y- prefix, for example *holpen*, and a form with the prefix: *yronne*.

The pronouns used in this extract show that Chaucer used just one of the ON derived forms: *they*, alongside forms inherited from OE, *hem* 'them' and *hir* 'their'. The use of *his* in line 1 shows the use of this form for the third singular neuter pronoun equivalent to PDE 'its'.

Now we have looked in brief at some of the key features that characterize Middle English, and Chaucer's own variety of this language, we may turn to a more detailed consideration of the individual levels of language. However, before doing so, it is worth pausing to consider the nature of the available evidence for a study of Chaucer's language.

Evidence

Modern editions of Chaucer's works are based on handwritten documents known as manuscripts, which were copied by professional scribes. Chaucer's works survive in large numbers of manuscripts, although none of these is thought to have been produced during the poet's lifetime. The earliest surviving Chaucer manuscript is probably the Hengwrt manuscript of the *Canterbury Tales*, copied in the first decade of the fifteenth century. The scribe responsible for copying this manuscript has been identified as Adam Pynkhurst, a professional London scrivener who copied a number of Chaucerian manuscripts, as well as works by Gower, Langland and documents for the London Mercers' Guild. Given his evident close association with Chaucer, it is likely that Pynkhurst was also the Adam 'scriveyn' to whom Chaucer addressed his witty poem complaining about the errors and inaccuracies introduced into his works by the scribe's haste and carelessness:

Adam scriveyn, if ever it <u>thee bifalle</u>	happen to you
Boece or Troylus for to wryten newe,	
Under thy long lokkes thou most have the <u>scalle</u>,	a scaly disease
<u>But</u> after my <u>makyng</u> thou wryte more trewe;	unless; composition
So ofte adaye I mot thy werk <u>renewe</u>,	do again
It to correcte and eek to rubbe and <u>scrape</u>,	erase
And al is thorugh thy negligence and <u>rape</u>.	haste

Despite the close relationship between poet and scribe suggested by this familiar and teasing poem, Pynkhurst seems to have encountered problems in obtaining and arranging the various tales and links when copying and assembling his first copy of the *Canterbury Tales* (Blake 1985, Owen 1991).

Pynkhurst produced another complete copy of the poem, this time a more coherent and organized production, elegantly and expensively illuminated and illustrated. This manuscript is known as the Ellesmere manuscript and is now housed in the Henry E. Huntington Library in San Marino, California (MS El 26.C.9). While Pynkhurst was clearly a professional and accurate copyist, his work does contain errors, so that we cannot always be certain exactly what Chaucer wrote. Furthermore, as we have already seen above, when a scribe copied a ME text he frequently imposed his own spelling habits, although the consistency with which scribes made such changes often varied. So to some extent the language of Chaucer's manuscripts is the language of Adam Pynkhurst and other scribes. The text of most modern editions of the *Canterbury Tales*, including that of the *Riverside Chaucer*, is based upon the Ellesmere manuscript, copied by Pynkhurst using a spelling system that is probably similar, but not identical, to Chaucer's own. However, for other of Chaucer's works, such as the *Book of the Duchess* and the *House of Fame*, no early manuscripts survive, so that editors have to rely on copies produced in the middle of the fifteenth century as the basis of their editions. The language of these later manuscripts differs considerably from that of the Hengwrt and Ellesmere manuscripts, and cannot be considered simply as evidence of Chaucer's language.

When editing an ME manuscript for a modern edition, editors introduce certain changes to the language and spelling of their texts to make them more accessible to their readers. This often includes imposing certain PDE spelling conventions, such as the introduction of <j>, a letter not found in ME, regularizing inconsistencies, and imposing modern punctuation on the text. To demonstrate some of the differences between the text found in a modern edition of the poem and that of a medieval manuscript, I have included a transcription of the above extract from the opening of the General Prologue as it appears in the Ellesmere manuscript:

Transcription from the Ellesmere manuscript

Whan that Aprill with hise shoures soote
The droghte of March / hath perced to the roote
And bathed euery veyne / in swich licour
Of which ver*tu* / engendred is the flour
Whan Zephirus eek / w^t his sweete breeth
Inspired hath / in euery holt and heeth
The tendre croppes / and the yonge sonne
Hath in the Ram / his half cours yronne
And smale foweles / maken melodye
That slepen al the nyght / with open eye
So priketh hem nature in hir corages
Thanne longen folk / to goon on pilg*ri*mages
And Palm*er*es / for to seken straunge strondes
To ferne halwes / kowthe in sondry londes
And specially / fram euery shires ende
Of Engelond / to Caunterbury they wende
The hooly blisful martir for to seke
That hem hath holpen / whan þ^t they were seeke

Perhaps the most obvious difference here concerns the use of italics, which I have used to mark where the scribe has employed an abbreviation mark rather than spelling the word out in full. Editors commonly expand such abbreviations but do not use italics to record this, so that it is not clear where such expansions have been implemented. There are differences in spelling between the transcription and the edited text, such as the use of <u> for [v] in *euery*. This is a common feature of ME spelling, where <v> was used initially and

<u> medially, although most modern editors replace this with PDE practice. Another difference is the use of the letter <þ> in *þᵗ*, an abbreviation for *that*. This letter is commonly replaced with the PDE equivalent <th> in modern editions of Chaucer's works.

There are also instances of the editor adjusting the spelling of words found in his base manuscript. For example, the word *hise* in line 1 is spelled *his* in the edited text, the manuscript spelling *eye* has been replaced with *ye*, and *seke* 'sick' is spelled *seeke*. Changes of this kind are common in modern editions and are usually made silently, so that it is only through comparison with the manuscript that we can observe where such changes have been carried out. Other significant differences between the manuscript and edited texts concern punctuation and capitalization. The manuscript does contain some punctuation, but it is generally much lighter and less consistent than PDE practice, so that modern editors customarily introduce PDE punctuation as a guide for their readers. The scribe uses capital letters to emphasize certain nouns, although this is not always in line with modern practice, as is shown by the spelling of *Palmeres* in line 13.

As further evidence for the variation and lack of regularity in ME scribal practice, it is worth briefly comparing the above transcription from the Ellesmere manuscript, with the older Hengwrt manuscript copied by the same scribe:

Transcription from the Hengwrt manuscript

Whan that Aueryll wᵗ his shoures soote
The droghte of March / hath perced to the roote
And bathed euery veyne in swich lycour
Of which vertu engendred is the flour
Whan zephirus eek wᵗ his sweete breeth
Inspired hath in euery holt and heeth
The tendre croppes / and the yonge sonne
Hath in the Ram / his half cours yronne
And smale foweles / maken melodye
That slepen al the nyght with open Iye
So priketh hem nature / in hir corages
Thanne longen folk to goon on pilgrimages
And Palmeres for to seeken straunge strondes
To ferne halwes / kouthe in sondry londes

And specially / from euery shyres ende
Of Engelond to Caunterbury they wende
The holy blisful martir for to seke
That hem hath holpen whan þ^t they weere seeke

While the two extracts are very similar, they are not identical, showing how a single scribe may vary his spelling and punctuation practices. The use of abbreviations differs in the two extracts, as does the spelling of certain words, for example *his/hise, licour/ lycour, eye/Iye, seken/seeken, kowthe/kouthe, fram/from, shires/ shyres, holy/hooly, were/weere*. While these spelling variants may not seem very significant, it is worth being aware of this kind of variation as it is an important aspect of Chaucer's language. While variation of this kind, and the inconsistencies introduced by his scribes, may have led to confusion and corruption in the copying and transmission of his works, it also provided him with considerable flexibility in his writing. This will become more apparent in the following chapter, as we come to look in greater detail at Chaucer's spelling and pronunciation practices.

Further reading

It is a good idea to situate your study of ME within the development of the English language as a whole by reading an account of the history of English, such as Barber (1993), Baugh and Cable (2002), Blake (1996). Horobin and Smith (2002) focuses exclusively on the ME period, while Burrow and Turville-Petre (2004) provides a useful collection of annotated ME texts and has a helpful introduction. Blake (1992) presents an extremely comprehensive and detailed survey of ME, which is indispensable for more advanced students. Davis (1974) is a useful introduction to Chaucer's linguistic context.

The development of London English and the process of standardization is discussed by Samuels (1963) and Horobin (2003, Chapter 2). Facsimiles of the Hengwrt manuscript are available in printed form in Ruggiers (1979) and in electronic form in Stubbs (2000). McCarren and Moffat (1998) provides a good collection of essays dealing with the theory and practice of editing ME texts.

4 Spelling and pronunciation

Reading Chaucer's works today is generally a silent activity, in which we pick up a printed copy of his works and read it quietly to ourselves. For Chaucer and his contemporary audience, poetry was primarily an oral encounter, in which a poem was read aloud to a group of listeners. One of the manuscripts of Chaucer's *Troilus and Criseyde* contains an illustration of Chaucer reading aloud to a group of noble men and women. While this picture is likely to be a fictional representation rather than a record of an actual event, it does suggest how Chaucer's first audience might have encountered his poetry. It thus suggests that Chaucer's works were written to be read aloud, so that knowing how to pronounce the words correctly is an important part of appreciating and understanding Chaucer's poetry. This is particularly true of the *Canterbury Tales*, where a variety of characters are given different voices, and their language is part of their characterization. Moreover, Chaucer wrote poetry with regular metre and rhyme and it is important to know how the words are pronounced to be able to appreciate and assess his skill as a versifier. In this chapter we will look at how Chaucer's language was pronounced and how this affects our understanding of Chaucer's skill as a poet.

Whenever I read a section of Chaucer aloud, I am often asked the question "How do you know that it is supposed to be read that way?" This is a good question and one which I will begin by trying to answer.

Spelling evidence

One kind of evidence used by scholars to determine how Chaucer would have pronounced his words is the way in which they are spelled. The relationship between writing and speech, and the way that sounds map onto letters, is a complex issue. Take the word *cat* as an example. This word is composed of three separate sounds, or 'phonemes': /kæt/ and these are represented in the written language by three equivalent letters, or 'graphemes': <cat>. This is a simple example and it is not the case that all words are comprised of individual phonemes mapping onto individual graphemes. If we replace the initial /k/ with /ð/, then the word is spelled <that>, with the initial phoneme being represented by a combination of two graphemes: <th>. As well as the use of combinations of graphemes to represent single phonemes, we are also accustomed to single graphemes representing more than one sound. For instance, the grapheme <y> in PDE can be used to represent the sound [j] in words like *yes* and an [ɪ] sound in words like *very*. A further complication is that single sounds can be represented by more than one grapheme, as in the case of [k] which is spelled <c> in some words and <k> in others.

Because we have a fixed, or standard, spelling system these conventions are learned and followed by all users of English; where a speaker is uncertain as to the correct spelling of a particular word, s/he may turn to a dictionary for guidance, or to an electronic spellchecker. In the ME period there was no standard spelling system and as a result users of English were free to adjust their spelling system to reflect their own particular pronunciation. Thus the spelling systems found in ME texts show considerable variation in the way they represent particular sounds. Some of this is simply spelling variation with no implication for pronunciation, such as the many different ways in which the phoneme [ʃ] could be represented, including <ch, sc, sch, sh, ss>.

But in some cases such variation testifies to different pronunciations, giving us important access to regional differences in the pronunciation of ME. For instance, some southern dialects of ME pronounced the sounds [f] and [s] as [v] and [z], as is still the case in some parts of southwest England today, as caricatured by reference to the 'Zummerzet' (Somerset) accent. In the ME period these different pronunciations were reflected in the spelling system, so that texts from these dialect areas spell words like *fox* and *sit* as *vox* and *zit* to reflect this pronunciation. While such pronunciations persist in the present-day dialects of the southwest, they are no longer reflected in the spelling system. We are aware of them through contact with speakers of other dialects, or through exposure to these accents via the media, but linguists of the future analysing texts written in English of the twenty-first century would be unaware that such differences existed. So in the ME period there was a much closer relationship between the spoken and written languages and it was possible for speakers to adjust their spelling system to reflect their own pronunciation, rather than conforming to a national norm.

In the sixteenth century, English spelling became increasingly fixed so that changes in the spoken language were no longer reflected in the written language, meaning that the spelling system we have inherited today more closely reflects the pronunciation of the ME period than it does that of PDE. This explains apparent oddities in the PDE spelling system such as silent letters, which testify to a ME pronunciation that has since changed. While it may be frustrating for learners of English to have to remember many apparently arbitrary rules concerning the spelling of words, such as 'knight', the preservation of such spellings provides important clues to the ways such words were once pronounced. In the case of the word 'knight', its spelling indicates that it was once pronounced with an initial [k] and with the <gh> pronounced like the sound in the German word *nicht*. Over a period of time, the pronunciation of the word has changed, while the spelling has remained fixed. So, by using the evidence of PDE spelling, we are able to derive important insights into how such words were pronounced in the Middle Ages.

Rhyming evidence

The example of the word 'knight' raises a further fundamental issue, namely that the pronunciation of words changes over time; a concept known to linguists as 'sound change'. This is perhaps most obvious to us when we look at the way in which Chaucer rhymes certain words in his verse. For instance, Chaucer rhymes the words *glass* and *was*, two words that survive into PDE but no longer rhyme. Some other examples of rhyming pairs that no longer rhyme in PDE are *town* and *region*, *good* and *blood*, *nice* and *malice*. Such instances suggest that, assuming that Chaucer was a competent poet aiming at exact rhymes, these words rhymed in ME but their pronunciations have since changed.

An important aspect of sound change is that it is frequently regular, and often affects specific sounds in an ordered way. For instance, the word *town* was pronounced in ME with a vowel sound like that in PDE *goose*, and this vowel was subsequently replaced by the PDE pronunciation. But this was not an isolated instance, as may be indicated by the similar change in words like *house*, *mouse*, *how*, *down* and so on. So, from such examples, we may deduce that words pronounced like *house* in PDE were pronounced like *goose* in ME. Some speakers may be aware of this difference today in the Scots pronunciation of these words, which retains the ME sound, as in the modern Scots pronunciation of *house* that sounds like 'hoos'.

In fact, this change in the pronunciation of words like *town* is part of a larger structural change in the English long vowel system, which marks a major difference between the pronunciation of ME and PDE. This major sound change is known today as the 'Great Vowel Shift'. The Great Vowel Shift is a process which occurred in the fifteenth and sixteenth centuries, and is the cause of the most significant differences in pronunciation of vowel sounds between ME and PDE. While a detailed understanding of the Great Vowel Shift is unnecessary for an understanding of Chaucer's pronunciation, it is often helpful to remember the basic correspondences between ME and PDE that it created, such as the general rule that words now pronounced like *town*, *gown*, *cow* and so on should be pronounced with the vowel in *goose*, or that the words like *wife* and *life* were pronounced with the vowel in *bee*.

Despite the huge significance of the Great Vowel Shift for English pronunciation, the Shift happened after the spelling system had become standardized and therefore did not affect the way such words were spelled. If we compare the spelling of affected words in ME and PDE, we find that these are often identical, revealing the surprising fact that PDE spelling is often a helpful guide to the pronunciation of ME vowel sounds, as is frequently the case with consonant sounds, as mentioned above. For instance, words spelled with a medial <oo> in PDE are pronounced with a long *o* sound in ME, like the sound in PDE *vote*, as might be expected from such a spelling. However, subsequent sound changes have obscured this relationship between spelling and pronunciation, as may be seen in the different ways in which many people now pronounce words like *blood*, *good*, *mood* and so on; in Chaucer's English all these words were pronounced with the same long *o* sound.

Comparative evidence

In addition to the primary evidence of spellings and rhymes, there are certain other types of evidence that can be used to enable scholars to reconstruct Chaucerian pronunciation. Such evidence involves the comparison of ME forms with other stages in the history of English and with related languages. For an example let us return to the word 'knight' with which we began. This is a Germanic word also recorded in Old English where it has the spelling *cniht.* While this is a different spelling to that of ME *knight,* it evidently implies a similar pronunciation to that represented by the ME spelling. Other Germanic languages provide further comparative evidence; for instance, we might compare Old High German *kneht,* Middle Dutch *knecht,* Old Saxon *knecht* and Old Frisian *kniucht.* These related languages show different spellings, but all testify to a similar pronunciation. This does not mean that all these words sounded exactly the same, but it does make it highly likely that the broad pronunciation we have suggested for ME *knight* is likely to be correct. Evidence of this kind can therefore be used to compare with our ME spellings and reconstructions, in order to provide further support for our theories of how such spellings should be pronounced.

One final kind of comparative evidence may also be mentioned. It may have already become apparent that comparison with later stages in the development of English can provide important information concerning Chaucer's pronunciation. The widespread use of rhyme in post-Chaucerian poetry makes this kind of evidence especially valuable. The Early Modern English period also witnessed the beginnings of phonetic descriptions of English, by so-called 'orthoepists' and spelling reformers. These two groups have provided us with important evidence concerning the pronunciation of Early Modern English, although their desire to prescribe a partic-ular kind of accent which they perceived to be prestigious means that their evidence must be treated with care.

Chaucer's sound system

Soun ys noght but eyr ybroken;
And every speche that ys spoken,

Lowd or pryvee, foul or fair,
In his substaunce ys but air;

(*House of Fame*, 765–8)

Having discussed the ways in which it is possible to reconstruct Chaucer's pronunciation from his spelling system, we can now look at the sound system he employed in detail. We will start by looking at the vowel sounds used in Chaucer's spoken system, and how these were spelled. In this section I have used the International Phonetic Alphabet (IPA) to represent individual sounds. This is an international standard alphabet which enables speakers of different languages and dialects to recognize the sounds being discussed. However, not all students will be familiar with the IPA and so I have added a table below which gives a PDE word which contains a vowel sound similar to that represented by the phonetic symbol. The following is an inventory of all the single vowel sounds, known as 'monophthongs', found in Chaucer's system, comprising both short and long vowels:

[iː, ɪ, eː, ɛː, ɛ, aː, a, ɔː, ɔ, oː, uː, ʊ]

The short vowels [ɪ, ɛ, a, ɔ, ʊ] were generally spelt <i/y, e, a, o, u> respectively.

The long vowels [iː, eː, ɛː, aː, ɔː, oː, uː] were generally spelt <i/y/, e/ee, e/ee, a/aa, o/oo, o/oo, ou/ow> respectively.

It is often the case that single vowels before single or double consonants were short, if they are still short vowels in PDE, and that single vowels or 'digraphs' were long if they remain long today. Thus the PDE system remains a good guide to the length of vowels in ME. There are some exceptions to this general rule, such as words spelled with <ea> in PDE that are now short, but in ME were pronounced with the long vowel [ɛː], for example *dead*, *breath*. Another exception concerns words spelled with <oo> in PDE. In ME all such words were pronounced with the long vowel [oː], although some, such as *good* and *foot*, have since become short, while others, for example *food*, have remained long.

You will notice from the above that there were two long vowel sounds represented by the spellings <e/ee> in ME: [eː, ɛː]. This use of a single spelling for two sounds can be confusing when reading Chaucer, although once again PDE spelling practices come to our aid. In most cases the sound [e:] was used in words with PDE <e, ee>, such as *green*, *free* and so on, while the [ɛ:] sound was found in words now spelled with <ea>, for example *death*, *heath*. It is important to remember, however, that this correspondence is concerned with the *distribution* of these different vowels, not the vowels themselves. Subsequent sound changes have obscured these correspondences, so that the Chaucerian distinction between [me:tən] *meet* and [mɛ:tə] *meat* has now been lost and both words are pronounced with [i:], although relics such as *great* and *break* can help to remind us that such words were once pronounced differently.

A similar situation is found with the two long vowel sounds represented by <o, oo>: [ɔ:, o:]. The vowel [o:] should be used in words that are pronounced in many accents with [u:, u, ʌ] in PDE, that is words like *mood*, *good* and *blood* respectively. The vowel [ɔ:] should be used in words that are now pronounced with [əʊ], words like *boat* and *holy*.

Table 4.1 Comparison of ME and PDE vowels

ME	Pronunciation	ME spelling	PDE	PDE example
[ɪ]	*sit*	kyng, is	[ɪ]	king, is
[ɛ]	*bet*	bed	[ɛ]	bed
[a]	*man*	nat	[æ]	cat
[ɔ]	*hot*	oft	[ɒ]	hot
[ʊ]	*put*	but, sonne	[ʊ, ʌ]	but, sun
[i:]	*bee*	wyf, wif	[aɪ]	wife
[e:]	*fate*	mete	[i:]	meet
[ɛ:]	*fare*	mete	[i:]	meat
[a:]	*father*	name, taak	[eɪ]	name
[u:]	*goose*	toun, town	[aʊ]	town
[o:]	*vote*	mo(o)d	[u:]	mood
[ɔ:]	*hoard*	bo(o)t	[əʊ]	boat

Diphthongs

ME	ME spelling	ME examples
[aɪ]	<ai, ay, ei, ey>	day, wey
[ɔɪ]	<oi, oy>	joye, Troie
[ʊɪ]	<oi, oy>	destroye, anoye
[aʊ]	<au>	taught, lawe
[ɔʊ]	<ow>	knowe, trowe
[ɛʊ]	<ew>	lewed, fewe*
[ɪʊ]	<ew>	newe, trewe

Note: Very few words were pronounced with [ɛʊ] in ME; the most common examples are *lewed*, *fewe*, *shewe*, *beautee*.

Table 4.1 presents a comparison of these ME sounds with their PDE equivalents, as well as some examples of their use and spelling. It is intended to provide a helpful summary of the information discussed above, as well as a basic guide to the pronunciation of Chaucer's vowels.

In unstressed syllables, like the <e> in the second syllable of *wynne*, the vowel now known as schwa [ə] was used, pronounced as the final unstressed sound in *china*. This sound was generally spelled <e>, although <i, y> were also possible alternatives. Spellings with <i, y> could also reflect a slightly different pronunciation, as is implied by their use in rhyme with words like *is*, *Alis* (D 40, 319) and so on. While such spellings were most common in northern dialects of ME, they were used frequently by earlier London poets and were clearly acceptable variant pronunciations during Chaucer's lifetime.

Consonants

As we have already noted above, the system of consonants used by Chaucer does not differ substantially from that of PDE. There are, however, some important differences in the way these spellings were pronounced in ME. Perhaps most important is the fact that there were no silent letters in ME as there are in PDE. We have already noted in our discussion of *knight* that both <k> and <gh> were pronounced. However, the pronunciation of <gh> varies according to its use. Where <gh> appears after a front vowel, as in *knight*, it is pronounced as [ç] as in German *nicht*, where it is after a back vowel as in *thoght*, it is pronounced as [x], like Scots *loch*. All consonant clusters are pronounced in Chaucer's system, no matter how odd these may sound to our ears, or how difficult they may be for us to get our tongues around. So when we read Chaucer, we must pronounce the initial <w> in words like *write*, the initial <g> in *gnawen*, initial [ʍ] in *which*, <l> in *half*, the <r> in *hard* and the <g> in *ring*. While many of these pronunciations may seem unusual to us today, some do survive in certain dialects of English, and in Scots. For example, compare these Chaucerian usages with northern English pronunciations of *singing*, and with Scots and General American *hard*, and Scots *which*.

Another difference between the pronunciation of ME and PDE concerns the pronunciation of the <f> and <s> at the ends of words like *his*, *was*, *of*. This group of weakly stressed grammatical words are all pronounced with a [z] or a [v] sound in PDE, whereas in Chaucer's language the pronunciation would have followed the spelling, as is shown by rhymes such as 'was: cas', 'was: glas'. The same process has also affected the initial <th> sound in the words *the*, *this*, *that*, which in Chaucer's accent were all pronounced with the sound like that in *thin*.

Other slight differences concern the pronunciation of words derived from French. Initial <h> was not pronounced in French words, as in Modern French words like *hôtel*, and as is often implied by the ME spelling, for example *onour* 'honour', *oost* 'host', nor was the <g> in words like *compaignye*, which is also spelled without the <g> as *companye* and rhymes with words like *hostelrye*. In French words spelled with <gh> in PDE, such as *delight*, the <gh> is not pronounced, as is shown by their ME spellings, for example *delit*, and their use in rhyme, for example 'delit: despit' (F 1371–2). These differences should present students of Chaucer with few difficulties in reading Chaucer aloud.

There are few major differences between the alphabet used in Chaucer's ME and that of PDE. A letter known as 'thorn', written <þ>, which was used in Old English, continued to appear in ME as an alternative to <th>. The Old English letter 'yogh', <ȝ>, also continued to be used throughout the Middle English period, to represent a number of different sounds depending on its position in the word. Where 'yogh' is used at the beginning of words, it is pronounced like an initial <y> in words like *year*. It can also appear in the middle of words, where it is used as an alternative to <gh>, and pronounced like the <ch> in Scots *loch*. The letters <ȝ> and <þ> are often replaced by modern editors with their PDE equivalents and so will not generally trouble students of Chaucer.

The letters <u> and <v> had a different distribution in Chaucerian ME than in PDE, although this difference is often removed by modern editors. In ME both letters could be used to represent both the vowel and consonant sounds, with the choice between them governed by their position in the word. The letter <v> tended to be used in initial position, for example *vp*, *vntil*, and <u> was used medially, for example *loue*, *euery*. The letters <y> and <i> were also used interchangeably in ME to represent the same sound, [i], with the choice of letter often conditioned by the immediate environment. The letter <y> was often used alongside the letters <u, n, m> which were written as a series of minim strokes, short vertical strokes similar to the letter <i>, which could otherwise be confusing. The avoidance of this potential confusion explains the ME practice of using <o> in such environments instead of the more common <u>, in words like *sonne* and *loue*, where a number of minims could also result in confusion.

Patterns of stress

The major difference between Chaucer's ME and PDE concerns the stressing of words derived from French, many of which retained their native stress patterns. For example, the word *corage* is derived from French and Chaucer's use of the word in rhyme shows that it retained its French stress pattern, with accent on the second syllable, in contrast to our PDE pronunciation of its reflex *courage*. A good example of this is found at the opening of the General Prologue, where the use of French words with French pronunciations adds to the high style of this important opening passage:

> Redy to wenden on my pilgrymage
> To Caunterbury with ful devout corage   (A 21–2)

Some French words could be pronounced with stress on either the first or the second syllable. A similar situation is found in PDE in the variant pronunciations of words like *research*, which may have stress on either the initial or second syllable. So while the word *manere* is stressed on the second syllable when rhyming with words like *chiere*, *heere*, *deere*, it can also be pronounced with initial stress when not in rhyme, for example A 71. Other examples are the words *vertu* and *nature*, which may be stressed either way, according to the demands of metre and rhyme. A similar kind of variation is also found, less commonly, with words of native origin. For instance, the word *millere* is used in rhyme with stress on the second syllable, while it has initial stress elsewhere. Compare, for instance, the following examples of its use:

> What sholde I moore seyn, but this Millere
> He nolde his wordes for no man forbere,   (A 3167–8)

> The Millere, that for dronken was al pale   (A 3120)

There are even instances where Chaucer draws on a pronunciation of present participles with stress on the second syllable for the purposes of rhyme, as follows:

> Sownynge alwey th'encrees of his wynnyng.
> He wolde the see were kept for any thyng (A 275–6)

Some scholars have suggested that such rhymes indicate Chaucer invoking a poetic licence, although it is instructive that such rhymes were already common in works written in London before Chaucer.

There are many other aspects of pronunciation studied by modern linguists that cannot be reconstructed for Chaucer's ME, given the limitations of the evidence. These features include things like intonation, pitch and voice quality, which cannot be reconstructed from purely written evidence. Chaucer does make some glancing references to these features of pronunciation, revealing an awareness of them, as in his reference to the lisping Friar's 'sweete' voice quality in the General Prologue (A 264–5) and the 'soft' speech of the Friar of the Summoner's Tale (D 1771). One final factor which may affect pronunciation in ME, as in PDE, is drunkenness, as the Miller is only too aware:

> But first I make a protestacioun
> That I am dronke; I knowe it by my soun.
> And therfore if that I mysspeke or seye,
> Wyte it the ale of Southwerk, I you preye.
>
> (A 3137–40)

Variation

I mentioned earlier that Chaucer used the London dialect of Middle English, and this has implications for our understanding of his poetic practices. An important feature of the London dialect in this period is its variety, which is a direct result of its prominence as a metropolitan centre. During the fourteenth century there was a large amount of immigration into London from all over the country, which had a huge impact upon the language spoken in the capital. London English began to adopt features of the dialects spoken by these immigrants, bringing about a number of important changes, many of which will be discussed elsewhere in this book. One implication of this process of immigration is that the London dialect came into contact with different accents of English that had alternative pronunciations to Chaucer's own. For instance, in an official London document from the Mayor's office, dated 1422, the writer uses the form *gayttys* 'goats'. Chaucer's own spelling of this word was *goot*, a spelling which reflects a southern pronunciation. The spelling *gayttys* shows a pronunciation which was largely restricted to northern dialects during this period. The fact that the form was used in an official London record demonstrates the level of acceptance of this kind of variation within London English of this period.

Variation in pronunciation of this kind was particularly useful for a poet writing rhyming verse, as it provided greater flexibility in finding rhyme words. This is a feature of the London dialect that Chaucer exploited for exactly this reason, as can be seen by looking at his employment of certain variant forms. A simple example of this kind of variation concerns the use of either <a> or <o> in words like *hand* and *land*. Chaucer draws on this variation in rhyme, allowing him to rhyme *hand* with both *garland* and *bond*, as in the following examples:

> That wered of yelewe gooldes a gerland,
> And a cokkow sittynge on hir hand;   (A 1929–30)

> Com neer, and taak youre lady by the hond.
> Bitwixen hem was maad anon the bond   (A 3093–4)

In the above discussion of Chaucer's sound system, we looked at the distinction between variant pronunciations of long *o* and long *e*. However, this distinction is not always maintained by Chaucer and there are certain cases where Chaucer rhymes the two variant pronunciations. Compare, for example, the following couplet that rhymes *do* and *so*, despite the fact that these were pronounced with [o:] and [ɔ:] respectively in Chaucer's system:

> And for to pleye as he was wont to do;
> For in this world he loved no man so,   (A 1195–6)

In a similar way, the distinction between the vowel sounds of *bifore* and *moore* is ignored by Chaucer when rhyming these two words in a couplet that occurs several times in his verse:

And tolde hire al the cas, as ye bifore
Han herd; nat nedeth for to telle it moore. (C 229–30)

Compare similar pairs of lines with the same rhymes in the Franklin's Tale at F 1465–6 and F 1593–4.

Chaucer's exploitation of these variant pronunciations of long *o* is paralleled in his treatment of certain words with the long *e* vowels. For instance, the following couplet shows the word *street*, which normally rhymes on the [e:], rhyming with the vowel [ɛ:].

And criden 'Out' and 'Harrow' in the strete.
The neighebores, bothe smale and grete, (A 3825–6)

We might also compare the rhyming of *dede* 'deed', which usually rhymes on [e:], with the [ɛ:] sound in *rede* 'red':

Out renneth blood on bothe hir sydes rede.
Som tyme an ende ther is of every dede. (A 2635–6)

These examples show that, even though Chaucer probably did not use such variant pronunciations himself, he heard them spoken around him on the streets of London, and drew upon them as convenient alternatives in his rhymes.

A similar kind of situation may be demonstrated by examining a group of words with variant spellings and pronunciations in different dialects of ME. This group of words includes *merry*, *busy*, *church*, *hill*, which all had the same vowel sound in Old English. The East Midlands dialect of ME, which included that of London, pronounced this group of words with [ɪ, i:] and spelled them with an <i> or a <y>. In the West Midlands, these words were spelled with <u>, while in the southeast and East Anglia they were spelled with <e>. As a result of immigration into the capital from these various areas, all three pronunciations and spellings were available in the London dialect and Chaucer used all three. The distribution of these different spellings across Chaucer's works shows that he drew on these variant forms for the purposes of rhyme, as may be shown by the following examples concerning the word *merry*:

And thus I lete hym sitte upon the pyrie,
And Januarie and May romynge myrie. (E 2217–8)

Whan that we come agayn fro Caunterbury.
And for to make yow the moore mury,   (A 801–2)

His palfrey was as broun as is a berye.
A Frere ther was, a wantowne and a merye.   (A 207–8)

It is apparent that Chaucer drew on different pronunciations of this word depending on the rhyme word, an option which was clearly of considerable benefit to him as a poet.

Some words are used most frequently in their East Midland spelling, but appear occasionally in their southeastern form in rhyme. An example of this is found in the forms of the word *thin*, which is commonly used in rhyme in the form *thynne* (for example G 740–1 'wynne: thynne'), but also appears in a single instance in rhyme in the form *thenne* (A 4065–6 'renne: thenne'). A similar example is found in the spellings of the word *dint*, which appears within the line and in rhyme in its East Midland spelling *dynt* (for example D 276, HF 534), but also appears in one instance in rhyme in its southeastern form *dent*, rhyming with *yblent* (A 3807–8). These examples suggest that Chaucer preferred to use the form with <i, y>, but would use the <e> forms when the rhyme scheme demanded it.

A similar distribution is found with the spellings of the word *kin*, which is found just once with the spelling *ken* in rhyme, in the *Book of the Duchess* (lines 437–8). This poem is one of Chaucer's early works and it is probable that he was willing to use this variant early on in his career, but subsequently dropped it in favour of the more common *kyn*. Similarly, the spelling *stere* is limited to appearances in rhyme in *Troilus and Criseyde* (3.910, 4.1451) and does not appear elsewhere in Chaucer's works. It seems that Chaucer favoured the East Midland spelling *stire* and that the use of *stere* in the *Troilus* was necessitated by the demands of a more complex rhyme scheme. The fact that the spelling *stente* is only recorded in rhyme in the Knight's, Clerk's and Monk's Tales may be explained in a similar way. The Clerk's and Monk's Tales both employ rhyme schemes which are more demanding in terms of finding rhyme words, while the Knight's Tale is known to have been composed early in Chaucer's career. This distribution in the *Canterbury Tales* appears to be reinforced by the use of the form *stente* in Chaucer's other works. This form appears in rhyme in a total of 10 instances in

Troilus and Criseyde, often rhyming with the common words *wente*, *sente* (for example 4.340). Other appearances of the form in Chaucer's works are two instances in the *Book of the Duchess*, where *stente* rhymes with the verb *wente* (BD 153–4, 357–8). This distribution outside the *Canterbury Tales* seems to reinforce the use of *stente* observed above. It appears to be restricted to certain rhyming contexts, such as *stente*: *wente*: *sente*, and is found only in earlier works and those composed in more demanding verse forms, such as the rhyme royal of the *Troilus*.

So the variation inherent within the London dialect of this period furnished Chaucer with a useful tool, providing variant forms that could be exploited for rhyming purposes. The status of these variants appears to have varied and to have been subject to change, highlighting the dynamic nature of fourteenth-century London English and Chaucer's response to such changes. There are a handful of other variants that, although found in earlier London writings, cannot be explained with reference to dialectal variation. A good example are the half-rhymes that appear sporadically in Chaucer's verse, but which are a common feature of earlier London works, for example *sike*: *endite* (TC 2.884–6), *abiden*: *yeden* (TC 2.935–6).

As well as tolerating variation in pronunciation, we have seen that the London dialect of ME also allowed spelling variation, and this is also reflected in Chaucer's works. For example, a common word like *not* appears in two different spellings in the *Canterbury Tales*, *nat* and *noght*, and there is no evidence that Chaucer preferred one form over the other. There are two different spellings of the word 'though', *thogh* and *though*, and the two appear to have been interchangeable. An older form of 'though', *theigh*, is also found in some Chaucer manuscripts but not in others. This form was evidently less acceptable than the others and was in the process of being replaced by the more common spellings *thogh* and *though*.

While these variants appear to have been used without significance, Chaucer did draw upon spelling variation for metrical purposes. As an example we can compare the spelling of the word *April* in the opening line of the General Prologue, with a different spelling that appears in *Troilus and Criseyde*:

Whan that Aprill with his shoures soote (A 1)

Of Aperil, when clothed is the mede (*Troilus and Criseyde* 1.156)

The difference in the two spellings allows Chaucer to use both disyllabic and trisyllabic forms as necessary. It is impossible to deduce
from this evidence which was Chaucer's preferred form, if indeed he
had a single preferred form. What we can say for certain is that variation in spelling of this kind was exploited by Chaucer to suit the
demands of his metre: a disyllabic or trisyllabic form could be
selected according to need.

A similar situation is found in the use of two variant spellings of
guiltless, with differing numbers of syllables:

And ofte tymes giltelees, pardee.   (A 1312)

That giltlees were? By yow I seye the same,   (G 1005)

In each of the above examples the differences in spelling reflect
distinct pronunciations of the word. In the following examples we
can see how Chaucer selected different forms of the verb *had* to
enable particular rhymes:

And therto brood, as though it were a spade.
Upon the cop right of his nose he hade   (A 553–4)

By ounces henge his lokkes that he hadde,
And therwith he his shuldres overspradde;   (A 677–8)

Have ye nat seyn somtyme a pale face,
Among a prees, of hym that hath be lad
Toward his deeth, wher as hym gat no grace,
And swich a colour in his face hath had
Men myghte knowe his face that was bistad   (B1 645–9)

Despite all this variation and its availability to Chaucer for rhyming
purposes, he still complained about the scarcity of rhyme words in
English, as compared to French: 'Syth rym in Englissh hath such
skarsete' (*Complaint of Venus*, 80).

Further reading

Basic descriptions of Chaucerian pronunciation can be found in editions of
Chaucer's works, such as that by Norman Davis in the *Riverside Chaucer*

(Benson 1988, xxv–xli). A useful general guide is provided in a short pamphlet by Kökeritz (1978). There is a more advanced discussion in Part 1 of Sandved (1985). More detailed information concerning the different systems of pronunciation operating in ME can be found in Horobin and Smith (2002, Chapter 4). For more advanced discussions of the reconstruction of ME phonology and the relationship between speech and writing, see Smith (1996, Chapter 2) and Samuels (1972, Chapter 1).

When learning to read Chaucer aloud, it is especially valuable to have access to recordings of his works read by experts, and many of these are now freely available on the World Wide Web. The Chaucer pages at Harvard University contain a pronunciation tutorial with detailed examples, accompanied by sound files giving examples of individual words and complete lines, as well as a reading of the short poem 'Truth': (http://icg.fas.harvard. edu/~chaucer/pronunciation/section1.html). A number of extracts from Chaucer's works read by various scholars can be accessed from the links listed on the Chaucer Metapage (http://academics.vmi.edu/ english/audio/ audio_index.html). Recordings of readings of complete poems have been produced by the Chaucer Studio, and can be downloaded or purchased on cassette from their website (http://english.byu.edu/ chaucer/). The Chaucer Studio cassettes are also available for purchase from bookshops.

5   Vocabulary

The words that make up the vocabulary, or lexicon, of Middle English are derived from four main sources: Old English, Old Norse, French and Latin. The words inherited from OE comprise the core of ME vocabulary and many of these words survive into PDE. These include many core vocabulary items such as the kinship terms *father*, *mother*, *brother* and *sister*. Other words have been introduced as a result of 'borrowing', a term used by linguists to describe the process whereby a language adopts a word from another language, although it is not an entirely appropriate one as the word is, of course, never returned. The kinds of words borrowed from these languages differ according to the kind of contact, and the subsequent interaction between the donor and recipient languages.

In many cases borrowing is a straightforward process in which a new word is adopted in order to express a new concept. However, there are also instances where new words are borrowed whose meanings overlap with existing words in the language. In response to this overlap, the meaning of one or both words may change to create a distinction, or a distinction in connotation or register may be introduced. The first process is demonstrated in the case of the English words *skirt* and *shirt*. The word *skirt* was borrowed from Old Norse and had the same meaning as the Old English *shirt*, with both words deriving ultimately from the same Germanic form. Once the ON word was borrowed, it developed a different meaning so as to distinguish it from the existing word *shirt*, a distinction still found in PDE. The second process is demonstrated by the adoption of the French verb *commence* in the ME period. This verb's meaning overlapped considerably with the existing verb *begin*, derived from OE, and was distinguished according to register rather than meaning. This register distinction is still found in PDE, as can be seen from the difference in formality between the two sentences: 'You may commence' and 'You may begin'.

OE does not appear to have been susceptible to the borrowing of words from other languages, and only a few loanwords appear in OE. These include words of Latin origin, such as *abbod* 'abbot', *deofol* 'devil', *engel* 'angel' and *cirice* 'church', whose adoption is evidently related to the introduction and spread of Christianity. It is likely that words of ON origin were also adopted into OE, as a result of the Scandinavian invasions and settlement, although there are few examples of these in the OE written records. ON words recorded in OE belong to a specialized register associated particularly with the Viking invasions, comprising words like *griþ* 'truce', *liþsmenn* 'sailors' and *utlaga* 'outlaw'. New words in OE were generally formed through the processes of compounding or affixation, in which new words were created from existing words within the language. 'Compounding' is a process whereby two words are joined together to produce a new word, as in the PDE formation *railway*, and as in the OE examples *sciprap* 'cable', a combination of *scip* 'ship' and *rap* 'rope'. 'Affixation' refers to the process whereby new words are formed through the addition of prefixes or suffixes to existing words. OE examples of this process include *ingan*, a combination of *in+gan* meaning 'enter', and *freondlic*, 'friendly', comprised of *freond+lic*.

In the Middle English period, the main source of new words was the borrowing of words from other languages; partly the result of the increased contact with other languages. It is during the ME period that the impact of ON on the English lexicon becomes apparent, although it is likely that many ON words were first borrowed in the OE period but remained part of the spoken, rather than the written, language. Old Norse is a Germanic language and thus shares a number of similarities with Old English. Because of these similarities, and the extended period of Viking settlement in England, Middle English shows the adoption of a considerable number of words borrowed from Old Norse. Many of the words derived from ON in ME were everyday words which became thoroughly assimilated into the English lexicon. These words often describe concepts which are basic to English language and culture, words like *egg*, *husband*, *knife*, *leg*, *neck*, *take*, *Thursday*, *ugly*, *want*, *window*. Because of a major pronunciation difference between ON and OE, many of the English words which begin *sk-* are derived from Old Norse, for example *sky*, *skin*, *skill*. The interaction between Old Norse and Middle English also led to the adoption into ME of the

ON third person plural pronouns, *they*, *their* and *them*, which were borrowed to remedy a lack of distinctiveness in the OE derived paradigm, and the present plural form of the verb *be*: *are* is also of ON derivation.

The adoption of ON vocabulary in ME varied according to geography, reflecting the patterns of Viking settlement in the Anglo-Saxon period. A result of this is that the adoption of ON borrowings differs according to dialect, with the dialects of the north and East Midlands showing the greatest number of ON loans. Thus ON borrowings such as *slik* 'such', *starn* 'star', and *kirk* 'church' are features of northern and eastern dialects, while the southern and western dialects continued to use the OE equivalents *swich*, *sterre* and *chirch*.

The number of words derived from Latin in the ME period is comparatively small, and these words tend to be associated with specialized areas such as religion and learning, including words like *scripture*, *history* and *allegory*. The use of Latin alongside French in the English administration also led to the adoption of Latin words in this area; examples include *client*, *conviction* and *executor*. Many words of Latin origin in ME entered English via French, and it is often difficult to determine whether a word was borrowed from Latin or French. This is because adjustments made to the form of Latin words in ME may in fact reflect earlier adjustments in the borrowing of such words into French. An example of this problem is presented by the verb *enclinen*, which may be spelled either *enclinen* or *inclinen* in Middle English. This variation means that it is difficult to determine whether it derives from French *encliner* or from Latin *inclinare*.

In the fifteenth century, a style of writing emerged known as 'aureate diction', which employed numerous Latinate words to create an elevated style. While this style was artificial and poetic, and many of the words introduced in such works have not been adopted into English, it does prefigure the process of classical borrowing which occurred on a much larger scale in the Early Modern English (EModE) period. During the EModE period large numbers of Latin words were adopted in English, a direct result of the revival of interest in classical texts and learning associated with the Renaissance. In addition to the need for new words to express new concepts, this period also witnessed the adoption of Latinate words as an ostentatious display of learning. Such words were branded 'inkhorn terms' by the opponents of such practices, who were concerned with restricting the number of needless borrowings from foreign sources.

The largest group of words borrowed in the ME period is from French, a direct result of the Norman Conquest and the imposition of French culture and government that followed. Borrowing of words from French during the Middle English period can be divided into two main stages. During the first stage, borrowed words are of Norman French origin and often relate to areas of most importance to the Norman conquerors. This includes words relating to the law and government, such as *justice*, *chancellor*, *prison*, *noble*, *crime*, *court*, although the words *law* and *by-law* are both of ON derivation. Another area which saw the importing of large numbers of French words was the church; during this period we see the first use of words such as *mercy*, *pity*, *preach*, *clergy* and many other words of this kind. In some cases the Norman French origin of a word is still apparent in its English form, as in the ME *werre* 'war', which is derived from Norman French *werre* rather than the standard French form *guerre*. In other cases both Norman French and central French forms have been adopted into English, as in the case of *warranty* and *guarantee*, where the former term has become restricted to specialized legal contexts.

In the second stage of borrowing, we see the introduction of words from the central French dialect which are not restricted to any specific area. As French speakers remained the aristocratic class during this period, it is not surprising that these words generally relate to refined and elevated areas of English culture, including the arts, for example *paint*, *music*, *verse*; fashion, for example *robe*, *gown*; and food for example *mutton*, *beef*. It is during this second stage of borrowing that the greatest number of French borrowings occurred, peaking around 1400, and then dropping off in the fifteenth century. While many of the French words borrowed in the ME period were stylistically elevated, a number were also quickly assimilated into the language. This is demonstrated by the practice of 'derivation', in which these French borrowings were subjected to the processes of compounding and affixation described above. For example, the word *gentle* is a French borrowing which was combined with other English words to produce new terms, such as *gentleman* and *gentlewoman*, while many French adjectives formed adverbs through the addition of the English ending *-ly*, for example *courteously*. Similarly, French endings were added to English words to create new formations. The French ending *-able*, found in French words like *reasonable*, was added to English roots to produce new

adjectives such as *believable* and *knowable*. The profound way in
which French affected ME vocabulary is also demonstrated by the
replacement of OE words with French synonyms, especially in core
concepts such as kinship terms, for example *uncle*, *aunt*, *nephew*,
niece and *cousin* are all of French origin. The number and nature of
French borrowings in this period often varies according to the type
of text. Courtly literary works tend to employ many more French
loans, and this is particularly true of works which are translations of
French originals.

A small number of words of Celtic origin are first recorded in ME,
although they are likely to have been used in the spoken language in
the OE period. These include words associated with Celtic culture,
such as *bard* and *clan*, as well as topographic terms, such as *crag* and
glen. Trading links with the Low Countries led to the introduction of
a number of words of Middle Dutch origin into ME. These words are
generally concerned with trade and shipping, and include *skipper*,
pump, *bung*, *grot* and *tub*.

Chaucer's lexicon

Now that we have examined the origins of the ME lexicon, we can
turn to a consideration of Chaucer's vocabulary. As we might expect
from the above discussion, Chaucer's vocabulary consists of words
derived from each of the languages which contributed to the ME
lexicon. To consider the significance of these groups of borrowings
we will examine each in turn.

A large proportion of Chaucer's vocabulary is made up of words
of OE origin, and these tend to be words that make up the core of his
vocabulary, words used frequently which refer to everyday concepts.
However, even in this area of the lexicon French influence can be
seen, and in some cases Chaucer uses both French and OE
synonyms. For example, Chaucer uses the OE *em* alongside *uncle*,
even though the French word had been available in ME since at least
1300. Chaucer's exploitation of such pairs of words is worth investigating more fully, as the choice between an OE or a French synonym
in a particular context provides useful evidence concerning their
relative status. A good example of such a pair are the words *stevene*,
inherited from OE, and *vois*, borrowed from French. *Vois* is the more
common form in Chaucer, with *stevene* appearing just four times in

the *Canterbury Tales*. The French loan is recorded in ME from 1300, so Chaucer's use of the OE *stevene* seems likely to be marked in some way. These uses of the word *stevene* seem not to be designed to achieve a particularly archaistic effect but to be for metrical reasons. In each case the word appears in rhyme with the word *hevene*, suggesting that Chaucer's usual word was *vois* but that he was willing to employ *stevene* as a metrical convenience.

A similar pair are the words *routhe* and *pitee*, both of which can be used to mean 'compassion', 'sorrow' or 'grief'. *Pitee* is of French origin and is the more common of the two, appearing 52 times in the *Canterbury Tales*, where the OE *routhe* appears 19 times. There seems to be little semantic distinction between the two words in Chaucer's usage, as is seen in several instances where both are used together as doublets, for example 'for routhe and for pitee' (E 893), 'but he hadde rowthe/And pitee of my sorwes smerte' (BD 592–3). Of these 19 instances of *routhe*, seven are in rhyme, suggesting that the choice between them may be partly one of metrical convenience as we saw with the use of *stevene*.

It is interesting to compare the use of these two synonyms with another word that has a similar semantic range. This is the word *misericorde* which means 'compassion, mercy, pity'. However, despite the similar range of meanings, the occurrences of this word are almost exclusively restricted to religious contexts. It appears in the Tale of Melibee to describe Christ's 'erys of misericorde', and in the Summoner's Tale the work of friars is said to include 'wepynge, misericorde, and clennesse' (D 1910). It is also used in Chaucer's *ABC*, where he refers to the Virgin Mary as 'thou queen of misericorde' (*ABC* 25). This word is evidently a specialized term belonging to religious discourse, as is further indicated by the Parson's use of the word 11 times, including a detailed discussion of the quality of *misericorde*, its origins in Christ, who 'suffred deeth for misericorde', and its relationship to *pitee* (I 805–10). An awareness of this specialized usage, and its peculiarly religious associations, makes its sole appearance in a non-religious context all the more striking. Criseyde's response to Troilus' begging for mercy in Book 3 employs this word in a secular context, although perhaps responding to Troilus' spiritualizing of his emotions: 'Of gilt misericorde!/That is to seyn, that I foryeve al this' (3.1177–8).

Another word whose meaning overlaps with this group is *debonairete*, as indicated by its use alongside *pitee* in the Tale of

Melibee, describing acts of Christian charity (B2 2811). But this word also seems frequently to be restricted to religious contexts: seven of its nine occurrences are in the Parson's Tale. By studying the distribution of groups of synonyms in this way, we can build up an understanding of the relative status and connotations of Chaucer's words, the kinds of association they had for him and his contemporary audience.

As well as exploiting the native lexicon to provide synonyms that could be used in rhyme, Chaucer also drew upon words derived from OE in other interesting ways. While it is certainly true that many of the OE words used by Chaucer were unmarked everyday terms, it is important not to overstate this claim. There are a number of technical words derived from OE, whose use by Chaucer provides an interesting insight into his stylistic practices. According to the *MED*, Chaucer is the first ME writer to use a number of words that appeared in Old English but were not used by earlier ME authors. For example, the *MED* cites the Parson's Tale as the earliest use of the word *thurrok*, a technical term for the hold or bilge of a ship. Chaucer evidently recognized the word's technical status, as he supplied it with a gloss the first time he used it: 'the smale dropes of water, that entren thurgh a litel crevace into the thurrok, and in the botme of the ship' (I 363). Having introduced this unfamiliar word in this way, Chaucer evidently felt able to use it in a figurative sense later in the same text, where *ydelnesse* is described as 'the thurrok of alle wikked and vileyns thoghtes, and of alle jangles, trufles, and of alle ordure' (I 714).

Another technical shipping term whose first literary appearance is in Chaucer's works is the word *last*, which refers to a ship's load, as well as to a measure of wool. Chaucer worked as controller of the wool customs and it is likely that his knowledge of this word derives from this connection. While Chaucer's use of the word is the earliest literary example, there are numerous contemporary appearances of this word in official documents, demonstrating its use in technical contexts. Given the word's connection with shipping, it is interesting that Chaucer's only use of the word is in the host's response to the Shipman's Tale of the cheating and adulterous monk. The host praises the shipman for his tale and then pronounces a curse upon the monk: 'God yeve the monk a thousand last quade yeer!' (B2 1628), which may be translated 'God give the monk lots of bad years'. But it seems particularly appropriate that the host should choose the technical shipping term *last*, so that the phrase means more specifically 'a ship load of bad years'.

Another example of Chaucer's practice of drawing upon words belonging to specialized registers is found in the Host's use of the word *drasty* in his brusque interruption of Chaucer the pilgrim's Tale of Sir Thopas: 'Myne eres aken of thy drasty speche', 'Thy drasty rymyng is nat worth a toord!' (B2 2113, 2120). These two occurrences of this word are the only uses Chaucer makes of it, suggesting that it was not a word in widespread use. This is backed up the evidence of the *MED*, which records just three other instances, where *drasty* is used in more specialized contexts to refer to sediment or dregs. The evidence suggests that *drasty* was a word associated exclusively with the process of fermentation, used by brewers to refer to the sediment or dregs at the bottom of the barrel, and is thus a particularly appropriate adjective to be used by the taverner Harry Bailly. Chaucer's innovation is taking a word that was a specialized brewing term and reappropriating it as a term of literary criticism and putting it in the mouth of an innkeeper.

I mentioned earlier that OE favoured the processes of affixation and compounding for the coining of new words, and Chaucer employed a number of words formed in this manner. The prefix *for-* was added to verbs in OE to add greater intensity to the verb's meaning, and is found in verbs like *fordronke* 'completely drunk' (C 674), *forlost* 'disgraced' (TC 4.756) and *fortroden* 'trampled upon' (I 190). Despite the traditional nature of such formations, Chaucer exploited this method of word formation so that a number of such words make their first appearance in his works. For instance, Chaucer's use of *forwrapped* in the Parson's Tale (I 320), where it describes covering up a sin instead of openly confessing, is the first attestation of this word, which may have been coined for this particular occasion. The verb *forwelked*, meaning 'withered' or 'shrivelled up', is first used by Chaucer in the *Romaunt* (RR 361), where it describes the personification of *Elde* 'Old Age' in a memorable description. The only other appearance of the word in ME is by John Lydgate, and it is probable that Lydgate's knowledge of the word derives from Chaucer's earlier work. The verb *forsongen*, meaning 'completely exhausted from singing', is recorded just once in ME in Chaucer's *Romaunt* (RR 664), and also seems likely to have been coined by Chaucer for this specific occasion. Another example from the *Romaunt* (RR 323), *forcracchen* or 'severely scratched', shows just how useful Chaucer found this method of word formation early in his career. Chaucer's is the first attestation of the verb *forpassing*, meaning 'surpassing', which he uses just once, in the first of the descriptions of Criseyde: 'Nas noon so fair, forpassynge every wight' (1.101). The phrase 'al hoors forshright', 'hoarse and exhausted from shrieking', is a particularly apt description of Criseyde's tearful response to *Troilus*, and the earliest use of the word *forshright* (4.1147).

A particularly nice example of Chaucer's ability to exploit this method of word formation to produce striking effects is found in the short poem 'The Former Age'. This poem begins by describing a golden age that is past, where people had simple tastes and needs and were not *forpampred with outrage* (line 5), 'overpampered with excess'. This is the only instance of this word in ME, and its suitability in this specific context makes it seem likely that Chaucer coined it specifically for this occasion. Other examples of words formed in this way are recorded first in Chaucer but then appear subsequently in other ME texts, such as the word *forbrused* 'severely bruised' (B2 3804). Chaucer is also the first to employ the phrase *forweped and forwaked*, 'exhausted from weeping and lack of sleep' (BD 126), although it appears elsewhere in contemporary texts and is therefore unlikely to be Chaucer's own coinage.

Chaucer's vocabulary comprises a substantial number of words of ON derivation, the majority of which represent core concepts such as *housbonde*, *law*, *sky*, *skile*, *though*. However, as a Londoner, Chaucer did not use the many ON-derived words found in more northerly dialects. Chaucer has OE *swich* not *slik*, *chirch* not *kirk*, *ey* not *egg*, and he used only the nominative third person plural pronoun from ON, *they*, alongside *hem*, not *them*, *hir/her*, not *their*. The only appearance of the forms *them* and *their* in Chaucer's works is in the northern dialect of the students in the Reeve's Tale, indicating that Chaucer considered these forms to be northern, despite the fact that they would replace the OE forms in London English in the fifteenth century. Chaucer appears to have been familiar with some ON words of predominantly northern origin and to have used them only infrequently. A good example is the word *bown*, meaning 'ready' or 'prepared', which has a clear northern provenance in ME and appears just once in Chaucer's works (F 1503). In some cases Chaucer used ON words alongside OE equivalents, for example *same/thilke*; *give/yive*; *against/ayeinst*. Chaucer's preference for the OE form in such cases may be demonstrated by the distribution of the verbs *clepe* and *calle* in Chaucer's works. The OE-derived *clepe* is found on 106 occasions in the *Canterbury Tales*, while *calle* is recorded in 55 instances. More significant is the distribution of these 55 instances. Many examples of *calle* are in rhyme with *alle*, suggesting that Chaucer used the form largely for metrical convenience. *Calle* also appears three times in the speech of the northern students in the Reeve's Tale (A 4111, 4264, 4287), implying that it had northern dialect associations for Chaucer.

In certain cases of pairs of words, or doublets, there was a distinction in meaning or use which is significant for our interpretation of Chaucer's work. As an example we may examine Chaucer's use of the pair *cherl* and *karl*. The first of these words is of OE origin, while the second is from ON. Both words were used by Chaucer to signify a person of low social status, or someone with the lack of manners and morals associated with the peasant class. The Miller and the Reeve are both called *cherls* in the Miller's prologue, while in the Wife of Bath's Tale, the old hag claims that whoever behaves like a peasant is a *cherl*, irrespective of rank: 'He nys nat gentil, be he duc or erl./For vileyns synful dedes make a cherl' (D 1157–8). The word *carl* has a similar range of meanings in ME, but Chaucer used it much less frequently, just four times in the *Canterbury Tales*. The distinction is not one of dialect, as we might expect of a word of ON origin. It is first used in the General Prologue in the description of the Miller, who we are told was a 'stout carl for the nones' (A 545). In the Miller's Tale the carpenter's servant is also described as a *carl* (A 3469). In the Friar's Tale the devil uses the word to refer to a peasant, and in the Pardoner's Tale one of the drunken revellers addresses the old man as *carl* in an extremely rude and brusque greeting. It appears from the restricted uses of the word that Chaucer considered *carl* to be a more contemptuous term of abuse than *cherl*. More specifically, these instances suggest that the use of the word was designed to reflect badly on its user as well as the person to whom it was addressed. This is most clear in the case of the Friar's Tale where it is used by the devil himself, and in the Pardoner's Tale where the debauched young men use it to insult an innocent and elderly man. In the Miller's Tale it is the Miller who uses the word to describe the carpenter's knave, and this is perhaps also designed to reflect on the character of a man who we are told is himself a *carl*. So, while many words of ON origin were everyday, unmarked words, others, like *carl*, appear to have had particular connotations of which we need to be aware.

As in our previous discussion of Chaucer's native vocabulary, it is important not to view all words derived from ON as everyday words. Some Norse words could also have a technical status in certain contexts. For instance, the common English word *happy* is often used by Chaucer with the PDE meaning 'pleased' or 'glad'. But the word is derived from an ON word *hap,* which means 'chance', and in Middle English often has a more specialized sense of 'favoured by fortune', 'lucky', as in the phrase 'his happy day' in *Troilus* (2.621). This meaning does not survive into PDE, except in archaic phrases like 'by happy chance' and in the word *mishap*, an unlucky or unfortunate event. Another example of a word of ON origin, which has technical connotations in Chaucer's works, is the verb *flitte*, meaning 'move, change', which is used frequently in *Boece* and *Troilus* to describe the changeable and unstable nature of Fortune.

In some cases the connotations of a word vary according to the particular context in which it is used, forcing us to be particularly alive to subtle shifts in association and register. An example of this is *semely*, a word of Norse origin used by Chaucer with three main meanings: 'attractive', 'suitable', 'honourable'. In Chaucer's early works, the word *semely* is employed as a conventional epithet of praise, as in the idealized courtly description of Ydelnesse in the *Romaunt of the Rose* (563, 586). There is a single occurrence of the word in another early poem, *The Book of the Duchess*, where the Man in Black describes his lady as 'so semly on to see' (1177). However, Chaucer's subsequent use of the word is more restricted and less clearly an unqualified term of praise. In the *Canterbury Tales* it is used to describe the Host in the General Prologue, a man with aspirations of courtliness but surely not of the same class as the lady White. It is used three times in just 30 lines in the description of the Prioress, referring to the way she sings the liturgy, reaches for her food and the pleating of her wimple. While the Prioress is of a higher social and moral standing than Harry Bailly, the description of her focuses on her misplaced courtly aspirations and satirizes both her worldliness and striving for outdated modes of fashionable behaviour. Perhaps the clearest indication of its lowly and outdated stylistic connotations is found in the use of *semely* to describe Chaucer's anti-hero, Sir Thopas, who had a 'semely nose' (B2 1919).

Discussions of Chaucer's vocabulary have tended to focus most on his borrowings from French, and principally on those French words that are first recorded in his works. Such words have frequently been seen as an index by which we can measure Chaucer's contribution to the establishment of English as a literary language. This approach is most evident in Joseph Mersand's book *Chaucer's Romance Vocabulary* (1937), which calculates that Chaucer's complete vocabulary was 8,072 words, of which 4,189 are derived from Romance sources. Drawing on the evidence of the citations provided by the *Oxford English Dictionary (OED)*, Mersand computed that 1,180 of these words were first recorded in Chaucer's works, and therefore represent Chaucer's 'gifts to the English language' (Mersand, 1937, 56). There are, however, problems with this kind of approach. Mersand's figures were based on the first citations recorded in the *OED*. Many of the words cited as first occurring in Chaucer's works in the *OED* are in fact found in earlier texts, as recorded by the *Middle English Dictionary (MED)*. Mersand's approach also assumes that the earliest use of a particular word will always be recorded in our surviving records, overlooking the likelihood that earlier instances have been lost, and that many words would have been used in speech before they appeared in writing. Another objection to Mersand's approach is the assumption he makes that Chaucer's tendency to borrow words from French and Latin was new, ignoring the fact that earlier ME writers made considerable use of this same practice.

Mersand's statistics also fail to take sufficient account of the question of Chaucer's sources. Where a work is a translation of a French text, as in Chaucer's *Romaunt of the Rose*, it is not surprising that Chaucer borrowed numerous words from his source text. If we look at the vocabulary used by Chaucer in his *Romaunt*, we find a large number of borrowings from French. In just the opening 100 lines we find numerous words derived from French such as *fable*, *apparaunt*, *warraunt*, *avisioun*, *signifiaunce*, *covertly*, *delitous*, *aguyler*, *outrageous*. The presence of these many French loanwords is hardly surprising when we remember that this work is a translation of a French poem, *le Roman de la Rose*. In some instances it is apparent that Chaucer adopted the French word where no suitable English equivalent was available, as in the case of *aguyler*, meaning a 'needle case'. It is interesting to note that when translating the French *aguille* at lines 97 and 100, Chaucer opted for the English word *nedyl*. In addition to such functional borrowings, Chaucer adopted numerous words from his source text into his English translation.

The importance of such borrowings for Chaucer's language and for the English language as a whole is worth investigating in some detail. For instance, the use of *delitous* at line 90 is clearly suggested by the appearance of *deliteus* in the French source, and this is the first occurrence of the word in the *MED*. However, following this introduction into English, the word had a very brief career, appearing just once more in the *Romaunt* (line 489) and then never again in any English work. A similar situation is found with the word *saverous*, used in rhyme with *amorous* in line 84 of the *Romaunt*, the first recorded use in English. However, the word never appears again in Chaucer's works, and its subsequent career is limited to two further appearances in fragment B of the *Romaunt* and a handful of occurrences in later ME texts. Chaucer's use of the word *apparaunt* in line 5 was no doubt influenced by the form *aparent* in *le Roman de la Rose*, and this is the first instance of this word in ME. It seems unlikely, however, that the borrowing was in any way stylistic, but was rather a practical solution to the need to find a rhyme for *warraunt* in the following line. This is reinforced by the fact that the word never appears again in Chaucer's works, suggesting that its use was simply a question of expedience. The adverb *covertly* is suggested by *covertement* in the *Roman* and is the first occurrence of this word in ME. However, Chaucer's decision to adopt this word into his text would have received further encouragement from the existence of the noun *covert*, which is recorded in ME from the middle of the fourteenth century.

Alongside these first occurrences, there are also many instances of French words used by Chaucer that appear in his source text, but which are also found in other earlier, or contemporary, ME texts. For instance, the words *fable*, *signifiaunce*, *avisioun*, *ryme*, *gree*, *mater*, *attempre*, *prys*, *amorous* all appear in Chaucer's source, suggesting that his decision to adopt them was influenced by the French *Roman*. However, these words also appear in earlier ME works, so we cannot see Chaucer's decision to borrow such words as innovative. Of course we do not know whether Chaucer was aware of these earlier uses of these words, and it may be that when he used them in the *Romaunt,* he was unaware of their earlier introduction into English. Nevertheless, it is apparent that, in introducing such words from his source text, Chaucer was simply following a practice of lexical borrowing that he had inherited from earlier vernacular authors. The findings of this analysis of the vocabulary of the first 100 lines of the

Romaunt is representative of much of the remainder of the text. Throughout the text we find Chaucer introducing words from his French source, many of which are recorded in earlier English works in the *MED*. Those words that are first recorded in the *Romaunt* often seem to be borrowed for practical purposes, and many do not reappear in Chaucer's works, such as *delectable*, *endouted*, *habyten*, *resemblable*. Other words represent specialized concepts, adopted for a specific purpose but not required again: words like *alyes* 'service berries', *amourettes* 'love-knots', *date-tree* 'date palm', *scochouns* 'shield-shaped ornaments'. Another feature of many of these words that appear only in the *Romaunt* is that they are frequently in rhyming position, suggesting that Chaucer found it useful to preserve words used in rhyme in the *Roman*. Borrowing of technical terms for specific purposes accounts for a number of Romance words in Chaucer's works. There are many technical hunting terms in the *Book of the Duchess,* which are borrowed from French and do not appear elsewhere in Chaucer's works. These include words such as *embosed* 'taken refuge in a wood', *forloyn* 'a horn call made by a hunter when separated from the rest of the hunt', *lymere* 'a hound trained to be led on a leash', *soures* 'bucks in their fourth year'.

The above discussion emphasizes that, when analysing Chaucer's use of Romance words, it is important that we do not treat all French words used by Chaucer as of equivalent status. The simple fact that a word is of French origin tells us very little about its status in Chaucer's language; we need to consider the word's history and its use, both by Chaucer and his contemporaries. In assessing Chaucer's Romance vocabulary, we must distinguish between French words used by Chaucer that had been borrowed into English early in the ME period and would therefore have been perceived as fully assimilated into the English language, and French words that were more recent borrowings. The importance of this distinction is made apparent by Chaucer's treatment of the French word *seraines* in his translation of the *Roman*. Here Chaucer introduces the word *sereyn*, but prefaces it with an explanation that the English equivalent is *meremaydens* 'mermaids'. Evidently Chaucer felt that the French word *sereyn* would have been unfamiliar to his audience and so he provided an English gloss: 'Though we mermaydens clepe hem here,/In English, as is oure usaunce,/Men clepe hem sereyns in Fraunce' (RR 682–4). Chaucer's concern about his audience's lack of familiarity with *sereyn* is reinforced by the evidence of the *MED*, which shows that this is the earliest recorded use of the word in ME. In contrast, Chaucer's discussion of the word *fruit* shows a French word thoroughly assimilated into the English lexicon. In the Parson's Tale Chaucer refers to the word *fruyt* as the English equivalent of the Latin *fructus* (I 869). The word *fruyt* is ultimately of French origin, although it is recorded in ME from the early thirteenth century, and by Chaucer's time it was clearly well assimilated into the English lexicon. A similar example is found in the Second Nun's Tale, where *peple* is given as the English word for the Greek *leos* (G 106). *Peple* is also a French loanword, but it is one that is found in ME from the late thirteenth century and thus well established within the English lexicon by the late fourteenth century. To these two words we might add a number of others which are of French origin but recorded in English from the twelfth or thirteenth centuries, such as *counseil*, *courteisie*, *debonaire*, *dettour*, *dignite*, *diligence*, *enchesoun* and so on.

So how can we distinguish between French words that were wellestablished parts of the English lexicon and those which were recent acquisitions? An important resource is the *MED*, which provides evidence of a word's history throughout the ME period, allowing us to see when a word was first recorded and assess how widespread it was in the late fourteenth century. However, we must always remember that the earliest recorded usage does not necessarily represent the first time a word was used, nor is the *MED* a complete record of the occurrences of a word in the ME period. While the patchy nature of the written record means that we cannot always be sure that a word is a recent coinage, the *MED* does help us to identify words that were likely to have been considered new to Chaucer's readers. For example, the Old French (OF) loanword *conservacioun* is first recorded in Chaucer's *Boece*, but is also found in several contemporary late fourteenth and fifteenth-century texts. The fact that it does not appear in any earlier texts suggests that it was a recent borrowing, although the contemporary occurrences indicate that Chaucer was not responsible for introducing it into English. The verb *consideren* shows a similar kind of distribution. It is first recorded in Chaucer but also appears in numerous contemporary texts, indicating that it was a recent borrowing in fairly widespread circulation. No doubt Chaucer's adoption of such words helped to secure their future, especially in the works of his followers such as Hoccleve and Lydgate, but he cannot be credited with introducing them into English.

In some cases Chaucer acknowledges the unfamiliarity of certain words by providing a gloss or brief explanation, as in the case of *mansuetude*, meaning 'gentleness' or 'humility'. This word appears for the first time in ME in the Parson's Tale, where its meaning is explained by means of a gloss: 'The remedie agayns Ire is a vertu that men clepen mansuetude, that is debonairetee' (I 654). It is interesting that the gloss provided, *debonairetee* is another French word, but one which is first recorded in *MED* in a text of the mid thirteenth century, indicating that it was a more familiar part of the English lexicon. A similar example is found in Criseyde's use of the word *misericorde* at 3.1177–78. Here Criseyde responds to Troilus begging for mercy by granting him forgiveness in the following terms: 'Of gilt misericorde!/That is to seyn, that I foryeve al this'. Here we see Chaucer using a comparatively rare and technical religious term of French origin in a courtly love context, and providing a gloss to ensure that his readers understood it.

We must also distinguish between those French words that express a concept for which there was no obvious English alternative, and those used in preference to an English synonym for the purpose of stylistic ornament. Earlier we saw that the fourteenth century witnessed a decline in the ability to speak French, and this caused a corresponding increase in the adoption of French words by English speakers as a means of marking their social status. Given that Chaucer wrote courtly literature for an aristocratic audience, it is not surprising that his vocabulary consists of large numbers of words derived from French. French loanwords comprise a large proportion of Chaucer's words concerned with courtly concepts, such as *gentillesse*, *curteisye*, *chivalrye*, *honour*, *pitee*, *mercy*. As well as using French words associated with aristocratic and courtly culture, Chaucer employed a number of French words belonging to specialized areas of discourse. As Chaucer is one of the first writers to discuss the practice of literary composition in the vernacular, his works contain many first occurrences of technical literary terms, all derived from French; including words such as *balade*, *compilatour* 'compiler', *compleinte*, *poetrie*, *tragedie*, *comedie*. There are many other instances of technical terms of French origin being introduced by Chaucer into English, such as the word *concentrik*, first recorded in the *Treatise on the Astrolabe*, and *corrosif*, first employed in Chaucer's description of alchemy in the Canon's Yeoman's Tale. In these cases the reason for the borrowings is that discussion of specialized domains such as science had previously been carried out in French or Latin.

Many words first used by Chaucer have a technical sense in ME that has since been lost, so that the word's technical sense or connotations are often missed by modern readers. The word *consequence* is first recorded in Chaucer's *Boece* ,where it is used in its technical philosophical sense referring to 'something which follows logically from a premise'. The generalized sense of 'a result' only appears in the fifteenth century. Similarly, the adjective *effectif* is a term derived from Aristotelian philosophy and is thus found only in technical philosophical contexts, such as Chaucer's *Boece* and Tale of Melibee.

Our analysis of the status of French words used by Chaucer must also be alive to the different connotations a word may have depending on the context in which it is used. This is apparent when we look at the distribution of certain French words across Chaucer's works. Chaucer employed a large number of French words in the *Romaunt* whose use is much more restricted in his later works, suggesting that their status changed during his career. A good example is the word *fetys*, which appears frequently in the *Romaunt* meaning 'handsome, pretty, elegant'. Chaucer used the word to describe a range of noble and attractive characters, such as the personification Beauty, where it is used twice (1017, 1031), and that of Mirth, who is also twice described as *fetys* (821, 829). Given this, we would expect the word to appear frequently in Chaucer's other works, especially his courtly romances such as *Troilus and Criseyde* and the Knight's Tale. However, there are no occurrences of this word in either work. In fact the word is only used of characters whose social and moral qualities are decidedly dubious. It is used in the Pardoner's Tale of a group of dancing girls, described by the Pardoner as the devil's officers who tempt people to lechery (C 478). It is also used to describe the cloak worn by the Prioress in the General Prologue, part of a portrait that is full of details satirizing her misplaced morality and her sentimentality.

A similar distribution is found for the adverb *fetisly*, which describes the Prioress's provincial pronunciation of French, the Merchant's boots, the arrangement of Nicholas' bedroom and Absolon's trousers in the Miller's Tale, Perkyn Revelour's hairstyle in the Cook's Tale and the pen used by the Friar in the Summoner's Tale to record the names of those who present him with gifts. None of these characters can be considered equivalent in status to Mirth and Beauty in the *Romaunt*, and it seems that the word had since become old-fashioned and compromised, appropriate only for characters of low social and moral standing. It is also interesting that, outside the General Prologue, the word is only found in fabliaux, where the language and conventions of romances are undermined and satirized. So the example of *fetys* has shown us that the distribution of a word across Chaucer's works can provide insights into its status. Where a word is found in positive contexts in the *Romaunt*, but is later restricted to fabliaux, it is likely that its status changed so that it was no longer considered worthy of serious literary use.

Another word with a similar range of meanings and distribution is *gent*, 'noble, attractive, graceful', which is also used to describe Beauty in the *Romaunt* (1032). Elsewhere the adjective is used by Chaucer to describe Alison's waist in a striking and rather unflattering comparison: 'As any wezele hir body gent and smal' (A 3234). It is used of Sir Thopas in Chaucer's parody of the conventions of chivalric romance, and in the *Parliament of Fowls,* the goose's speech is described as a *facounde gent*, 'a noble eloquence' (558), although this is immediately undermined by reference to the goose's *kakelynge* (562). A similar loanword is *prys*, used frequently in the *Romaunt* to denote qualities such as 'high rank, nobility, excellence'. The word most commonly appears in the phrase 'of prys', meaning 'excellent' or 'noble', or with stock intensifiers such as 'of michel prys', 'of heighe prys', 'peerles of prys'. Outside the *Romaunt*, the phrase is used in Sir Thopas to describe the very romances that Chaucer is parodying in this tale: 'Men speken of romances of prys ...' (B2 2087). It would appear from this use that the phrase 'of prys' was one that Chaucer employed only in his early work and later rejected as part of the hackneyed diction of popular romance. There is a third instance of the phrase in the Franklin's Tale, where it is used without any suggestion of parody to describe the excellence of the garden in which Dorigen and her friends go to enjoy themselves: 'That nevere was ther gardyn of swich prys/But if it were the verray paradys' (F 911–2). This instance shows that, while Chaucer appears to have seen the phrase as highly conventional and to have avoided it in most instances, he was prepared to employ it in a serious courtly context when it suited him to do so. Presumably the rhyme with *paradys* contributed to his decision to employ the phrase here, although it could be that its use in the description of a garden was deliberately intended to evoke the language of the description of the garden of the *Romaunt of the Rose*.

As well as taking into account the connotations of each of Chaucer's French borrowings, we also need to consider the status of a word's individual senses. An example of this is the word *meyne*, which is used by Chaucer to describe a noble household, such as Criseyde's (1.127), as well as a household of regular religious such as monks and friars, termed the 'special meignee of God' in the Parson's Tale (I 894). But it can also be used to refer to less noble and worthy groups, such as the rabble of dodgy characters with which Perkyn Revelour is associated in the Cook's Tale, or even the band of rebellious peasants implicated with Jack Straw in the Peasants' Revolt:

And gadered hym a meynee of his sort
To hoppe and synge and maken swich disport   (A 4381–2)

Certes, he Jakke Straw and his meynee   (B2 4584)

Chaucer's use of the word *joly* also alerts us to the importance of being aware of the full range of senses and connotations that a particular word may have. The *MED* records three principal senses for this word in ME: (1) merry, glad, joyful; (2) vigorous, youthful, lecherous; (3) pleasing, comely, beautiful. There are many instances of the word in serious courtly contexts in Chaucer's works, where it signifies 'noble' or 'handsome', including several in the *Romaunt*, such as the following description of Mirth: 'So fair, so joly, and so fetys' (829). There are also examples where Chaucer uses the word in the second of the *MED* senses, as in the narrator's description of Alison in the Miller's Tale as 'Wynsynge she was, as is a joly colt' (A 3263), or the Pardoner's boast of a 'joly wenche in every toun' (C 453). But other instances, particularly those in the fabliaux tales where the word is quite common, are much less easy to categorize. In the Miller's Tale the word is used to describe Absolon who 'jolif was and gay' (A 3339) and, more specifically, his hair: 'Ful streight and evene lay his joly shode' (A 3316). In the Reeve's Tale it describes the miller's wife, perhaps significantly, at bedtime: 'To bedde he goth, and with hym goth his wyf./As any jay she light was and jolyf' (A 4153–4). Her husband Simkin carries a small dagger in his pocket that is termed 'a joly poppere', which may also carry sexual overtones. In the Shipman's Tale the wife is described as being as 'jolif as a pye' having made arrangements with Daun John, while her subsequent pledge to her husband to repay the money 'abedde' with her 'joly body' has a clear sexual reference.

A similar kind of usage is found in the distribution of the word *corage*. This word has three main senses in Middle English. The first sense concerns the 'heart', 'spirit' or 'disposition', while the second concerns 'inclination' or 'desire', including 'sexual desire' or 'lust'. The third sense involves 'valour' or 'courage' and is the sense of the word which survives as PDE *courage*. The first meaning is found in the high style opening of the General Prologue, describing the way small birds are inspired to sing: 'So priketh hem nature in hir corages' (A 11). *Corage* is also found frequently in Chaucer's *Boece* in a technical philosophical sense referring to the heart as the seat of the emotions, often as a translation of the Latin word *animus*. However, in other contexts the word's precise meaning is more diffi-cult to gauge, especially where the division between desire and sexual desire is unclear. It is used in the Clerk's Tale to refer to Griselda's father's belief that, once he had satisfied his desire, Walter would discard his wife, suggesting that here it refers to sexual desire:

For out of doute this olde poure man	
Was evere in suspect of hir mariage;	
For evere he <u>demed</u>, sith that it bigan,	judged
That whan the lord fulfild hadde his corage,	
Hym wolde thynke it were a <u>disparage</u>	dishonour
To his estaat so lowe for <u>t'alighte</u>,	descend
And <u>voyden</u> hire as soone as ever he myghte.	drive out
	(E 904–10)

However, in the Merchant's Tale, Chaucer appears to draw delib-erately on this ambiguity. Here a rich old man called January decides to marry a pretty young girl called May, a decision which he justifies on moral and spiritual grounds. Despite the spiritual justification, January's use of *corage* at line E 1759 clearly refers to his sexual appetite, as he feigns anxiety for the poor young woman who must endure the full strength of his ardour:

> Allas! O tendre creature,
> Now wolde God ye myghte wel endure

Al my corage, it is so sharp and <u>keene</u>!   eager
I am agast ye shul it nat <u>susteene</u>.   withstand
                                                                        (E 1757–60)

But how should we interpret its use at the beginning of the tale, when
the narrator recounts January's sudden desire, following his sixtieth
birthday, to get married?

And whan that he was passed sixty yeer,
Were it for hoolynesse or for <u>dotage</u>,   senility
I kan nat seye, but swich a greet corage
Hadde this knyght to been a wedded man
That day and nyght he dooth al that he kan
T'espien where he myghte wedded be,

                                                                        (E 1252–7)

This instance is glossed by the *MED* under 'inclination or desire' but
surely this ignores the strong sexual overtones associated with an
elderly man's desire to marry, and the image of him studying the
local talent?

Another feature of Chaucer's use of French vocabulary is his
tendency to draw on words associated with particular registers and
introduce them into unusual contexts. Chaucer was the first literary
writer to employ certain words belonging to the legal register,
which would have carried a specific technical connotation for his
contemporary audience. In some cases we have no difficulty
noticing a word's legal connotations as such words are still used
only in the law, such as *assise* or *sessions*, both of which refer
specifically to a judicial or court session, as in the expression 'in
session'. However, in other cases, especially where a word has
since become adopted in more widespread usage, it is harder for us
to spot its former legal status. An example of this is the word *collu-
sioun*, meaning 'fraud' or 'trickery', used by Chaucer in his short
poem 'Lack of Steadfastness'. This is not the first instance of this
word in an English text, as it appears earlier in a London guild
return, dated to 1389, and there are many subsequent occurrences of
it in legal documents. What is significant about Chaucer's use is that
he is the first writer to use the word in a literary context, and was
subsequently followed by later writers such as John Capgrave and
John Lydgate.

Chaucer used a number of technical legal terms that are not recorded elsewhere outside legal contexts, such as the word *reconyssaunce*, meaning a bond acknowledging some obligation, such as a debt. It is used to describe the financial dealings of the merchant in the Shipman's Tale, who is bound in a *reconyssaunce* and thus forced to make a *chevyssaunce*, or 'loan'. These technical legal terms are appropriate here in evoking the mercantile and economic context within which the tale operates, and creating a parallel to the alternative means that the merchant's wife uses to raise capital. Other words have remained in English only in the legal register and are thus known only to those with legal training. For instance, the word *champartie*, derived from OF *champart*, is used in legal language to refer to the practice of aiding a litigant in return for a share of the property in dispute, and this usage survives into PDE. But Chaucer is the first writer in English to use the word in a non-legal context, to urge the preeminence of Venus in the description of her temple in the Knight's Tale:

> Thus may ye seen that wysdom ne richesse
> Beautee ne <u>sleighte</u>, strengthe ne hardynesse,   dexterity
> Ne may with Venus holde champartie
>
> (A 1947–9)

Another such word is *replicacioun*, a legal term meaning 'an answer to a suit', or 'a reply to an answer'. Chaucer is the first writer to use this word in a literary text when he used it in the *Parliament of Fowls* as one of a number of legal terms, such as *verdit*, *pletynge*, *juge*, which help to portray the legal process that is being invoked in this debate. The word *esement* is used in Middle English to refer to comforts and conveniences such as accommodation, entertainment and food and drink, but it also had a legal sense referring to the right or privilege of using something not one's own, such as a piece of land. Chaucer uses the word twice, in the Reeve's Tale, where Aleyn the student claims that as they have been tricked by the miller they have a right to 'som esement' (A 4179, 4186). This word is often glossed as 'compensation' or 'redress', although the technical legal sense is surely also being invoked in this instance. Aleyn's way of gaining *esement* is by sleeping with the miller's wife, thereby asserting his right to use another person's property. These are the kinds of technical senses that it is easy to miss when reading

Chaucer, but which would have been apparent to Chaucer's audience, many of whom had some form of legal training. Chaucer draws on legal vocabulary for specific effects elsewhere, such as in Criseyde's response to her uncle's insistent arguments on behalf of Troilus. Criseyde replies with a *protestacioun* in response to Pandarus' *proces*, both of which are legal terms. *Protestacioun* can be used to mean a 'declaration', but also has a more technical legal sense referring to a type of pleading where a party affirms or denies a matter, or raises a question of law or jurisdiction, which cannot be ignored. The word *proces* can mean simply 'discourse' or 'subject matter', but also had a technical sense of 'course of legal proceedings' or 'lawsuit'. By using these terms Criseyde invokes the law in her own case for her defence, agreeing to her uncle's request that she be sympathetic towards Troilus but on her own terms, that is, on the understanding that her uncle goes no further with the case. An interesting comparison with Criseyde's ability to use and exploit technical legal jargon is provided by the Miller's use of the word *protestacioun* in his prologue, where he uses it to enter a plea of being drunk: 'But first I make a protestacioun/That I am dronke' (A 3137-8). By affirming his drunkenness before he begins his tale in a formal legal manner, the miller argues that he cannot be held accountable for what he says.

The number of Latin words borrowed into English during the ME period is not as large as that derived from French, and those Latin words that were adopted in this period tend to belong to specialized registers with which the Latin language was associated. A number of words of Latin origin have become fully assimilated into the English language, such as *delicate*, *direct*, *indeterminate*, *inordinate*, *submit*, *vulgar*, while others remain associated with more technical registers, such as *testament*, *scripture*, *horoscope*, *psalm*, *retraction*. Chaucer's Latin vocabulary tends to be technical and often relates to the specialized domains in which Latin was used. For instance, the word *elongacioun* is a Latin word used as a technical astronomical term to refer to an 'angular distance', first recorded in Chaucer's *Astrolabe,* and can also be used as a medical term meaning 'extension' or 'spreading'. Another such example is the word *tropik*, a Latin loan used only in astronomical contexts to signify 'either of the points at which the sun appears farthest from the equator'. The word *pregnaunt* is adopted from Latin during this period, and could be used in medical texts to mean 'with child', as well as in learned discourse to mean 'full of meaning' just as it can in modern usage. As well as scientific and medical terms, Latin was also a major source of religious vocabulary in the ME period, giving us words like *ecclesiaste*, *curat* and *renegat* meaning an apostate, or someone who forsakes his religious beliefs. Words derived from the academic register are also found, such as *conclude* and *conjecte*, meaning 'suppose' or 'speculate'.

It is important to be aware of the likelihood of Latin loanwords having technical or specialized meanings, especially in the case of words that have since been adopted into more general usage. A good example is the verb *dissolve,* which is in common use in PDE to mean 'soften' or 'melt'. However, Chaucer's only use of this verb is in the *Boece*, where it has a technical sense referring to the soul's departure from the body, as made clear through the use of a gloss: 'that is to seyn, whan the soule departeth fro the body' (Book II, prosa 3). The word *fatal* is now used generally to mean 'deadly', although it is derived from Latin *fatalis* and is thus related to the word *fate*. In Middle English it retains a technical sense of an event being predestined, or fated to occur, and it is used in this way in several instances in the *Boece* and in the opening line of Book 5 of *Troilus*: 'Approchen gan the fatal destyne'. The word *diffyne*, which in PDE is used to mean 'specify', has a technical sense in ME that refers to a concluding statement. It is used in this sense in the *Boece* and also by Criseyde, to bring a formal close to her self-defence in response to the rumour that she is in love with Horaste.

Just as we have seen Chaucer exploiting the connotations of specialized English and French terms by using them in unexpected contexts, we find similar examples in his use of Latin vocabulary. A good example of this occurs at the end of the Wife of Bath's lengthy prologue, which the Friar refers to as a 'long preamble of a tale (D 831)'. The Summoner reacts to the Friar's comment by questioning his right to interfere: 'What spekestow of preambulacioun?' (D 837). Elsewhere in ME the word *preamble* is used to refer to a formal prologue to a literary work, such as a saint's life, and its use to refer to the idiosyncratic monologue by the wife seems intended to be ironic.

Earlier we saw that it is often difficult to determine whether a word was borrowed directly from Latin or via French. In some cases both Latin and French forms are adopted, as in the case of *equal* and *egal*. Despite their similar origins and an obvious overlap in their meanings, the words do have a different range of senses. *Egal* is used to mean 'equivalent', 'proportionate' and 'impartial', while *equal* can mean 'identical in amount' or 'smooth of surface'. The two words are further disambiguated in their use, with the Latin-derived *equal* being reserved for technical contexts, such as Chaucer's *Astrolabe* and Parson's Tale, while the OF equivalent *egal* is of wider currency in Chaucer's works.

I mentioned above that it is not until the aureate diction of the fifteenth century that we see the introduction of Latin loanwords into English on a large scale, a style of writing best associated with the poet John Lydgate (*c*.1370–1449), one of Chaucer's most important followers. Aureate diction is a self-consciously stylized and highly artificial poetic language designed to enrich vernacular poetic vocabulary by introducing Latin words, mostly from religious sources, into English. Poems written in aureate diction tend to deal with religious themes, and it is particularly favoured in poems addressing the Virgin Mary. Although Chaucer's career preceded the flourishing of this style of writing, the beginnings of this stylistic mode of writing can be seen in certain examples in Chaucer, such as the prologue to the Prioress' Tale.

The Prioress' Tale recounts a miracle performed by the Virgin Mary, and the prologue is an invocation to the Virgin which adopts many words of Latin and French etymology. In the following extract, I have placed the words of French and Latin origins in italics, to emphasize the reliance on such words:

O mooder Mayde, O mayde Mooder free!	
O bussh <u>unbrent</u>, brennynge in Moyses sighte,	unburned
That <u>*ravyshedest*</u> doun fro the *Deitee*,	drew down
Thurgh thyn *humblesse*, the <u>Goost</u> that in th'alighte,	Holy Spirit
Of whos *vertu*, whan he thyn herte lighte,	
Conceyved was the Fadres *sapience*,	
Help me to telle it in thy *reverence*!	
Lady, thy <u>*bountee*</u>, thy <u>*magnificence*</u>,	goodness; glory
Thy *vertu* and thy grete *humylitee*	
Ther may no tonge *expresse* in no *science*;	
For somtyme, Lady, <u>er</u> men *praye* to thee,	before
Thou goost biforn of thy <u>*benyngnytee*</u>,	graciousness
And getest us the lyght, of thy *preyere*,	
To *gyden* us unto thy Sone so deere.	

My konnyng is so <u>wayk</u>, O blisful Queene,   weak
For to *declare* thy grete worthynesse
That I ne may the weighte nat *susteene*;
But as a child of twelf month oold, or lesse,
That kan <u>unnethes</u> any word *expresse*,   hardly
Right so fare I, and therfore I yow *preye*,
Gydeth my song that I shal of yow seye.

                                                              (B2 1657–77)

While a number of the italicized words were borrowed into English from French rather than Latin, they are ultimately of Latin origin. These include: *sapience*, *reverence*, *magnificence*, *science*, *deitee*, *benygnytee*, *humylitee*. So, while aureate diction did not flourish until the fifteenth century, the beginnings of this style, and its association with poetry in praise of the Virgin Mary, can be traced in Chaucer's work.

Further reading

The major primary resources for the study of ME vocabulary are the *Oxford English Dictionary* and the *Middle English Dictionary*, now available online via the *Middle English Compendium*, with flexible search facilities. An excellent overview of ME vocabulary is provided by Burnley (in Blake 1992), while Burnley (1979) presents a more specialized study of Chaucer's philosophical background. The methodology adopted by Joseph Mersand in his *Chaucer's Romance Vocabulary* (1937) has been scrutinized and criticized by Cannon (1998). Useful glossaries of Chaucer's works can be found in Benson (1987) and Davis et al. (1979).

6 Grammar

In this chapter we will examine Chaucer's grammar, and more specifically the areas of morphology and syntax. 'Morphology' is concerned with the form of a particular word, and the special endings that are commonly added to words, such as the -s ending that is added to most nouns in PDE to indicate they are plural, or the -'s that is added as an indicator of possession. 'Syntax' deals with word order, and the various rules that operate concerning the way words can be combined to form clauses and sentences. So, this chapter will consider the kinds of special endings, known as 'inflexions', that were used in Chaucer's language, and the rules by which individual words were ordered and combined to create larger units.

Determiners

The system of determiners used by Chaucer is similar to that found in PDE. The definite article is *the*, which does not change, while the indefinite article is *a(n)*, with *an* used before vowels, just as in PDE. *An* is also used before words beginning with <h>, a usage found in some formal contexts in PDE but not commonly observed. Here is an example from Chaucer:

> Paraventure an heep of yow, ywis   (F 1493)   perhaps

The other major category of determiners in ME are the demonstratives, which functioned in a similar way to their PDE equivalents: *that* 'that'; *tho* 'those'; *this* 'this'; *thise/these* 'these'. The ME distinction between 'this' and 'these', *this* and *thise*, seems to have been a purely written one, as metrical evidence suggests that the final <-e> was not pronounced. This means that in speech there was no distinction between the two forms. Another demonstrative, not found in PDE, is *ilke/thilke* which means literally 'the same' but is often best translated simply as 'that', as in the following example:

And thilke same nyght this kyng was <u>slawe</u> (B2 3426)   slain

Here the use of *thilke* as the demonstrative 'that' is made clear by its use with the adjective *same*, which could be translated literally as 'the same same night', but should be rendered: 'that same night'.

ME also differs from PDE in having a further demonstrative, *yon*, which literally means 'yonder'. Its use in ME was largely confined to the northern dialects, and it survives into PDE in northern dialects and in Scots. Chaucer's only use of this form is in the dialect speech in the Reeve's Tale:

If that I may, yon wenche wil I <u>swyve</u>   (A 4178)   copulate with

One further demonstrative, unknown in PDE, is the use of the third person singular pronoun *hym* alongside a proper noun in phrases such as 'hym Daryus' (D 498), 'hym Olofernus' (B1 940), 'hym Mardochee' (E 1373), where the pronoun should be translated as 'that Daryus' and so on.

While the function of the demonstrative in ME is broadly similar to that in PDE, *this/thise* is used more frequently by Chaucer as a means of controlling and organizing a piece of narrative. For instance, *this* commonly appears at the beginning of a new section in the narrative to refer back to the previous mention of a particular character, such as in the following sequence of examples from the Knight's Tale, where a new piece of narration begins with a reference back to the subject:

This duc, of whom I make mencioun   (A 893)

This gentil duc doun from his courser sterte   (A 952)

Thus <u>rit</u> this duc, thus rit this conquerour   (A 981)   rides

Whan that this worthy duc, this Theseus   (A 1001)

And whan this worthy duc hath thus <u>ydon</u>   (A 1025)   done

A similar technique is employed in the following passages where the knights Palamon and Arcite are introduced, with each new section beginning 'This Palamon' or 'This Arcite', to avoid any confusion concerning the referent. A similar use of the demonstrative is found in the Miller's Tale, where the hapless lover Absolon is often introduced as 'This Absolon', or 'This parissh clerk, this amorous Absolon', 'this joly lovere Absolon'. It is tempting to read such constructions as expressing contempt for Absolon, or as being deliberately patronizing, but it is clear from the earlier examples from the Knight's Tale, which concern noble characters such as Duke Theseus, that they have a purely syntactic function.

Despite this, there are other instances where the demonstrative is used to refer to a person or a group of people who have not been previously mentioned, and who are not the subject of the narration, and in such cases a contemptuous or patronizing attitude may be implied. An example of this is the narrator's misogynistic dismissal of Dorigen's grief and that of women in general:

> For his absence wepeth she and <u>siketh</u>,   sighs
> As doon this noble wyves whan <u>hem liketh</u>. (F 817–8)   it pleases them

Another example in the Franklin's Tale is the clerk of Orleans' lighthearted teasing of Aurelius' love-sickness and his need for an early night:

> 'Go we thanne <u>soupe</u>,' quod he, 'as for the beste.   sup
> Thise amorous folk somtyme <u>moote</u> han hir reste.'   must
>
>   (F 1217–18)

Nouns

In PDE the noun phrase generally consists of a noun and one or more modifiers, such as determiners, adjectives or numerals. An important feature of PDE syntax concerns agreement between the noun phrase and other elements, such as the verb phrase. For example, we say 'I write', but 'the boy writes', where the change of subject necessitates a change in the form of the verb. The same rules apply in ME, although in ME there is also agreement within the noun phrase. In ME there were four inflexional categories which were inherited from OE, although in ME their formal distinctiveness and their range of function were much reduced. The basic noun declension in ME is shown in Table 6.1.

Table 6.1 Basic noun declension

Number	Singular	Plural
Case		
Nominative	stoon	stoones
Accusative	stoon	stoones
Genitive	stoones	stoones
Dative	stoon(e)	stoones

As in PDE, nouns were inflected for number (that is, to show the distinction between singular and plural) and the most common inflexion was <-s, -es> as in PDE, thus: *herte* (sg.), *hertes* (pl.). While the <-es, -s> inflexion is the most common in Chaucer's usage, he also made use of a variant form <-is, -ys>. This was originally a northern form, although it was known in London English of the late fourteenth century. It appears frequently in the Hengwrt manuscript of the *Canterbury Tales*, although it is less common in the Ellesmere manuscript. For instance, the Hg manuscript has 9 instances of *yeris* and 6 of *yeres*, while El has 14 occurrences of *yeres* and just 1 instance of *yeris*. It is therefore difficult to be certain as to Chaucer's own use of this variant, although its appearances in rhyme show that Chaucer was willing to draw on it on specific occasions. Here is an example where the <-ys> inflexion has been used to allow the word *wyvys* to rhyme with the verb *is*:

> Which yifte of God hadde he for alle his wyvys!   gift
> No man hath swich that in this world alyve is. (D 39–40)   such

A similar example appears elsewhere in the Wife of Bath's Prologue, where the form *talys* is selected to rhyme with *Alys*:

> Taak youre disport; I wol nat leve no talys.   enjoy yourself
> I knowe yow for a trewe wyf, dame Alys.   (D 319–20)

One further variant is found in the case of words which end in <t>, which form their plural by adding <-z>, as in *tirauntz*, *servantz*, *instrumentz*, *argumentz*.

This is the most common noun paradigm in ME, derived from the OE strong noun declension, although, as in PDE, some nouns take the <-en> plural derived from the OE weak noun declension, for example *children*, *oxen*. Some nouns take the <-en> plural in ME which have since adopted the <-es> plural, for example *eyen* 'eyes', *doughtren* 'daughters'. A number of nouns could form their plural with either <-es> or <-en> inflexions, such as *toon*, *toos* 'toes', *shoon*, *shoes* 'shoes', *sustren*, *sustres* 'sisters'. Once again, Chaucer was able to exploit variation of this kind for rhyming purposes, as in the following examples from the Nun's Priest's Tale:

His <u>byle</u> was blak, and as the <u>jeet</u> it shoon;   beak; jet
Lyk <u>asure</u> were his legges and his toon   (B2 4051–2)   azure

This Chauntecleer stood hye upon his toos,
Strecchynge his nekke, and heeld his eyen cloos (B2 4521–2)

Some nouns, especially those ending in <-s>, take no inflexion, and their number can only be gleaned from the forms of accompanying verbs or adjectives. For instance, in the following line from *Troilus,* the word *vers* is plural, as can be seen from the plural form of the verb *wepen* as well as the form of the determiner *thise*: 'Thise woful vers, that wepen as I write' (1.7). Similarly, in the next example, the noun *hors* is plural, as can be deduced from the plural verb and the inflected adjective *goode*: 'His hors were goode, but he was not gay' (A 74). It is common to find nouns without inflexions after numbers, as in the following example where the uninflected form is used in rhyme:

Whan ended was the lyf of Seinte Cecile,
<u>Er</u> we hadde riden fully fyve mile   (G 554–5)   before

We may compare this form with another instance of the plural of *mile* later in the same tale, where it does not appear in rhyme:

It semed as he had priked miles three   (G 561)

One further variant form is the mutated plural, also found in PDE, such as *goose* (sg.), *geese* (pl.), or *foot* (sg.), *feet* (pl.).

The above paradigm shows that the plural inflexion was identical with the genitive inflexion, which was <-es, -s> for example *myn hertes queene* 'my heart's queen'. The <-es, -s> inflexion is the ancestor of the modern genitive inflexion with -'s as in heart's. As in PDE, the genitive case could also be indicated using a construction involving the preposition *of*, as in 'the queen of my heart', a construction partly influenced by the French construction using *de*, as in 'la reine de mon coeur'. A slightly more complex construction which does not survive into PDE is found in examples such as *the wifes tale of Bath*, which in PDE should be rendered 'the Wife of Bath's tale'. It should also be noted that, unlike PDE which distinguishes between the *boy's book* and the *boys' book,* there was no distinction between genitive singular and plural inflexions in ME. Some nouns, especially kinship terms like *fader* and *brother*, are endingless in the genitive singular, thus 'Now, by my fader soule that is deed' (A 781), although they can take the <-s> inflexion where the uninflected form would lead to potential confusion:

> And thus Lyno hath of his faders brother
> The doughter wedded, and ech of hem hath other.   (LGW 2608–9)

Dative inflexions are also found after prepositions in some constructions, such as *on honde*, *in londe*, although these tend to be fossilized and archaic usages.

Pronouns

As in PDE, ME pronouns were inflected according to number, case and gender. Third person pronouns were selected according to natural gender, that is, real world sex distinctions, as in PDE, rather than according to grammatical gender as found in OE. The only significant difference between the ME and PDE pronoun systems is the use of the ethic dative in ME, which was used to reinforce the subject, as in 'I wol me haste' (A 2052), a usage which does not survive into PDE. The forms of the personal pronouns used by Chaucer are shown in Table 6.2.

Table 6.2 shows that there was no formal distinction between the accusative and dative cases in ME; these two cases had merged so that the same pronoun was used for both. The different forms of the first person singular nominative pronoun, *I*, *Ich*, and *Ik*, represent dialect distinctions. *Ik* is an East Anglian form which is used by Chaucer only in the speech of the Reeve, a pilgrim whose origins are in Bawdeswell in Norfolk. Chaucer evidently introduced this variant form as part of the characterization of the provincial Reeve. *Ich* was originally a southern form which was in the process of being replaced by *I* by Chaucer's time. *Ich* survived longer in the more conservative dialects of the south, which accounts for its appearance in Chaucer's works, where it is much less common than the dominant form *I*.

Table 6.2 Personal pronoun paradigms

First person

Case	Singular	Plural
Nom.	I (Ich, Ik)	we
Acc.	me	us
Gen.	my(n)(e)	our(e)(s)
Dat.	me	us

Second person

Case	Singular	Plural
Nom.	thou/thow	ye
Acc.	thee	you/yow
Gen.	thyn(e)	your(e)(s)
Dat.	thee	you/yow

Third person | | Singular | |

Case	Masc.	Fem.	Neut.
Nom.	he	she	it, hit
Acc.	hym, him	hir(e), hyr(e)	it, hit
Gen.	his	hir(e)(s)	his
Dat.	hym, him	hir(e), hyr(e)	it, hit

Plural | All genders |

Case	All genders
Nom.	they
Acc.	hem
Gen.	hir(e)(s)
Dat.	hem

Another difference between ME and PDE in Table 6.2 is the two forms of the second person pronoun: *thou/ye*, equivalent to PDE *you*. This distinction is inherited from OE, but in ME it took on additional functions through contact with French. French maintains a pragmatic distinction in the use of the singular and plural pronouns when used to address a single individual. The plural *vous* form is used to indicate respect and formality, while the singular form, *tu*, is reserved to signal familiarity or a lack of respect. A similar distinction is found in Chaucer's use of *thou* and *ye*, and an understanding of this distinction is important in appreciating the subtleties in the shifting relations between characters in Chaucer's works. It was conventional for courtly men and women to address each other using the plural pronoun, and this is even found in contexts where the power in the relationship is extremely one-sided. For instance, when the marquis Walter sets out the terms of the agreement by which he is willing to marry the humble Griselda in an extremely unromantic marriage proposal, he addresses her using the polite form:

> I seye this: be ye redy with good herte
> To al my lust, and that I frely may,
> As me best thynketh, do yow laughe or <u>smerte</u>,   suffer
> And nevere ye to <u>grucche</u> it, nyght ne day?   complain
> And <u>eek</u> when I sey 'ye,' ne sey nat 'nay,'   also
> Neither by word ne frownyng <u>contenance</u>?   expression
> Swere this, and heere I swere oure alliance.
>
> (E 351–7)

The singular form is used by socially superior people when addressing people lower down the social scale, or by members of the older generation to younger people. As an example we may compare Walter's use of the polite form in addressing Griselda above, with his use of the singular form to address her father Janicula, whose social inferiority is clearly marked:

> Janicula, I neither may ne kan
> Lenger the plesance of myn herte hyde.
> If that thou <u>vouche sauf</u>, what so bityde,   promise
> Thy doghter wol I take, <u>er</u> that I wende,   before
> As for my wyf, unto hir lyves ende.
>
> (E 304–8)

As well as expressing social superiority, the use of the singular form can also be an expression of disrespect or contempt, as in the Host's abrupt interruption of Chaucer's Tale of Sir Thopas:

> 'Namoore of this, for Goddes dignitee,'
> Quod oure Hooste, 'for thou makest me
> So wery of thy verray <u>lewednesse</u>'   ignorance
>
> (B2 2109–10)

In some instances it is not always possible to decide precisely why a particular form is being used, as in the Franklin's use of the singular form in addressing the Squire when praising his efforts: "In feith, Squier, thow hast thee wel yquit/And gentilly. I preise wel thy wit … considerynge thy yowthe" (F 673–5). Here the Franklin emphasizes the Squire's youth and the use of the singular pronoun is presumably a means of flagging the age gap, although there is also a suggestion here that the Franklin is deliberately patronizing the Squire.

The singular form may also be used to express familiarity and intimacy. Troilus uses the polite form when addressing Criseyde throughout the entire poem, switching to the singular form on just one occasion, when he pledges his commitment to his lady: 'For I am thyn, by God and by my trouthe!' (3.1512). The same is true of Criseyde, whose sole use of the singular pronoun occurs at a similar moment of high emotional intensity: 'Syn I am thyn al hol, withouten mo' (4.1641). These courtly conventions of formal address are deliberately undermined by Nicholas in the Miller's Tale, whose decidedly uncourtly advances on Alison are marked by the use of the singular pronoun: 'For deerne love of thee, lemman, I spille' (A 3278). Alison's outraged response, although it lasts only a few lines, includes the formal pronoun as part of her attempt to maintain decorum and distance in their relationship. Absolon, who is trying to play the role of the courtly lover, addresses Alison with the plural form, although she always responds with the singular form, indicating her contempt for his advances. Like Troilus, Absolon switches to the singular form at the crucial moment of intimacy, as he prepares to receive a kiss from his lady: 'Lemman, thy grace, and sweete bryd, thyn oore!' (A 3726), while his use of the singular form the next time he addresses her is full of contempt: 'I shal thee quyte'.

Switching from *ye* to *thou* as an expression of disrespect and contempt is also found in the Second Nun's Tale, where Cecilia begins by addressing Almachius with the more respectful pronoun, despite the scornful way in which he addresses her, and assures him that she is of noble birth:

'What maner womman artow?' tho quod he.
'I am a gentil womman born,' quod she.
'I axe thee,' quod he, 'though it thee greeve,
Of thy religioun and of thy <u>bileeve</u>.'   faith

'Ye han bigonne youre questioun folily,'
Quod she, 'that wolden two answeres conclude
In o demande; ye axede <u>lewedly</u>.'   ignorantly
                                                   (G 424–30)

Having defended herself in an outspoken and unapologetic fashion, she then proceeds to mock Almachius and his demand that she worship his gods and renounce her faith, switching to the singular pronoun to signal the increased contempt and scorn:

'O juge, confus in thy <u>nycetee</u>,   foolishness
Woltow that I <u>reneye</u> innocence,   renounce
To make me a wikked <u>wight</u>?' quod shee.   creature
                                                   (G 463–5)

We see a similar switching between polite and impolite usages in the way the old woman addresses the summoner who tries to extort money from her in the Friar's Tale. Her initial response to his knocking on her gate is polite and decorous and employs the plural form of address: 'God save you, sire, what is youre sweete wille?' (D 1585). However, she adopts a more aggressive and contemptuous tone when responding to his false accusations of adultery, switching to the singular pronoun: '"Thou lixt! ... Unto the devel blak and rough of hewe/Yeve I thy body and my panne also!"' (D 1618–23).

Another, more specialized, use of the singular pronoun occurs when addressing God, as in the following example from the Franklin's Tale: 'Which mankynde is so fair part of thy werk/That thou it madest lyk to thyn owene merk' (F 879–80). This usage is still found today in the archaic language used in certain liturgical contexts, as in the Lord's Prayer: 'Thy will be done/Thy kingdom come'. The factors that determined which form a person would use in any particular social situation are many and complex, and a reader of Chaucer needs to be sensitive to the potential significance of switching between these forms of address.

The neuter form of the third person singular pronoun remained identical with the masculine form *his*, as in OE. The replacement of this form with its PDE equivalent *its* did not occur until the EModE period. This usage is an important one to remember when reading Chaucer, as it is easy to read *his* as the masculine pronoun 'his', when it is in fact the neuter pronoun 'its', for example 'Whan that Aprill with his shoures soote' (A 1).

The third person plural pronouns are the other major difference between Chaucer's pronoun system and that of PDE. This is because Chaucer's system represents a transitional stage in the replacement of the OE pronouns *hie*, *hiera*, *him* with forms derived from ON: *they*, *their*, *them*. Towards the end of the OE period, the native third person plural pronoun system became increasingly indistinct, particularly in situations where the pronouns were not stressed. In addition to this, the replacement of grammatical gender with natural gender added to the ambiguity and the need for a formally distinct pronominal system. These problems were resolved by the adoption of the ON third person plural pronouns, which began with <th-> rather than <h->, and therefore helped to avoid confusion with other pronouns. As we have seen elsewhere in this book, the influence of ON was greatest in areas of densest Norse settlement, the north and East Midlands, and these pronouns appear earliest in texts copied in those areas. The earliest recorded appearance of the ON pronouns in English is in a text called the *Ormulum*, written in the East Midlands *c*.1200. It is not until the fourteenth century that we see these forms appearing in texts copied in London, and Chaucer used only the nominative form *they*, alongside the forms *hem* and *hir* derived from OE. This suggests that the need for a formally distinct pronoun was greatest in the nominative case, the subject of the sentence, and that *their* and *them* may have been adopted later by analogy rather than through necessity. The use of the same form for both 'her' and 'their' in Chaucer's ME is a frequent cause of confusion for students and it is important to remember the possibility that the form *hir(e)* could be translated as either, depending on the context. For instance, compare the following lines: 'So priketh hem nature in hir corages' (A 11), where *hir* is the plural pronoun 'their', referring back to the *smale foweles* 'small birds', and 'She leet no morsel from hir lippes falle' (A 128), where *hir* is the feminine singular pronoun referring back to the pronoun *she*, the Prioress. The only occurrences of the ON forms *their* and *them* in Chaucer's usage are in the Reeve's Tale, where they form part of the northern dialect of the two students John and Aleyn. This highlights the fact that these forms were still considered to be northern by Chaucer, despite the fact that they were adopted in London English in the fifteenth century and subsequently formed part of the standard language. For more detailed discussion of Chaucer's use of the northern dialect in the Reeve's Tale, see Chapter 3.

Adjectives

The function of an adjective is to modify a noun, and adjectives usually appear within noun phrases, as in 'a worthy man', where *worthy* is an adjective modifying the noun *man*. More than one adjective may appear in a noun phrase, as in 'a gentil parfit knight'. Adjectives can also function as the headword of an adjective phrase in both ME and PDE. ME differs from PDE in that there is commonly agreement within the noun phrase, so that adjectives agree with the noun they are modifying according to number. The most common adjective inflexion was <-e>, as in the following example: 'a smal hound', 'smale houndes', where the adjective *smal* takes an <-e> ending when modifying a plural noun.

Another feature of adjective agreement existed in some varieties of ME, including Chaucer's own, but has not survived into PDE. This is the distinction between weak and strong adjectives which was inherited from OE. The weak paradigm is used when an adjective is modified by a determiner, that is, the definite article: *the*, a demonstrative: *this*, *that*, or a possessive pronoun: *his*, *her*, while the strong paradigm is used in all other instances. The weak/strong distinction only applied to adjectives derived from OE which are monosyllabic and end with a consonant, such as *good*, *old*, *yong*. The weak paradigm differed from the strong paradigm in the addition of a final <-e>, in both singular and plural. Thus the weak/strong paradigms may be compared as shown in Table 6.3.

Table 6.3 Weak/strong paradigms

	Weak	Strong
Singular	goode	good
Plural	goode	goode

Here are some examples of these distinctions in Chaucerian usage:

- *Weak singular:*
  And whan this goode man <u>saugh</u> that it was so (A 850)   saw
- *Weak plural:*
  Soothly, the goode werkes that he hath lost   (I 232)
- *Strong singular:*
  With good swerd and with <u>bokeler</u> by hir syde (A 4019)   shield
- *Strong plural:*
  His <u>hors</u> were goode, but he was nat gay   (A 74)   horses

It is important to recognize that the indefinite article *a(n)* is not followed by the weak paradigm, thus 'A good man was ther of religioun' (A 477).

The weak declension is also used when an adjective modifies a proper noun, or forms part of a vocative expression, where someone is being directly addressed, as in the following examples:

And, goode <u>lemman</u>, God thee save and <u>kepe</u>! (A 4247)   lover; protect

O goode Custance, allas, so wo is me   (B1 817)

The weak paradigm is also used in some genitive expressions, as in the following: 'Of goode Arcite may best ymaked be' (A 2855). The weak/strong distinction was increasingly being lost in ME in the late fourteenth century, and had been completely lost in northern dialects by this time. Chaucer's retention of this distinction was thus rather archaic, and it is not surprising that we find some inconsistencies in the observance of these distinctions in manuscripts of his works. The loss of the distinction between weak and strong adjectives would have occurred earliest in the spoken language, so it is perhaps inevitable that we find most instances of inconsistency in vocative expressions. For instance, Criseyde addresses Pandarus as 'O good Em', while he retains the weak distinction in his address to her as 'goode Nece'.

As noted above, the weak/strong distinction applied only to words of OE derivation that were monosyllabic and ended with a consonant. Other adjectives, such as those ending in <-e>, for example *clene*, those which are polysyllabic, for example *litel*, and those which are derived from French, for example *gent*, *gentil*, do not show this distinction, and do not decline at all. The only other kind of adjective inflexion found in ME is derived from French usage and affects a small number of French loanwords. This is the addition of an <-s> inflexion, on the model of French practice, in phrases such as *weyes espirituels* or *places delitables*, although such phrases are few and rather specialized.

One further inflexion which survives from OE is found in just a few fossilized constructions. This is the form *aller*, which derives from the OE genitive plural *ealra*, and is found where *all* is modifying a plural noun in the genitive, as in the following:

Shal have a soper at oure aller cost (A 799). This expression should be
rendered 'at all our cost'.

Comparison of adjectives follows a similar pattern to PDE, with
the addition of <-er> and <-est>, for example soft, softer, softest.
Like PDE *mo*, *moore* 'more' and *moost(e)* 'most' could also be used
to indicate comparatives and superlatives, and these variants could
be exploited for metrical purposes, as in the following line: 'Was
roialler ne moore curius' (B1 402). The following examples show
the basic types of comparative and superlative constructions:

Is moore strong than whan it is <u>toscatered</u>   (D 1969)   dispersed

But he be stronger than Sampson, and hoolier than David,
and wiser than Salomon   (I 955)

The hyeste rokke in Armorik Briteyne   (F 1061)

Which was the mooste fre, as thynketh yow? (F 1622)

Verbs

As with the noun phrase, agreement is also an important aspect of
the verb phrase. The principal difference between ME and PDE is
that there are a greater number of different verb forms, as may be
seen in Table 6.4.

Table 6.4 Present tense forms

	ME	**PDE**
Singular	loue	love
	louest	love
	loueth	loves
Plural	loue(n)	love

Variation in this paradigm occurs in the forms of the third person
singular of certain verbs whose stem ends in a dental consonant, that
is, <d> or <t>, which are often contracted. So the third person
singular of *ride* appears as both *rideth* and *rit*. Other examples are
sit, *sitteth*; *writ*, *writeth*; *bynt*, *byndeth*. It is important to be aware of

such forms as their similarity with preterite, or past tense, forms often causes students difficulty. This is particularly true of the contracted form of the third person singular of the verb *wend*: *wente*, which is identical with the preterite form of the verb *go*: *wente*. Another verb which is commonly written in its contracted form is *come*, which may appear as *cometh* or *comth*. While the <-eth> ending is the dominant form used by Chaucer, another ending in <-(e)s> was also available, although this was a predominantly northern dialect form. Chaucer's use of this form is limited almost exclusively to the depiction of northern dialect in the Reeve's Tale (see Chapter 3), although some instances in rhyme in the *Book of the Duchess* suggest that it was a feature of London English during Chaucer's lifetime, for example:

That never was founde, as it telles,		
<u>Bord</u> ne man, ne nothing elles.	(BD 73–4)	plank

And I wol yive hym al that <u>falles</u>		belongs
To a chambre, and al hys halles	(BD 257–8)	

The <-es> ending also appears as the ending for the second person singular indicative in a single example in the *House of Fame*, also in rhyming position:

Whych than be, loo, these tydynges,		
That thou now thus <u>hider</u> brynges,	(HF 1907–8)	here

These examples suggest that these variants were features of London English, but ones which Chaucer avoided where possible. Another variant to the above paradigm is the ending <-es> for the plural, which is found exclusively in the northern dialect in the Reeve's Tale.

In ME, as in PDE, verbs also take different inflexions to indicate tense. ME had strong and weak verb conjugations, with weak verbs forming their preterite through the addition of the <-(e)d> inflexion, and strong verbs changing their stem vowel, as in the PDE distinction between *love*, *loved*, and *bind*, *bound*. The preterite paradigms for the weak and strong verb conjugations are shown in Table 6.5.

Table 6.5 Preterite forms

	Weak	**Strong**
Singular	louede	bounde
	louedest	bounde
	louede	bounde
Plural	louede(n)	bounde(n)

The variation between forms of the present plural in <-e> or <-en> was a useful metrical device for Chaucer, which he frequently exploited. When followed by a word beginning with a vowel or <h>, a present plural form ending in <-e> would be elided, while the <-en> ending was not elided, thus preserving an additional unstressed syllable, as can be seen in the following examples:

Men loven <u>of propre kynde</u> newefangelnesse (F 610)   by nature

I <u>rede</u> that we make of sorwes two   (A 3071)   advise

There were two participles in ME: the present and past participles, which were formed as follows:

Present	louyng(e)	bindyng(e)
Past	(y)louede	(y)bounde(n)

The <y-> prefix derives from the OE <ge-> prefix and was in the process of being dropped during Chaucer's lifetime. This is reflected in Chaucer's inconsistent use of the prefix, which he frequently manipulated for metrical purposes. Compare for example the two following examples of the past participle:

But finally ycomen is the day   (E 1700)

That streight was comen fro the court of Rome (A 671)

As with the present plural forms discussed above, Chaucer also drew upon the possibility of adding a final <-n> for metrical effect. In the first of the following examples the <-n> is added to avoid elision with the following vowel, while the second is without <-n> to allow elision:

The day is comen of hir departynge   (B1 260)

At nyght was come into that hostelrye   (A 23)

A number of verbs which are conjugated weak in PDE were strong in ME, such as *climb* (PDE *climbed*, ME *clombe*), *creep* (PDE *crept*, ME *crope*) and *help* (PDE *helped*, ME *holpe*).

Some verbs had variant forms, such as the strong verb *bere*, which could form its past participle in any of the following ways: *ybore*, *yborn*, *bore*, *born*. Such variation was particularly useful for Chaucer in rhyme, as in the following examples:

'Allas,' quod he, 'that day that I was bore!'   (A 1542)

He seyde, 'Allas that day that I was born!'   (A 1223)

The third singular forms of the preterite tense of *bere* also vary depending on their use, as in the following examples:

Of smal coral aboute hire arm she bar   (A 158)

Under his tonge a trewe-love he beer   (A 3692)

Some verbs had both weak and strong forms, such as *weep* which appears as *wept* and *wopen* in the past participle:

For, God it woot, I have wept many a teere   (E 1544)

Til he so longe hadde wopen and compleyned (F 523)

Chaucer's exploitation of variant forms of the principal parts of certain verbs can be seen in the forms of the verb *clothen*. The usual preterite form of this verb is *cladde*, as in the following line from the Knight's Tale:

And of the same suyte he cladde Arcite   (A 2873).

However, Chaucer also drew on the variant form *cledde* in rhyme, as in the following example from *Troilus and Criseyde*:

This Troilus up ros, and faste hym cledde   (TC 3.1521)

Another variant form is *clothed*, which is used by Chaucer before a word beginning with a vowel or <h>, when the metre requires a disyllabic form. In the following line from the prologue to the *Legend of Good Women*, the form *cladde* would be elided with the following *hym*, so the form *clothed* has been selected to prevent elision:

> And clothed hym in grene al newe ageyn   (LGW G 117)

A similar use is made of variant forms of the past participle of this verb, where the form *cled* is used in rhyme in the *Book of the Duchess*:

> I wil yive hym a fether-bed,
> Rayed with gold and ryght wel cled   (BD 251–2)

The form *clothed* also appears as the past participle, and is used under the same conditions as outlined above for the preterite form:

> And they were clothed alle in o <u>lyveree</u>   (A 363)   livery

As well as these types of verbs ME also had a number of irregular verbs, the most important of which is the verb *be*, shown in Table 6.6.

Table 6.6 The irregular verb *be*

Indicative		
Singular	**Present**	**Preterite**
	am	was
	art	were
	is	was
Plural	be(e)(n)/ar(e)(n)	were(n)
Subjunctive		
Singular	**Present**	**Preterite**
	be	were
	be	were
	be	were
	are(n)	were(n)
Imperative	be (singular), beth (plural)	
Participles	**Present**	**Past**
	beyng(e)	been

Table 6.6 shows that there was considerable variation in the forms
of the present plural, although forms with *be-* are much more
common than forms with *ar-*. There are just a handful of the latter
forms in the *Canterbury Tales*, none of which are in rhyme, and two
instances of *ar* are found in the Reeve's Tale, suggesting that
Chaucer considered this form to be principally a northern one:

Wommen are born to <u>thraldom</u> and penance	(B1 286)	slavery
Thise arn the wordes that the <u>markys</u> sayde	(E 342)	marquis
I is as <u>ille</u> a millere as ar ye	(A 4045)	poor
Now are we dryve til <u>hethyng</u> and til scorn	(A 4110)	contempt

Another variant form used by Chaucer is *ware* for the preterite
plural. This form derives from the Essex dialect and is found in
earlier London texts, but was not in widespread use in the later fourteenth century. In fact the form never appears in Chaucer's later
works, but is found in rhyme in the *Romaunt*:

<u>Th'assemble</u>-God kepe it fro care!-		the assembly
Of <u>briddis</u> whiche therynne ware,	(RR 505–6)	birds

Another method of indicating tense in ME, also found in PDE, is
the use of complex verb phrases, such as an auxiliary followed by a
main verb: for example *I have loved* and *I had loved*. In the case of
transitive verbs (verbs which take a direct object) the construction
have + past participle is used, while for intransitive verbs (that
cannot take a direct object), be + past participle is used:

This mayden bright Cecilie, as hir <u>lif</u> seith,		legend
Was comen of Romayns, and of noble <u>kynde</u>,	(G 120–1)	family

A difference between ME and OE is the use of the verbs *will*,
shall to indicate future tense, as in PDE, as shown in the following
examples:

'But los of tyme <u>shendeth</u> us,' quod he.		ruins
It wol nat come agayn, withouten <u>drede</u>,'	(B1 28–9)	doubt

Men seyde eek that Arcite shal nat dye;
He shal been heeled of his <u>maladye</u>.   (A 2705–6)   sickness

In OE, these verbs had a purely lexical function indicating volition, that is, wishing or wanting, or obligation, and this older usage is still retained in some instances in ME. For example, the following use of *wole* is clearly intended to express desire rather than the future tense:

Chaste goddesse, wel <u>wostow</u> that I   you know
Desire to ben a mayden al my lyf,
Ne nevere <u>wol</u> I be no love ne wyf.   (A 2304–6)   wish

while this example shows the use of *shal* to convey obligation:

Whoso be rebel to my juggement
<u>Shal</u> paye for al that by the wey is spent.   (A 833–4)   must

ME had a further auxiliary verb that could be used to indicate past tense: *gan*, which was followed by the infinitive: 'This Absolon gan wype his mouth ful drie' (A 3730), which is an alternative to 'This Absolon wyped his mouth ful drie'. The construction *gan* + infinitive functioned as an alternative to the simple use of the preterite tense, and had obvious metrical advantages. Not only does the use of *gan* alter the number of syllables in the line, it also allows the main verb to be moved, often to a position in rhyme. For instance, in the following line *gan* supplies an unstressed syllable between two stressed syllables:

This Palamon gan knytte his browes <u>tweye</u>   (A 1128)   two

In the next example this construction allows the main verb *espye* to be rhymed with *ye* in the preceding line:

But as she <u>saugh</u> a whit thyng in hir <u>ye</u>.   saw; eye
And whan she gan this white thyng espye,   (A 4301–2)

The metrical advantages of this construction do not account for all its uses in Chaucer's works. This is clear from the use of *gan* in the two prose tales, where metrical considerations do not apply. While it is much less common in these prose texts, its use suggests that it carried a semantic, as well as a purely syntactic significance. In the following example, *gan*, which literally means 'began', is used to describe an action which had just begun:

> Whan Melibeus retourned was into his hous, and saugh al
> this meschief, he, lyk a mad man <u>rentynge</u> his clothes, gan   tearing
> to wepe and crie.   (B2 2162)

Here the construction *gan* + infinitive seems to have been selected to convey the sense of Melibee beginning to weep and cry, as a response to what greets him on his return. A similar sense is implied in a use of this construction at the end of the tale, when Melibee finally begins to incline towards the advice offered to him by his wife:

> Whanne Melibee hadde herd the grete skiles and resouns of dame
> Prudence, and hire wise informaciouns and techynges, his herte gan
> enclyne to the wil of his wif.   (B2 3060–1)

So, as well as serving a grammatical function to indicate the past tense, *gan* may also be used to mark the beginning of an action.

The passive voice was expressed using the construction *be* + past participle, as it is in PDE:

> I sal been <u>halde a daf</u>, a <u>cokenay</u>!   (A 4208)   considered an idiot;
>   weakling

Another method, also found in OE, is the use of the indefinite pronoun *man*, as in the following: 'Which that men clepe in Englissh Ydelnesse': meaning 'which in English is called idleness' (G 2).

Subjunctive mood

The subjunctive mood is concerned with the speaker's attitude towards an utterance, rather than its content. Where the speaker is uncertain about what s/he is saying, or is expressing a possibility, or a desire, the subjunctive mood is used. In OE the subjunctive was marked through the use of inflexions, but these distinctions were increasingly blurred and subsequently lost in the transition from OE to ME. In Chaucer's ME the forms of the verb used to indicate the subjunctive are shown in Table 6.7.

Table 6.7 Subjunctive verb forms

Present		
Singular	loue	binde
	loue	binde
	loue	binde
Plural	loue(n)	binde(n)
Preterite		
Singular	louede	
	louede	
	louede	
Plural	louede(n)	

Examples of the use of the subjunctive in Chaucer's works include the following instances.

In conditional sentences, often beginning with *if* or *though*:

And if thou take a wyf unto thyn hoold
Ful <u>lightly</u> maystow been a <u>cokewold</u>.　　(E 1305–6)　　easily; cuckold

As smothe it was as it were <u>late</u> shave　　(A 690)　　recently

In optative sentences, expressing a wish or a desire, and after verbs expressing uncertainty, such as *hope*, *trowe* and *thynke*, as in the following:

For which I hope his soule be in glorie　　(D 490)

I <u>trowe</u> he were a geldyng or a mare　　(A 691)　　believe

Hym wolde thynke it were a <u>disparage</u>　　(E 908)　　degradation

Table 6.7 shows that the endings used to mark the subjunctive forms of the verb were not particularly distinctive. This is especially evident in the case of the first person singular form, which is identical with the indicative, as in the following example:

Thogh that I pleynly speke in this mateere   (A 727)

This similarity between indicative and subjunctive forms led to the increasing use of the indicative in contexts where the subjunctive was required, as in the following example:

If thou lovest thyself, thou lovest thy wyf   (E 1385)

Here the indicative mood has been used in a conditional clause, where we would expect the subjunctive. The indicative is also found after verbs expressing uncertainty, such as *trowe* and *thynke*:

I trowe thou woldest loke me in thy chiste!   (D 317)

And therfore me thynketh that pacience is good. (B2 2729)

There is another example in the description of the Parson where the verb *trowe* is followed by the indicative *ys* rather than the expected subjunctive *be*:

A bettre preest I trowe that nowher noon ys   (A 524)

The use of the indicative here may be further evidence for the loss of the subjunctive during the ME period, or it may be that Chaucer has deliberately used the indicative because of the rhyme with *nonys* in the line above. Another possible explanation is that Chaucer's use of the indicative here is a deliberate stylistic device to emphasize the Parson's qualities as a priest. The description of the Parson is one of the few unequivocally positive treatments in the General Prologue, so perhaps the use of the indicative here is designed to stress the lack of uncertainty in the narrator's assessment of the Parson's qualities.

As a result of this lack of formal distinctiveness, ME developed a new method of indicating the subjunctive mood using the verbs *may* and *might*, whose senses already overlapped with the subjunctive mood. In OE these verbs were used to mean 'can' or 'could', a usage which is found commonly in Chaucer's ME as in the following examples:

For many a man so hard is of his herte,
He may nat wepe, althogh <u>hym soore smerte</u>   he suffers painfully
                                                (A 229–30)

O destinee, that mayst nat been <u>eschewed</u>!   (B2 4528)   avoided

We may compare the certainty and inevitability of these usages with the uncertainty expressed in the following examples:

That by som cas, syn Fortune is chaungeable,
Thow maist to thy desir somtyme <u>atteyne</u>.   (A 1242–3)   attain

Thou myghtest <u>wene</u> that this Palamon   think
In his fightyng were a <u>wood</u> leon,   (A 1655–6)   angry

The uncertainty implied in the use of *might* is made particularly clear in the following example, where it is contrasted with *koude*:

Greet wonder is how that he koude or myghte (B2 3679)

Infinitive

The infinitive form of the verb takes the ending <-e(n)>, and these alternatives may be exploited for metrical purposes in the same way as the present plural forms discussed above. The infinitive may also be accompanied by the preposition *to*, or *for to*, and this variation may also be manipulated for metrical effect. The following list of examples of infinitive constructions involving the verb *make* gives an idea of the range of forms available to Chaucer:

He koude songes make and wel <u>endite</u>   (A 95)   compose

For he kan maken, at his owene <u>gyse</u>   (A 1789)   fashion

She peyneth hire to make good <u>contenance</u>   (B1 320)   expression

In purpos was to maken hire his heir   (A 3978)

And for to make yow the moore mury   (A 802)

The theatre for to maken and <u>devyse</u>   (A 1901)   contrive

Imperative

The imperative mood is used to express commands. In PDE verbs have just one imperative form such as *Move! Run!*, while in ME there were singular and plural forms depending on the number of people being addressed. The two forms were as follows:

Singular	loue	bind
Plural	loueth	bindeth

The choice between singular and plural forms was not based exclusively on number, as the plural form could be used to express deference or formality when addressing an individual, in a similar way as with the second person pronouns. When Harry Bailly is commanding elevated pilgrims such as the Knight and the Prioress, he uses the plural form of the imperative:

'Sire Knyght,' quod he, 'my mayster and my lord,
Now draweth <u>cut</u>, for that is myn <u>accord</u>.'   lots; decision
(A 837–8)

'Cometh neer,' quod he, 'my lady Prioresse.' (A 839)

This distinction was not always consistently maintained, and we find examples of switching between singular and plural forms when addressing an individual, as in the following address to the Wife of Bath:

'Dame, I wolde praye yow, if youre wyl it were,'
Seyde this Pardoner, 'as ye bigan,
Telle forth youre tale, spareth for no man,
And teche us yonge men of youre <u>praktike</u>.'   practice
(D 184–7)

Here the Pardoner uses the plural forms of the second person pronoun *yow*, *youre*, *ye* alongside both singular and plural forms of the imperative: *telle*, *spareth*, *teche*.

Impersonal verbs

Impersonal verbs are more common in ME than in OE, and consist of constructions such as *me thynketh* 'I think', *me semed* 'it seemed to me', *hym leste* 'it pleased him', where the pronoun is the object of the verb rather than its subject. For instance, in the following example *yow thynketh* means literally 'it seems to you' and thus should be translated 'you think': 'And if yow thynketh this is weel ysayd' (A 1867). In some cases a dummy subject *it* is introduced, as in the following: 'Me thynketh it acordaunt to resoun' (A 37). Impersonal verbs are rare in PDE, although they are found in constructions such as 'it is snowing' and in archaic usages such as 'methinks'.

Phrasal verbs

The ME period also saw the introduction of verbs that consist of two elements such as *stand up*, *go up*, which probably arose through contact with Old Norse. In PDE phrasal verbs tend to be associated with colloquial usage, and many have synonyms that are preferred in more formal situations. Compare, for instance, the following two sentences, whose meanings are similar but which belong to different registers: 'Do you give up?' and 'Do you surrender?' This colloquial association seems to have been attached to these verbs early in their histories, as is suggested by the following examples. Consider, for example, the following instance of *give up* in the good humoured banter between Pluto and his wife in the Merchant's Tale: 'I yeve it up!' (E 2312). Another example is the use of *look up* in the Host's disrespectful summoning of Chaucer the pilgrim to join the company and tell his tale: 'Approche neer, and looke up murily' (B2 1888).

Negation

ME inherited the system from OE whereby negation was indicated through the use of the negative particle *ne*, which is frequently emphasized using *nat*, *noght*, *nought*:

But he ne <u>lefte</u> nat, for reyn ne thonder   (A 492)   omit

However, it is also common to find examples in Chaucer where the particle *ne* has been omitted, and the negation is expressed simply by *nat*, *noght*, *nought*, as in the following two lines:

Oure <u>conseil</u> was nat longe for to seche.   decision
Us thoughte it was noght <u>worth</u> to make it <u>wys</u> (A 784–5)   worthwhile;
                                                                  difficult

Where the *ne* is followed by a verb beginning with a vowel or
<w>, the two are often elided, as in the following examples:

But, sooth to seyn, I noot how men hym calle (A 284) (ne+woot: noot)

And he nas nat right fat, I <u>undertake</u> (A 288) (ne+was: nas)   guarantee

As she that nyste what was best to rede (TC 1.96) (ne+wyste: nyste)

That ye n'arette it nat my <u>vileynye</u>   (A 726)   rudeness

But not all such instances are elided, as shown in the following:

In al this world ne was ther noon hym lik   (A 412)

The dropping of the *ne* particle is particularly associated with colloquial usage, as in the Wife of Bath's comment: 'What that he mente
therby, I kan nat seyn' (D 20), or the narrator's informal comment
about his source in *Troilus and Criseyde*:

But wheither that she children hadde or <u>noon</u>,   none
I <u>rede</u> it naught, therfore I late it goon.   (1.132–3)   read

It is important to emphasize that the stigmatization of double
negatives in PDE standard usage does not apply in ME, so that
double, or even triple negatives, often had a reinforcing effect, as in
the following line from the Wife of Bath's Prologue: 'Of myn estaat
I nyl nat make no boost' (D 98). One effect of such reinforcement is
to make clear the scope of the negation, whereas the use of a single
negative particle often causes some ambiguity in interpretation.
     A further way of marking emphasis in negation is the replacement
of the negative particle *nat/noght* with a stronger equivalent, such as
namoore, *nothyng*, *nevere*, *noon*:

I graunte it wel; I have noon envie   (D 95)

That <u>sith</u> that Crist ne wente nevere but <u>onis</u>   (D 10)   since; once

He nevere yet no <u>vileynye</u> ne sayde'   (A 70)   rudeness

Another type of negation worth mentioning is the construction *ne ... but*. This can be used to mean 'only', as in the following example: 'That I ne sholde wedded be but ones' (D 13). In other contexts there is an increased sense of inevitability, so that in Egeus' famous comment in the Knight's Tale: 'This world nys but a thurghfare ful of wo' (A 2847), the construction *nys but* may be rendered 'nothing more than'.

The emphasis may also be increased by placing the negative particle in a more marked position, either by moving it to a position before the verb, or by stressing it using the metre, as in the following:

And <u>biddeth</u> <u>ek</u> for hem that ben <u>despeired</u>   pray; also; in despair
In love, that nevere nyl recovered be   (TC 1.36–7)

Here the force of the negative is emphasized by the placement of *nevere* before the verb, in a position where it is further stressed by the metre.

Adverbs

Like PDE, many adverbs in ME are formed by the addition of the ending <-ly> to the adjective, thus: *swete* (adj)-*swetely* (adv); *trewe-trewely*; *nyce-nycely*. There are also many adverbs in ME that do not have the <-ly> ending, which are marked by the ending <-e>, for example *loude*, *cleere*, *faste*, *faire*:

And Frenssh she spak ful faire and <u>fetisly</u>   (A 124)   skilfully

Adverbs formed in this way are often indistinguishable from the related adjectives and may cause some confusion, as in the following example:

Of <u>orpyment</u>, brent bones, iren <u>squames</u>,   yellow arsenic;scales
That into poudre grounden been ful smal;   (G 759–60)

Here *smal* may be mistaken for an adjective modifying *poudre*, but it is in fact an adverb describing the process of grinding and should be translated 'finely'. Another example is the word *clene*, which is identical as both adjective and adverb. In the following example it is an adverb meaning 'completely', rather than an adjective modifying *love*:

That al his love is clene fro me <u>ago</u>	(F 626)	gone

Some adverbs may be formed in either way, such as *cleer,* which appears as both *cleerly* and *cleere*:

For he was riche and cleerly out of <u>dette</u>	(B2 1566)	debt
The fires <u>brenne</u> upon the auter cleere	(A 2331)	burn

Here the form *cleere* could cause confusion, as it is identical in form to the weak adjective, and thus may be understood to modify the noun *auter*, 'the bright altar', rather than as an adverb modifying *brenne*: 'burn brightly'. It is important to remember that such words may appear both with or without the <-ly> inflexion, as in the PDE expression 'loud and clear'. Another example of an adverb which could easily be mistaken for a weak adjective is *hye*. In the following example *hye* is an adverb, but could easily be mistaken for an adjective modifying *roof*:

Thanne shaltow hange hem in the roof ful hye (A 3565)

A less common adverbial ending is <-lich(e)>, which is often found alongside the more common <-ly> ending. For instance, compare the following two instances of the adverb 'namely':

And namely fro the white wyn of Lepe   (C 563)

And namelich in his counseil tellynge   (TC 1.743)

Some adverbs may take all three endings:

This carpenter hadde wedded newe a wyf   (A 3221)

This knyght was comen all newely   (RR 1205)

that oother of hem is newliche chaunged into a wolf (*Boece* IV, met. 3)

Variation of this kind was extremely useful for Chaucer and he frequently exploited it for metrical purposes.

Relative pronouns

Relative pronouns in ME function in a similar way to PDE, although there are some slight differences in their use. The main difference is that, where PDE distinguishes between human and non-human referents in the use of 'who(m)' and 'which', this distinction was not made in ME. So in ME *which* can be used to refer to both human and non-humans, as in the following examples:

… save Dorigen allone,
Which made alwey hir compleint and hir <u>moone</u> (F 919–20)   moan

That ye swiche meenes make it to destroyen,
Whiche meenes do no good, but evere <u>anoyen</u>? (F 883–4)   do damage

In the first of the examples, PDE would use *who*, as it refers back to Dorigen, whereas in the second example, PDE would also use *which*. The second example also shows that, where the referent is plural, the relative often takes an <-e> inflexion to show agreement. As well as the simple *which*, ME also employed the construction *which that*, as in the following example:

This squier, which that <u>highte</u> Aurelius   (F 1499)   was called

Another alternative construction is *the which* or *the which that*:

He fil in <u>office</u> with a chamberleyn   service
The which that dwellynge was with Emelye   (A 1418–9)

As in PDE, *that* also functioned as a relative marker on its own, both with human and non-human referents:

Aurelius, that his cost hath al <u>forlorn</u>   (F 1557)   lost

Quyt every <u>serement</u> and every bond   pledge
That ye han maad to me as heerbiforn   (F 1534–5)

Chaucer also used the relatives *whos* and *whom* much as in PDE:

Bifore whos child angeles synge Osanne,   (B1 642)

'My righte lady,' quod this woful man,
'Whom I moost <u>drede</u> and love as I best kan' (F 1311–2)   fear

However, unlike PDE, *who* is never used as a relative pronoun and is only found functioning as an interrogative, marking questions, as in the following:

'What, who artow?' 'It am I, Absolon.'   (A 3766)

Sentence structure

ME word order is similar to that of PDE, although it is more flexible and preserves some variant structures inherited from OE that do not survive today. As with PDE, the most common word order found in ME is subject-verb-object, where the verb is placed directly after the subject. However, it is also possible in ME for the verb phrase to be delayed to a later position in the sentence, as in the following example:

This Nicholas his dore faste <u>shette</u>   (A 3499)   shut

When complex verb phrases are used, it is common to find the main verb split from the auxiliary, so that it can appear in rhyming position:

And whan they han this blisful mayden <u>sayn</u> (B1 172)   seen

Another OE practice, not preserved in PDE, is the reversal of the subject and verb following an adverbial, as in the following example:

In Surrye <u>whilom</u> dwelte a compaignye   once
Of <u>chapmen</u> riche, and therto <u>sadde</u> and trewe (B1 134–5)   merchants;
                                                                          stable

The reversal of the subject and verb is also employed as a means of marking questions in ME, as in the following:

Why rise ye so <u>rathe</u>? Ey, <u>benedicitee</u>!   (A 3768) early; bless you!

This means of forming questions was particularly important in ME, as the construction using *do* found in PDE was only introduced in the Early Modern English period and so was not available in the ME period. Where subject and verb are reversed in questions of this kind, it is common to find the second person pronoun *thou/thow* joined to the verb. In the following example, the verb *wilt* and the pronoun *thow* have been elided:

'Why so?' quod I, 'why wiltow <u>lette</u> me'   (B2 2116)   prevent

In ME clauses can be combined using subordination and coordination just as in PDE. A subordinate clause is one that is dependent upon a main clause and cannot stand alone, as found in the opening of the General Prologue: 'Whan that Aprill with his shoures soote …' and 'Whan Zephirus eek with his sweete breeth …', both of which are dependent upon the main clause: 'Thanne longen folk to goon on pilgrimages'. There is little difference between the subordinating conjunctions used in ME and PDE, for example *whan*, *how*, *if*, *er*, *whil*, apart from the optional addition of *that* in ME: *whan that*, *how that*, *if that* and so on.

Coordinated clauses are main clauses which are linked by coordinating conjunctions such as *and*, *or*, *but* and differ little from PDE practices. The major difference between ME and PDE is the greater use made of coordination in ME, as will be discussed more fully in Chapter 7.

Further reading

General surveys of ME syntax and morphology are provided in most histories of the language, while more specific treatments of ME are found in Blake (1992) and Horobin and Smith (2002, Chapter 6). Key grammatical changes that characterize the transition from OE to ME are discussed at greater length in Smith (1996, Chapter 7). The standard survey of ME syntax is Mustanoja (1959).

7 Language and style

It is often argued that Chaucer's stylistic practices were based upon theories established for composition in Greek and Latin, which distinguished three levels of style: high, middle and low. High style was characterized as containing words which stand out, either as old-fashioned or as strikingly new, and thus contains many 'neologisms', or 'newly coined' words. In contrast, low style was intended to employ everyday vocabulary which would not stand out, so as not to interfere with, or distract from, the message. The middle style was intended for entertainment and comprised a balance of stylistic features designed to please the audience. These distinctions were reinterpreted to a certain extent in the Middle Ages, and the choice between the different levels of style became linked to subject matter. Thus the high style was employed when dealing with noble and courtly themes, while the low style was appropriate for the world of the fabliaux and other lowly subject matter. The middle style functioned as a kind of unmarked style that was to be used in all other general contexts.

It is important to emphasize that, although he probably knew of these distinctions, Chaucer never refers to three levels of style, nor does he discuss their relevance to composition in English. He does, however, refer specifically to two levels of style: high and low. We get a good insight into Chaucer's understanding of the differences between high and low style in the Clerk's Prologue, where the Host calls on the Clerk to tell a tale, asking him to use a plain style that they can all understand, rather than a learned high style which is more appropriate for writing to kings:

Telle us som <u>murie</u> thyng of aventures.	merry
Youre termes, youre <u>colours</u>, and youre figures,	rhetorical ornaments
Keepe hem <u>in stoor</u> til so be ye <u>endite</u>	in reserve; compose
Heigh style, as whan that men to kynges write.	
Speketh so pleyn at this tyme, we yow preye,	
That we may understonde what ye seye.	

(E 15–20)

This provides us with a useful definition of high style, which, according to the Host, incorporates a restricted vocabulary and rhetorical figures of speech and thought that are likely to create difficulties of comprehension for a general audience. It is significant that the Host felt a need to warn the clerk against using such a style, as this is clearly a learned style, associated with 'enditing', or 'written composition'. It is also apparent from this quotation that the choice of this elevated mode of writing was related to its function: it is appropriate for writing to a king but not for recounting an entertaining tale to a mixed audience. These levels of style are therefore similar to a modern linguistic concept known as 'register', which refers to the kind of language selected according to use, rather than according to the user, such as a dialect or a sociolect. A single speaker controls a wide range of registers, and shifts between these according to the circumstances of a particular utterance. A register is therefore associated with a specific kind of situation, so that a different register is appropriate for an essay, a personal letter, job application or email. The same kinds of distinctions are also found in Middle English, so that a particular linguistic register is appropriate for a particular context. Here the situation demands that the clerk use an unmarked register so that his entire audience can understand him, while addressing kings would call for a heightened linguistic register.

We get an insight into the nature of the formal linguistic register referred to here in the Physician's Tale, where Claudius presents a *bille*, or legal charge, claiming that Virginia his servant has been abducted by Virginius. As the *bille* is a formal legal document, it is written in a stylized rhetorical language, displaying features characteristic of the learned style associated by the Host with enditing:

> 'To yow, my lord, sire Apius so deere,
> Sheweth youre povre servant Claudius
> How that a knyght, called Virginius,
> Agayns the lawe, agayn al equitee,
> Holdeth, expres agayn the wyl of me,
> My servant, which that is my <u>thral</u> by right, servant, slave
> Which fro myn hous was <u>stole</u> upon a nyght, stolen
> Whil that she was ful yong; this wol I <u>preeve</u> prove
> By witnesse, lord, so that it nat yow <u>greeve</u>. grieve
> She nys his doghter nat, what so he seye.
> Wherfore to yow, my lord the juge, I preye,

<u>Yeld</u> me my thral, if that it be youre wille.'   return
Lo, this was al the sentence of his bille.

(C 178–90)

The first feature to notice is the forms of address that are employed:
the plural pronoun *youre*, *yow* and the repeated use of deferential
titles: *my lord*, *sire Apius so deere*, *lord*, *my lord the juge*. These
respectful titles are contrasted with the lowly position adopted by the
plaintiff who refers to himself as 'youre povre servant Claudius'.
The sentence structure is highly elaborate and includes numerous
short subordinate clauses, which add incrementally to the weight of
the complaint and the sense of injustice: 'which that is my thral by
right,/Which fro myn hous was stole upon a nyght,/Whil that she
was ful yong'. There is parallelism in the repeated phrases 'agayns
the lawe', 'agayns al equitee', 'express agayn the wyl of me', which
highlight both the personal and the public nature of the crime.
Following this complex use of subordination, the complaint is
expressed as a direct and straightforward claim, the simplicity of
which adds to its force: 'She nys his doghter nat, what so he seye'.
The actual request is delayed until the final sentence, and even then
the imperative 'Yeld me my thral' is couched in terms of begging and
respect: 'my lord the juge, I preye', and no attempt is made to coerce
the judge into acting against his will: 'if that it be youre wille'.

In this example we have observed some of the features that characterize Chaucer's high style in a formal legal document and in the rest
of this chapter we will look at what other features characterize the
various stylistic registers used by Chaucer. Let us return to the description of high style quoted above and the first feature mentioned by the
Host: the use of *termes*, groups of words associated with a particular
field of discourse. Such groups of words are similar to the technical
jargon associated with certain fields in our own society. For example,
terms such as *silly-mid-on*, *gully* and *slip* are all specialized terms
associated with cricket, while *surfing*, *hacking*, *downloading* are all
terms associated with the World Wide Web. In his writings, Chaucer
distinguishes similar groups of terms, such as those associated with
law, alchemy, astrology, medicine, the church, philosophy and love.
When discussing the practice of alchemy, the Canon's Yeoman uses a
number of scientific terms, such as *orpyment*, *squames*, *cucurbites*,
and *alambikes*, which he describes as 'so clergial and so queynte': 'so
learned and so complex'. An important aspect of such 'termes' was

that knowledge of the correct terminology was felt to guarantee an appropriate mastery of a subject, while a lack of understanding revealed ignorance.

Of course terms could be learned without any understanding and were thus potentially a means to deception, as shown by the Summoner's parroting of a few Latin terms which he picked up from an ecclesiastical textbook: 'A fewe termes hadde he, two or thre,/That he had lerned out of som decree' (A 639–40). A similar misuse of terms is revealed in the way that the Canon convinces his victims of his ability to turn base metal into gold: 'For in his termes he wol hym so wynde,/And speke his wordes in so sly a kynde' (G 980–1). This kind of misuse of terms may be contrasted with the honest Virginia in the Physician's Tale, who never adopted 'countrefeted termes' so as to appear wise, but spoke according to her rank and moral character:

> Hir <u>facound</u> eek ful wommanly and pleyn,   speech
> No <u>countrefeted</u> termes hadde she   affected
> To seme wys, but after hir degree
> She spak, and alle hire wordes, moore and lesse,
> <u>Sownynge</u> in vertu and in gentillesse.   tending to
>
> (C 50–4)

The knowledge of such terms was also a means of ostentatiously displaying your learning, especially to those who did not understand them. This is demonstrated by the false modesty of the Franklin's 'I kan no termes of astrologye' (F 1266), immediately followed by a lengthy list of learned and arcane astrological jargon, such as *tables Tolletanes* and *proporcioneles convenientz*. For those unable to master the correct terminology, it was a means of revealing your ignorance, as Harry Bailly demonstrates in his failed attempt to list the terms of medicine following the Physician's Tale, which includes the mala-propism *cardinacle* for *cardiacle* 'heart attack', and which leads to the desperate admission that 'I kan nat speke in terme' (C 311). So one aspect of high style was the use of the appropriate technical termi-nology which was associated with a particular field of discourse.

Malapropisms, or the incorrect use of such words, were a way of indicating a speaker's ignorance of the correct terminology. A good example of this occurs in the Miller's Tale, in John's warnings against the dangers of astronomy, which he twice mistakenly refers to as *astromye* (A 3451, 3457). John makes a similar kind of ignorant mistake in a reference to Noah's flood as 'Nowelis flood', confusing the words Noah and Noel (A 3818). A similar use of malapropism is found in a deliberate mistake in the Reeve's Tale in the form *phislophye*, intended to highlight the ignorance of Symkyn the Miller (Horobin 2001).

As well as mastering the appropriate terminology, it was also important not to mix up terminology from different registers, as Pandarus warns Troilus when he is composing his letter to Criseyde. Pandarus advises Troilus to avoid formal or artificial styles, and to ensure that he does not *jompre*, or 'muddle' his terms, by introducing medical terms rather than those appropriate to a love letter (2.1037–43). We are given a useful insight into the kinds of lover's terms to which Pandarus refers a few stanzas later, when we are told how Troilus addresses his lady:

First he gan hire his righte lady calle,	
His hertes lif, his lust, his sorwes <u>leche</u>,	healer
His blisse, and <u>ek</u> thise other termes alle	also
That in <u>swich cas</u> thise loveres alle seche;	such cases

(2.1065–8)

We also learn that 'he gan hym recomaunde unto hire grace' and 'pitousli gan mercy for to crye'. All these phrases and vocabulary belong to the linguistic register appropriate for a courtly lover to use when addressing his lady.

We may compare this appropriate use of terminology with a similar, yet ultimately doomed, attempt by Absolon to woo his lover Alison in the Miller's Tale. Absolon is attempting to adopt the role of the courtly lover, but is consistently satirized in this attempt. His clothes and physical appearance, especially his long flowing locks, associate him more with the conventions of the courtly lady rather than the heroic male lover. This inability to take on this role is further revealed by his attempt to employ the appropriate terminology in his love speech to Alison:

What do ye, hony-comb, sweete Alisoun,	
My faire <u>bryd</u>, my sweete <u>cynamome</u>?	bird; cinnamon
Awaketh, <u>lemman</u> myn, and speketh to me!	lover
… <u>Ywis</u>, lemman, I have swich love-longynge	truly
That lik a <u>turtel</u> trewe is my moornynge.	turtle-dove

(A 3698–706)

Here Absolon makes the very mistake that Pandarus warns Troilus of: he mixes up words from a variety of registers. Instead of the polite terms of affection used by Troilus in his letter, Absolon calls Alison his *lemman*: a word which elsewhere in Chaucer is used only of women of dubious moral and social standing. In the Merchant's Tale, the narrator refers to Phebus' wife's lover as her *lemman*, but then immediately retracts the word with the following elaborate apology:

And so <u>bifel</u>, when Phebus was absent,	it happened
His wyf anon hath for hir <u>lemman</u> sent.	lover
Hir lemman? Certes, this is a <u>knavyssh</u> speche!	churlish
<u>Foryeveth</u> it me, and that I yow biseche.	forgive
The wise Plato seith, as ye may rede,	
The word <u>moot</u> nede accorde with the dede.	must
If men shal telle proprely a thyng.	
The word moot cosyn be to the <u>werkyng</u>.	deed
I am a <u>boystous</u> man, right thus seye I:	plain
Ther nys no difference, trewely,	
Bitwixe a wyf that is of heigh degree,	
If of hir body <u>dishonest</u> she bee,	unchaste
And a <u>povre</u> wenche, oother than this-	poor
If it so be they werke bothe amys-	
But that the gentile, in <u>estaat</u> above,	rank
She shal be <u>cleped</u> his lady, as in love;	called
And for that oother is a povre womman,	
She shal be cleped his wenche or his lemman.	

(H 203–20)

Here the narrator is making the point that, while *lemman* and *lady* have the same referent, there is a key difference in their connotations. The word *lady* is used to signal a woman of high social class, while *lemman* is suitable for a woman of low social standing. It is therefore inappropriate to use the words *lemman* or *wenche* to refer to a noble woman, who must be referred to using a more elevated term such as *lady*.

This usage is reinforced by the appearances of these words elsewhere in Chaucer's works. For instance, the word *lemman* is used by the Miller's daughter in the Reeve's Tale, by the Parson to describe the concubines of lecherous priests (I 903), by the steward who threatens to rape Constance (B1 917), and to refer to extramarital lovers in the Summoner's Tale (D 1998). In each case the word's use is intended to reflect badly on the social and moral qualities of the user or the subject. The restricted use of the word *wenche* makes clear its social and moral connotations. It is used to describe Malkyn in the Reeve's Tale, the prostitutes employed by the corrupt Summoner in the Friar's Tale and the disreputable women of the town visited by the Pardoner. Its lowly social associations are made explicit by May's ironic assertion that she is 'a gentil womman and no wenche' (E 2202). Given these connotations, it is interesting that the narrator of the Miller's Tale uses it to describe Alison: 'There nys no man so wys that koude thenche/So gay a popelote or swich a wenche' (A 3253–4). Thus certain words were considered to have particular social and moral connotations, and to belong to specific registers. Just as it is clearly inappropriate to refer to an elevated lady as a *lemman* or *wenche*, so is the use of terms like *lady* and *madame* to refer to women of low social or moral status, as is implied by the pretensions of the guildsmen's wives to be called by the title *madame* (A 376). So, while words like *lady* and *madame* belong to the elevated stylistic register, words like *wenche* and *lemman* are part of the low register, what the Reeve calls *cherles termes*.

If we look more closely at Absolon's attempts to woo Alison, we can see further examples of words that are sociolinguistically stig-matized in this speech (Donaldson 1970). For instance, Absolon assures Alison of his *love-longyng*, a phrase that appears only once elsewhere in Chaucer, in the Tale of Sir Thopas. The Tale of Sir Thopas is a sophisticated parody of the romance genre, and this use of *love-longyng*, combined with its lack of occurrences elsewhere, highlights how Chaucer undermines and satirizes Absolon's attempts to play the courtly lover. Another example occurs at line 3726: 'Lemman, thy grace, and sweete bryd, thyn oore!' Here Absolon begs Alison to show him grace and mercy, using the word *oore*. While the request is a highly conventional one for a courtly lover, this is the only use in Chaucer of the word *oore*. In every other occurrence the words used are more elevated terms such as *mercy*, *benignitee*, *charitee* and *pitee*.

It is apparent from this analysis of the distribution of these words that terms like *lemman*, *wenche*, *love-longyng*, *oore* belong to Chaucer's low style, as they are found most commonly in fabliaux tales that deal with characters of low social and moral standing.

Another feature of Chaucer's low style is the use of colloquial, scatological and vulgar vocabulary, generally avoided in more polite discourse. Chaucer's fabliaux include words like *ers*, *pisse*, *fart*, *swyve*; words that do not appear in tales dealing with more elevated subjects told by socially superior pilgrims. Yet we must not assume that all fabliaux employ a consistently low style. Often fabliaux draw on a range of styles for specific effects. For instance, the verb *swyve* is found frequently in Chaucer's fabliaux, yet in the Merchant's Tale the narrator avoids using such an 'uncurteis' word by adopting an elaborate circumlocution in which Damyan 'dressed [May]/In swich manere it may nat been expressed,/But if I wolde speke uncurteisly' (E 2361–3). This modesty is clearly intended to be ironic, especially as the narrator has just previously described the same act in much cruder terms: 'this Damyan/Gan pullen up the smok, and in he throng' (E 2352–3). A similar joke is found in the Manciple's Tale where the text of the Hg manuscript reads:

> The <u>montance</u> of a gnat, <u>so moote I thryve</u>!   value; as I may be saved
> For on thy bed thy wyf I <u>saugh</u> hym et cetera.   saw
>
> (H 255–6)

Here the narrator appears to suppress the vulgar word *swyve* in order to maintain a more polite register, yet the rhyme makes the absent word clear, with the result that our attention is drawn to it, rather than deflected from it (Horobin forthcoming).

Another characteristic feature of Chaucer's low style is the use of colloquial vocabulary, although identifying such words is often problematic. While we may be reasonably sure that the scatological and vulgar terms mentioned above were not used in more courtly contexts, there are difficulties in identifying other words that belong to this register. One way of discerning such words is by examining their distribution across the corpus of Chaucer's works. Where certain words are found to appear only in fabliaux, it is likely that these words are also indicative of a low or colloquial register.

There are a number of examples of such words in the Miller's Tale that are recorded elsewhere in Chaucer's works only in fabliaux tales. A good example of this is the word *hende*, meaning noble, courtly or refined (Donaldson 1970). There seems to be a paradox here: why would a word meaning noble or courtly appear only in the Miller's Tale? Surely we would expect it to be used of Chaucer's courtly heroes like Theseus in the Knight's Tale, or Troilus? In fact the word appears a total of 13 times in Chaucer's works, and 11 of these instances refer to Nicholas. This seems a particularly odd situation. Surely there is nothing very courtly about Nicholas, particularly when compared to the heroes of other tales? Yet the way this word is used in the Miller's Tale suggests that it is so closely related to Nicholas, that he can hardly be named without his epithet: 'hende Nicholas'. The two appearances of this word outside the Miller's Tale are also interesting, as neither refers to noble or heroic characters. The word appears in the Wife of Bath's Prologue, where it is used of another Oxford student of dubious morals, the Wife of Bath's fifth husband Jankyn. It is also used by Harry Bailly in an attempt to appeal to the Friar's better nature when trying to settle a dispute between the Friar and the Summoner (D 1286–7). It is interesting that it should be Harry Bailly who uses the word, someone with pretensions to grandeur but hardly qualifying as noble. So despite the word's meaning, *hende* is never used by Chaucer of truly noble and courtly characters, who are generally *gentil*, *noble* or *worthy*. The word *hende* can also mean 'skilled' or 'crafty', as it does when describing *hende* Nicholas's skill in *derne love*: 'This clerk was cleped hende Nicholas/Of deerne loue he koude and of solas' (A 3199–200). Another potential meaning of *hende* is 'handy' or 'near at hand', a meaning which also applies to Nicholas, whose success as Alison's lover is aided by his being her lodger, as the narrator makes clear: 'Alwey the nye slye/Maketh the ferre leeve to be looth' (A 3392–3). So it seems that, for Chaucer, the word's connotations of true nobility and gentility have been lost so that the word may only be used ironically, describing characters whose morals and behaviour are quite the reverse of these qualities.

Another word that means 'noble', 'gracious', 'attractive', but which is restricted to fabliau contexts is *gent*. It appears in the Miller's Tale to describe Alison's waist in a strikingly unflattering comparison: 'As any wezele hir body gent and smal' (A 3234). The only other occurrence in the *Canterbury Tales* is in the parodic Tale of Sir Thopas, where the hero is described as 'fair and gent' (B2 1905). Sir Thopas is the ultimate Chaucerian anti-hero, through whom Chaucer parodies and satirizes the whole genre of Romance. So the use of the word to describe Thopas further hints at its dubious connotations. One further appearance of the word elsewhere in Chaucer's works confirms our suspicions of its lowly status. The word is used to describe the goose, the most uncourtly of the birds represented in

Chaucer's poem the *Parliament of Fowls*, who is said to speak with a 'facounde gent' (PF 558). So *gent* is clearly another term of approval, but one whose connotations undermined such approval, satirizing and mocking its object.

The word *fetys* means 'elegant, shapely, handsome, neat', but its usage suggests that for Chaucer the word belonged to a low register (Burnley 1983). The adjective *fetis* describes the *tombesteres*, or 'dancing girls', in the tavern in the Pardoner's Tale, as well as the Prioress's cloak in her description in the General Prologue. The adverb *fetisly* is also confined to similar contexts: it describes Nicholas's bedroom and Absolon's hose in the Miller's Tale; Perkyn Revelour's hairstyle in the Cook's Tale; the friar's *poyntel* in the Summoner's Tale; the Merchant's boots and the Prioress's mastery of French in the General Prologue. The word *tretis* has a similar range of meanings, 'slender', 'graceful', 'well-formed' and appears only with reference to the Prioress's nose.

The adjective *deerne*, meaning 'secret', shows an interesting distribution across Chaucer's works. It is used only in the Miller's Tale, where it appears three times: once by the narrator in his description of Nicholas cited above, once by Nicholas who tells Alison that: 'For deerne love of thee, lemman, I spille' (A 3278), and then by Alison when she is urging Nicholas to be careful so as not to arouse the suspicions of her jealous husband: 'Ye moste been ful deerne, as in this cas' (A 3297). In all other contexts Chaucer favours the adjectives *privee*, *secret*, or *discret*, as in *Troilus and Criseyde* where Criseyde particularly praises Troilus' ability to control himself and remain 'so discret in al,/So secret' (3.477–8). So Chaucer's use of the word *deerne* in the Miller's Tale is evidently a deliberate use of a word whose status was lower than that of the words *secret*, *discret* and *privee* used elsewhere. Elsewhere in Middle English, the word *deerne* has a long history in romances and love lyrics, where the lovers are of lower status and where the reason for the secrecy is less praiseworthy than Troilus' desire to protect his lady's reputation. In the romances and love lyrics, the word is used of the furtive liaisons between clerks and their lovers, where its sense is often illicit or immoral. Clearly Chaucer's use of this word in the Miller's Tale is intended to carry some of those same connotations of the illicit and immoral love shared by lowly clerks and their lovers. Rather than being a means of protecting a lady's reputation, the *deerne* love of the Miller's Tale is a necessary means of carrying out adultery.

This low style is most evident in Chaucer's Tale of Sir Thopas, which draws heavily on the stock phrases and vocabulary of the vernacular romances. This is immediately apparent from the opening few lines:

<u>Listeth</u>, lordes, <u>in good entent</u>,	listen; kindly
And I wol telle <u>verrayment</u>	truly
Of myrthe and of solas,	
Al of a knyght was fair and gent	
In bataille and in tourneyment;	
His name was sire Thopas.	

(B2 1902–7)

This extract contains a number of words and phrases that contribute to its parodic style. For instance, there are several words and phrases operating as empty intensifiers, such as *verrayment* which means 'truly', 'plainly' or often simply 'indeed'. This word is particularly common in rhyme and is used extremely frequently in romance literature. Chaucer, however, never uses the word outside this context, showing that he did not feel it appropriate in serious usage. Elsewhere in this short tale there are other instances of tag phrases that serve no purpose other than to make the rhyme. These include 'in good certayn', 'ywis', 'it is no nay', 'In towne' and 'In londe'. As well as using these tag phrases in rhyme, Thopas also makes frequent use of stock phrases, another characteristic of vernacular romances. For example, Thopas himself is described as 'fair and gent'. His lovers are 'bright in bour', a phrase which occurs five times in the single romance *Amis and Amiloun*, in contexts that are similar to that of Thopas, such as 'With leuedies and maidens bright in bour'. Similarly, 'game and glee', found in Thopas at line 2030, is a stock phrase in these romances, as in the following example from *Guy of Warwick*: 'Sethen thai went into the cite/with ioie & mirthe gamen & gle.' Similarly, the phrase 'listeth, lordes' with which the tale opens, and which is subsequently repeated, imitates the opening of a large number of ME poems. Despite the popularity of this phrase elsewhere, these are the only occurrences of the verb *listeth* in Chaucer's works; elsewhere he uses only *herkeneth* (see Burrow 1984).

The vocabulary of Sir Thopas contributes to the establishment of an informal style in a similar way as we have seen in the Miller's

Tale. A number of the words used in Thopas coincide with those discussed above in the Miller's Tale, such as *gent*, *lemman*, *love-longynge*, *rode*. Thopas also contains words whose use is restricted across Chaucer's works, and whose distribution elsewhere in ME suggests that Chaucer considered them to belong to the same literary register. Thopas is labelled a *swayn*, a word used to describe the retainers of noble knights in numerous earlier romances. However, the word appears just once elsewhere in Chaucer, in the Reeve's Tale, where it is used by John to describe a common servant: 'Hym boes serve hymself that has na swayn' (A 4027). Alongside the word *love-longynge*, found only in Thopas and the Miller's Tale, are two other words that do not appear at all in Chaucer's other works: *love-likynge* and *love-drury*. Both terms are used elsewhere in ME to describe serious forms of love, such as in the lyric directed to the Virgin Mary where the poet describes how 'A loue-likyng is come to me/To serue þat ladi'. *Drury* is a term used frequently outside Chaucer to refer to love, a lover or a love token and it appears in many serious courtly contexts as well as in religious lyrics, where it can even be applied to Christ: 'Ihesu, my dere & my drewrye'. But for Chaucer the connotations of these words were evidently much less positive and he used them only in parody.

Another group of words used by Chaucer could appear in both formal and informal contexts depending upon the sense in which they were being used. For instance the word *cors* has three principal meanings in ME: a dead body or corpse; a living body; an individual or person. Chaucer uses the word in all three of these senses but only the first of these is found in formal contexts, as it is in the Knight's Tale to refer to the dead body of Arcite: 'Swownynge, and baar hire fro the corps away' (A 2819). The second sense is found on just one occasion in Chaucer, where it is used by the Host to refer to the body of the drunken cook, which he fears the pilgrims will be unable to lift should he fall into the mud:

And if he falle from his <u>capul</u> <u>eftsoone</u>,　　　　　horse; again
Thanne shal we alle have ynogh to doone
In liftyng up his hevy dronken cors.

(H 65–7)

Clearly the more usual sense of the word, referring to a dead body, is also being invoked here as part of the satirical treatment of the cook,

while the context demonstrates that this sense belongs to Chaucer's
informal usage. The third sense of the word is found twice in Chaucer
and both instances indicate that this usage is a colloquial one. In his
reaction to the Physician's Tale, the Host offers the following blessing
to the Physician: 'I pray to God so save thy gentil cors' (C 304),
where the word *cors* means 'person' or 'self'. It is significant that
once again it is the Host who uses the word in this way, indicating
further its low and informal status. The only other instance of this
usage is in reference to Sir Thopas, where the narrator prays: 'God
shilde his cors fro shonde' (B2 2098). So, while the word *cors* may be
used in formal contexts to refer to a dead body, its other senses are
only appropriate in informal and colloquial contexts, such as in the
speech of the Host or in the Tale of Sir Thopas.

   In considering words belonging to Chaucer's low style, we have
so far concentrated on words that are predominantly literary, but
whose status changed during the fourteenth century, so that by
Chaucer's time they were considered to be unrefined and unfashionable. As well as these, there is another group of words that may be
considered colloquial, in the sense that they were probably more
common in spoken than written language. This group includes
words that are imitative or onomatopoeic, such as *chirken* 'twitter',
fnesen 'sneeze', *poupen* 'to make a gulping sound when drinking',
twiteren 'twitter, chirp', or *chuk*, 'a clucking sound'. This group
also consists of interjections like *buf* and *tee hee*. All these words
and expressions are first recorded in Chaucer's works, suggesting
that the introduction of colloquialisms into the literary register was
an innovative feature of Chaucer's low style, although it did have
precedents. For example, the onomatopoeic verb *chiteren* means
'twitter' or 'chatter' when used to refer to birds, although it is also
used by Chaucer to refer to the way alchemists speak about their
craft (G 1397). But the application of this verb to humans is not
unique to Chaucer; it is used to describe the mumbling of a prayer
in a text of the early thirteenth century.

   Another group of words that probably belong to the colloquial
register are those which appear very rarely in the ME written record
and whose etymologies are uncertain. An example of such words is
gnof, used just once by Chaucer, with reference to the carpenter in the
Miller's Tale: 'A riche gnof' (A 3188). The word's etymology is uncertain, although it is thought to be related to the Frisian words *knufe*
'lump' and *gnuffig* 'coarse'. This instance is the word's only appear-

ance in ME, making it difficult to assess its meaning and its connotations. However, the very fact of the word's failure to appear in the written record, combined with its use to describe a comic character in a fabliau tale, may indicate that its use was generally restricted to speech, and that Chaucer's use of it in written English was unusual.

A similar word is *knarre*, also found just once in Chaucer's works, where it describes the Miller in the General Prologue: 'a thikke knarre' (A 549). This word is attested in several other ME works, where it means 'crag' or 'swelling'; Chaucer's use is the only instance of it being applied to a human. This may indicate that Chaucer was the first to apply a word traditionally applied to rocks to a person, or it could be that this usage was common in speech and that Chaucer was the first to introduce it into the written language.

Another example is the word *virytrate*, used by the Summoner in the Friar's Tale to address the old woman in a characteristically abusive manner as 'thou olde virytrate' (D 1582). The origin of this word is unknown and, as this is its only appearance in the written record, it seems likely that it was a colloquial term of abuse for an elderly woman introduced by Chaucer into the written language on this one occasion. Another contemptuous term for an old woman of uncertain etymology used by Chaucer is *rebekke*, whose appearance in the Friar's Tale is its only instance in ME (D 1573). Later in the same tale the summoner addresses the old woman as 'olde stot', a word that more commonly refers to a bullock or a horse, but was also employed as a disparaging term for a woman. Chaucer's is the first instance of this word in the written record, and the few other recorded occurrences appear mostly in colloquial dialogue in plays, indicating that it was a term of abuse associated predominantly with the colloquial register.

There are other examples of such words which are attested earlier in ME, indicating that Chaucer was not the first writer to exploit the resources of the spoken language. For instance, the word *fonne* 'fool' is used by John in the Reeve's Tale: 'By God, Alayn, thou is a fonne!' (A 4089). However, it is recorded earlier in *Cursor Mundi*, showing that its introduction into the written language was not Chaucer's innovation. Another word for a fool, *daffe*, again used by John in the Reeve's Tale, is probably also derived from colloquial usage. But, as in the case of *fonne*, this word is attested in writing in earlier instances, indicating that Chaucer was not the first writer to adopt it.

An example of a verb that appears to derive from colloquial usage is *gabben*, meaning 'to talk nonsense' or 'to talk indiscreetly'. A look at Chaucer's uses of the word with this meaning indicates that it was also considered informal in ME, as is suggested by Troilus's exasperated 'Whi gabbestow' to Pandarus (4.481). Other uses of the word tend to confirm this, as in the promise given by the carpenter John to Nicholas that he will not tell anyone of the second flood in the Miller's Tale: 'I nam nat lief to gabbe' (A 3510), or the man in black's sudden interruption of his exuberant description of his wife's beauty with 'Nay, trewly, I gabbe now' (BD 1075). In ME the word may also be used to mean 'deceive', or 'mock', and here the informal connotations are also evident. In *Boece* it is used by Lady Philosophy in a direct address to Boethius (Book II, prosa 5): 'Gabbe I of this? Thow wolt sey "nay"' and in the Nun's Priest's Tale it appears as part of the lively exchange between Chantecleer and Pertelote: 'I gabbe nat, so have I joye or blis' (B2 4256). A good indicator that this word was considered colloquial is that it only ever appears in direct speech, and never in reported speech or narrative. In most of these cases, the informal nature of the conversation further suggests that *gabben* was considered colloquial. The exception is the example in the *Book of the Duchess*, where it appears in the midst of a highly wrought speech, full of classical allusions, spoken by a nobleman. However, what we know of the word's use elsewhere allows us to appreciate the switching in register that this sudden interjection represents. Without a detailed knowledge of the word's use and associations elsewhere, such stylistic shifts would be lost on us.

As well as the use of colloquial and informal vocabulary, Chaucer's low style is characterized by the adoption of a directness that avoids learned or stylistic ornamentation, in favour of the communication of a simple message. Such a style is often labelled *brode* or *rude* by Chaucer, as in the Host's direct appeal to the Nun's Priest to tell his tale (B2 3998–4005), where the style is a reflection of the social status of the speaker and a lack of respect for the addressee. This kind of direct and simple style is not solely the domain of rude and uncouth speakers, but may also be used as a simple expository or didactic style, as adopted by Chaucer for his *Treatise on the Astrolabe*. In the prologue to this work, Chaucer excuses his *rude endityng*, or plain style, on the basis that *curious endityng* is difficult for a child to understand. A similar contrast is made by the Franklin in the prologue to his tale, where he apologizes for his *rude speche*, blaming it on a lack of rhetorical training, which necessitates his adoption of a style that is *bare and pleyn*. Following the elaborate apology quoted above, the Manciple also attributes his inability to observe the codes of linguistic propriety to a lack of learning: 'I am a man noght textueel' (H 235).

So, Chaucer's low style consists of a group of basic terms, including scatological terms, combined with a number of colloquialisms, as well as outdated courtly terms that are used ironically. Yet to try to impose a simple category of low style on Chaucer's works would be an artificial and unsatisfactory task. We have seen that low style is particularly associated with the fabliaux, because of the lowly social and moral qualities of the characters they deal with. However, another characteristic feature of fabliaux is a tendency to switch between styles, as may be exemplified by the Miller's Tale where we find a mixture of both high and low styles. At the end of his tale the Miller concludes his story with 'Thus swyved was this carpenteris wyf' (A 3850), using the characteristically vulgar term. Yet when describing Nicholas and Alison in bed, the narrator uses the euphemistic phrase 'In bisynesse of myrthe and of solas' (A 3654).

A similar contrast is achieved through the use of the direct *ers* and the discreet euphemism *nether ye*. Nicholas grabs Alison by the *queynte*, a word that means a 'curious device' or 'ornament', but here puns on the similar-sounding *cunt*. The same word appears twice in the Wife of Bath's Prologue, with the same referent, where it forms part of a series of euphemisms referring to male and female genitalia. These include the Latin word *quoniam*, meaning 'since', used as a slang word for *cunt*, perhaps punning on the French word *conin*, 'rabbit'. The French phrase *bele chose*, meaning 'beautiful thing' is also used, as are *nether purs*, *harneys*, *sely instrument*, *thynges smale*. The Wife of Bath's Prologue displays a series of stylistic shifts, from an elevated style to a more conversational tone. The Wife's elevated discourse is characterized by the use of learned terms, generally polysyllabic words of Romance origins, and the frequent use of rhetorical questions, as in the following discussion of the functions of genitalia:

Telle me also, to what <u>conclusion</u>   purpose
Were membres maad of <u>generacion</u>?   reproduction

(D 115–6)

Her conversational style is marked by the frequent use of discourse markers and interjections, such as *lo* and *fy*, and the following lines in which she gathers her thoughts aloud:

> But now, sire, lat me se what I shal seyn.
> A ha! By God, I have my tale ageyn.
>
> (D 585–6)

A similar kind of register mixing is found in the Miller's Tale. Here a learned style is created by drawing on a similar group of recondite, technical terms, which are foregrounded by their use in rhyme: for example *conclusiouns*, *interrogaciouns*, *affecioun/ymaginacioun*, *impressioun*. Alongside this elevated stylistic register appears a conversational register best characterized by Alison's titter following Absolon's kiss: 'Teehee!', and also heard in Absolon's pathetic response: 'Fy! allas! what have I do?' (A 3739). Another nice example is Alison's abrupt and dismissive response to Absolon's attempt at elevated courtly speech: '"Have do," quod she, "com of, and speed the faste"' (A 3728).

Chaucer's prose style

Although he is known today principally as a poet, Chaucer also wrote a number of important prose works, including a prose translation of Boethius, known as *Boece*, an astronomical work, the *Treatise on the Astrolabe*, and two prose tales that form part of the *Canterbury Tales*: Chaucer's Tale of Melibee and the Parson's Tale. These texts are very different in genre and subject matter so that a general discussion of Chaucer's prose style may seem impossible, or at least misguided. However, as will emerge in the following discussion, there are various features that link all these works, so that it is possible to generalize about the characteristics of Chaucer's prose style. In order to demonstrate this, and to isolate the features of which this style is composed, I will examine several prose texts in turn, beginning with the Tale of Melibee.

Chaucer's Tale of Melibee is a translation of a French prose work, the *Livre de Mellibee et Prudence*, itself a translation of a Latin work known as *Liber consolationis et consilii*. The French translation employs a stylistic mode known as 'curial prose style', and many of these features are preserved by Chaucer in his translation of this work. The curial prose style derived not from literary composition but from legal writing, and consists of a set of formulaic features that were common in legal and diplomatic documents. So while Chaucer encountered this style in his French source for the Melibee, he was also familiar with it from the prose in which parliamentary and Chancery documents were composed. This style of writing is characterized by the frequent use of Latinate expressions, legal phrases and linking devices such as *the seyde*, modelled on the French *le dit*, which all contribute to a precision and clarity of expression that is an important feature of legal writing. Another common stylistic feature of curial prose is the use of doublets, pairs of words with similar meanings. At the level of syntax, curial prose relies principally on subordination rather than coordination (Burnley 1986a).

A useful way of gauging Chaucer's debt to the curial prose style is to compare the style of his Tale of Melibee with that of its immediate French source. This comparison reveals instances of Chaucer embellishing the curial prose features of his source by adding doublets not found in the French, such as 'crie and wepen', 'by license and assent', 'by leve and by conseil'. He also introduced some of the set phrases that characterize this style, such as 'for sothe', 'for this same cause', 'this is to seyn'. However, Chaucer's attitude to the curial style of his source is not straightforward, as some changes show him removing certain repetitions, and reducing doublets to single words or phrases. For instance, Chaucer renders the French 'secret et celé' as *secree*, 'fuir et eschever' as *eschewe*, 'droit et raison' as *resoun*. So while Chaucer evidently adopted many of the stylistic features of his prose source, as well as expanding upon these in places, his use of the curial prose style in the Tale of Melibee is not especially prominent. Despite this, some critics have argued that the Tale of Melibee was intended to be a burlesque of the curial prose style, in the same way that the Tale of Sir Thopas is a parody of the Romance style (Elliott 1974).

Having determined Chaucer's inconsistent attitude towards the curial style in the Tale of Melibee, it is interesting to note that the features associated with this style are more prominent in a completely different kind of work: the *Treatise on the Astrolabe*. This suggests that Chaucer considered this stylistic mode as more suited to instructional and expository prose: a 'technical' style. I noted above that, while Chaucer encountered this prose style in the French source for his Tale of Melibee, he would also have been familiar with it from its use in parliamentary and legal documents. The majority of such records were in French, and it is only after 1420 that we begin to see English texts using curial features appearing in the Parliamentary Rolls. Despite their being in Anglo-Norman, such texts could easily have provided a model for Chaucer's own stylistic practices and may have suggested to him its suitability to technical writing. The earliest example of curial prose in a document composed in English is the Mercers' petition, written in 1386. This document contains a number of features associated with the curial style, including the elaborate opening and closing addresses: 'To the moost noble & Worthiest Lordes, moost ryghtful & wysest conseille to owre lige Lorde the Kyng, compleynen, if it lyke to yow, the folk of the Mercerye of London', and in closing: 'moost worthy moost ryghtful & wysest lordes & conseille to owre lige lorde the kyng'. The text shows considerable use of doublets, such as 'bi gode & paisable auys', 'the wysest & trewest', 'fredam or fraunchise', 'thynges nedeful & lefful', 'symple & vnkonnyng men'. The text also relies heavily on linking devices such as 'the said', especially in reference to the London mayor Nicholas Brembre, the subject of the Mercers' complaint: 'the forseid Nichol', 'the same Nicol', 'hym Nichol', 'he Nichol'.

Despite encountering this style in legal and parliamentary contexts, Chaucer evidently considered it primarily as an expository and instructional mode of writing, as indicated by his greater use of it in the *Treatise on the Astrolabe*. This treatise is a translation of a Latin work, *Compositio et operatio astrolabii*, by Messahala. Chaucer adds a prologue of his own composition, in which he directs the work to his 10-year-old son Lewis, claiming to have translated it into 'light Englissh' because Lewis is unable to read Latin. This is also a useful narrative device, allowing Chaucer to direct the treatise to a general uninformed and uninitiated readership, unfamiliar with the nature and use of an astrolabe. Thus Lewis is as much a persona and a narrative device as he is Chaucer's son and recipient of the text. That the text was intended for a wider and more diverse audience is further implied by the reference in the prologue to 'every discret persone that redith or herith this litel tretys' (lines 41–2), and the fact that it now survives in 31 manuscripts indicates that it did indeed gain a wider readership. The primary function of this text is therefore to convey technical information concerning the astrolabe to the uninitiated. The curial style found in legal texts is thus an appropriate method of conveying such information, as it aims at specificity in reference and the avoidance of ambiguity.

Here is an example of the use of this style, where Chaucer draws on the same cohesive devices, such as *the whiche*, *the forseid*, noted in the Mercers' petition discussed above:

> This moder is dividid on the bakhalf with a lyne that cometh descending fro the ring doun to the netherist bordure. The whiche lyne, fro the forseide ring unto the centre of the large hool amidde, is clepid the south lyne, or ellis the lyne meridional.   (I/4)

The simple didactic style of this text is further achieved through the use of coordination rather than subordination, as shown by the number of clauses beginning *and*, *than*, *next*, *tho* 'then':

> I fond the day of the month in manere as I seid; tho leide I my rewle upon this forseide 13 day, and fond the point of my rewle in the bordure upon the firste degre of Capricorne a lite within the degre. And than had I of this conclusion the ful experience.   (II/1).

There is very little in the syntax of the text that suggests a deliberate attempt at ornamentation. The reversal of the subject and verb found throughout the text, as in the last sentence of the previous example, is not a stylistic device, but an instance of the common practice in ME of reversing the subject and verb after adverbials (see Chapter 6 for further discussion). The examples of adjectives appearing after the noun, such as *lettres capitals*, *sterres fixes*, are also common in ME, found elsewhere in Chaucer's works, and are not an attempt at stylistic ornamentation.

Chaucer's treatise lacks other rhetorical or stylistic devices, often found in vernacular prose. There is no alliteration, a common feature of Old English and other ME didactic and instructional prose. There is frequent use of repetition, but this serves a didactic rather than a decorative purpose. The didactic function of such repetition is underlined by Chaucer's explanation of his stylistic method in the prologue, where he states that 'sothly me semith better to writen unto a child twyes a god sentence, than he forgete it onys' (49), and in a direct address to Lewis: 'Now have I told the twyes …'. The frequent direct appeals and addresses to Lewis are an effective means of engaging the reader, and help to construct a fictional relationship between the author as teacher and the reader as pupil: 'And tak kep, Forget not thys, litel Lowys; But understond wel; tak kep … and forget it nat' and so on. The use of first and second person pronouns adds to this sense of immediacy and directness, for example:

> Thyn Astrolabie hath a ring to putten on the thombe of thi right hond in taking the height of thinges. And tak kep, for from henes forthward I wol clepen the heighte of any thing that is taken by the rewle 'the altitude,' withoute moo wordes.   (I/1)

This last example raises another important issue in considering the style of Chaucer's treatise: the treatment of technical vocabulary. As a technical treatise, translated from a Latin work, Chaucer's work inevitably contains a certain amount of specialized vocabulary. However, Chaucer's treatment of technical words differs considerably from other technical writing of this period in avoiding, or explaining such terminology to his readers, rather than assuming that they are familiar with such terms. Where contemporary authors, often writing in Latin rather than English, use specialized Latin terms without explanation, Chaucer sets out to use only 'naked wordes', that is, ones whose meaning is transparent and clear. For instance, the word *equidistantes* appears in Chaucer's Latin source, yet instead of simply borrowing the Latin word Chaucer translates it as 'ylike fer', thus explaining it in simple English terms. In the above example, we see how Chaucer introduces a technical term, *altitude*, with a full gloss, and then warns his readers that he will now use the word without further explanation. The practice of glossing hard words is common in this treatise, and where Chaucer does rely upon rare or specialized vocabulary, he often accompanies it with a gloss, as in the following instances: 'contened or bownded', 'contened or intercept'. These doublets are generally a feature of curial prose style, where they are designed to add ornamentation and elevation to the text; here they serve the more pragmatic purpose of aiding comprehension. As well as using doublets, Chaucer also provides glosses for technical terms, such as his definition of 'tortuose signes', those which rise at an oblique angle, as 'croked signes'. More explicit definitions and explanations of terminology are also found, as in Chaucer's explanation that

> this forseide hevenysshe zodiak is clepid the cercle of the signes, or the cercle of the bestes, for 'zodia' in langage of Grek sowneth 'bestes' in Latyn tunge.   (I/21)

The *Treatise on the Astrolabe* does, perhaps inevitably, contain a number of scientific terms that would have seemed unusual and technical to a contemporary reader. This is worth stressing, because many of these have since become common features of English vocabulary, and their technical status is not always apparent to a modern reader. The word *introductory* is used for the first time here, and its only other appearances in ME are in medical and religious treatises. Another example is the word *fortunat*, which is used here in a technical astrological sense, referring to a time when the stars are found to favour the success of a person, or an undertaking. This is the earliest instance of the word in this sense in the *MED*, suggesting that it would have been a relatively specialized and unusual sense for Chaucer's readers. Given this, it is interesting to note that the word appears in a similar sense, in a quite different context, in the Merchant's Tale: 'The hevene stood that tyme fortunaat' (E 1970), indicating the amount of scientific knowledge that Chaucer expected of readers of his poetry, as well as those of his astronomical treatise. Another word that has a specialized astronomical sense in the *Astrolabe* is *dignitee*, used to refer to the situation of a planet in which its influence is heightened, either by its position in the zodiac or by its aspects with other planets. There are a number of other terms whose technical status is more obvious to a modern reader, such as *fraccions*, *longitudes*, *meridian*, *almenak*, *ecliptik*, *latitude*, *practik*.

Another feature that we have noted of curial prose style is the use of short stock phrases, and these are also common in the *Treatise on the Astrolabe*, especially such expository and explicatory phrases as 'this is to seyn'. Chaucer's treatise differs from contemporary scientific texts in employing homely comparisons and similes, which serve as effective ways of engaging the reader and helping to relate complex concepts to familiar ones. For example, in describing a complex pattern, Chaucer resorts to invoking a more familiar visual pattern, likening the crooked lines to the claws of a spider or a lady's hairnet:

> From this cenyth, as it semeth, there comen a maner croked strikes like to the clawes of a loppe, or elles like the werk of a wommans calle, in kervyng overthwart the almykanteras.   (I/19)

A similar attitude towards technical terminology is displayed in another prose treatise by Chaucer: the Parson's Tale. The Parson's Tale is a treatise on penitence and the seven deadly sins, partly translated from a Latin source, the *Summa de poenitentia* by Raymund of Pennaforte. As a penitential tract, dealing with the nature of sin and its remedies, the Parson's Tale is a similarly technical work, although, as with the *Astrolabe*, Chaucer's style is simple and didactic. Technical terminology is frequently glossed, as in the earliest use of the word *essoine*, an excuse offered for non-appearance in court, which appears alongside the more familiar *excusacioun*:

> biforn the seete of oure Lord ... whereas no man may been absent. For certes there availleth noon essoyne ne excusacioun. (I 163–4)

Other technical terms are explicitly defined, as in the following explanation of *actueel synne*, sin which is committed by one's own act (as contrasted with original sin):

> And thus is synne acompliced by temptacioun, by delit, and by consentynge; and thanne is the synne cleped actueel. (I 357)

The simple didactic style used in the Parson's Tale is also achieved by the use of repetition, noted above as a feature of the *Astrolabe*. Here is an introductory passage dealing with the nature of penitence, where the word penitence is frequently repeated and defined to avoid any potential uncertainty or ambiguity:

> and this wey is cleped Penitence, of which man sholde gladly herknen and enquere with al his herte to wyten what is Penitence, and whennes it is cleped Penitence, and in how manye maneres been the acciouns or werkynges of Penitence, and how manye speces ther been of Penitence, and whiche thynges apertenen and bihoven to Penitence, and whiche thynges destourben Penitence.   (I 81–3)

The Parson's Tale shows greater use of rhetorical devices than the technical prose of the *Astrolabe*, such as the use of alliteration, a device frequently used in sermon literature of this period. A good example of this is the definition of sompnolence as *sloggy slombrynge,* which comes from *slouthe.* Chaucer also employs colloquial and idiomatic diction, another feature noted above in his technical prose, as in the following definition of the sin of *janglynge*:

> Janglynge is whan a man speketh to muche biforn folk, and clappeth as a mille, and taketh no keep what he seith.   (I 406)

Another lively passage, which draws on colloquial and proverbial language, is the celebrated condemnation of fashionable clothing:

> Allas, somme of hem shewen the boce of hir shap, and the horrible swollen membres, that semeth lik the maladie of hirnia, in the wrappynge of hir hoses; and eek the buttokes of hem faren as it were the hyndre part of a she-ape in the fulle of the moone.   (I 423–4)

So, despite the very different genres of writing represented by Chaucer's prose corpus, certain stylistic features are common to all the works discussed in this section. Each of these works shows the influence of features derived from the curial prose style, although Chaucer's use of these devices seems to have been a reflection of their usefulness for conveying complex technical content in a clear and expository manner, rather than a concern with stylistic embellishment and ornamentation.

Further reading

Chaucer's stylistic practices are discussed in detail by Burnley (1983, Chapters 7 and 8), while Donaldson (1970) provides a seminal account of Chaucer's use of the language of popular poetry. General discussions of Chaucer's prose style can be found in Elliott (1974, Chapter 3) and in Schlauch (1966). More specialized accounts of Chaucer's style in individual prose works are found in Eisner (1985) and Bornstein (1978).

8 Discourse and pragmatics

One aspect of Chaucer's work that is often praised by critics is his ability to represent speech, and it is sometimes claimed that Chaucer's works give us an insight into how people actually spoke in the Middle Ages. While it is possible to exaggerate the significance of this claim (after all, millers did not use learned vocabulary or speak in strict iambic pentameter), there is certainly an element of truth in it. This chapter is concerned with Chaucer's representation of speech and dialogue and in it we will employ some of the methods developed for the study of pragmatics to see how he achieves these effects. 'Pragmatics' is the study of how meaning is communicated and understood by a speaker and a listener, and focuses more on the context of the message than on the message itself. In this chapter we will be concerned with issues to do with the way speakers address each other, the way they convey respect or disrespect, social superiority or inferiority. To do this we will look in turn at a variety of pragmatic features, including forms of address, politeness, swearing and the use of discourse markers. Finally, we will integrate these various approaches in a consideration of different styles of speech.

Forms of address

In our society the way we address someone is determined by a complex range of social factors, including age, social position and degree of formality. Some of these factors remain relatively stable, such as age and social rank, while others, such as degree of politeness, may be fluid throughout a conversation. We might address an old friend in a formal manner, but become increasingly informal as the conversation progresses and the intimacy returns. Alternatively, a conversation may begin on friendly terms but become less polite as it progresses, perhaps as a direct result of something said. A useful indicator of politeness is the form of address used by a speaker in a conversation. We might begin addressing someone using a formal title and surname, but switch to first name address to indicate greater familiarity or intimacy. Medieval society maintained a hierarchical social structure and many of these same factors can be observed in the conversations represented in Chaucer's works. If we look at the way Harry Bailly addresses the pilgrims, we see that the polite form of address is Sir + professional name. This form is used for a range of pilgrims, such as Sire Knyght, Sire Clerk, Sire Man of Lawe and Sir Parisshe Prest. There are, however, certain instances when Harry Bailly refers simply to a pilgrim by their professional name. This form of address, where the *Sir* is deliberately dropped, is a less polite variant. This is shown in the Host's use of this form in addressing the Franklin, where he dismisses his pretentious musings on the nature of *gentillesse* and reminds him of the obligations of the tale-telling contract:

'Straw for youre gentillesse!' quod oure Hoost.	
'What, Frankeleyn! <u>Pardee</u>, sire, wel thou woost	by God
That ech of yow <u>moot</u> tellen <u>atte leste</u>	must; at least
A tale or two, or breken his <u>biheste</u>.'	promise

(F 695–8)

This form of address is also used by the Host to refer to the Squire, Merchant and Manciple in less confrontational situations, suggesting that in these cases the Host did not perceive the social distance to be as great as in the case of the Knight, Monk, Nun's Priest and others. This is further indicated by the form of address used by these pilgrims when addressing the Host. Most of the pilgrims use the simple form 'Hooste' to address Harry Bailly, while the Squire, Merchant and Franklin are the only pilgrims who employ the more polite form 'Sire Hooste'. The form Sir + first name is also recorded, although it is more restricted in its use. It is a conventional way of addressing a priest, and it is also used to refer to the judge in the Physician's Tale: 'sire Apius' (C 178). This title is never used to refer to knights, such as Troilus; its avoidance seems to be an imitation of French polite usage, as evidenced in the works of Chaucer's contemporary Jean Froissart where sire + name is never used of knights

(Burrow 1984). The only time Chaucer does use this title of a knight is for the hero of his own Tale of Sir Thopas, where it is clearly intended to be a disparaging and mocking title.

A less polite form of address, commonly found in the *Canterbury Tales*, is *thou* followed by a professional name, as used by the host when calling on the drunken cook to tell a tale in the Manciple's Prologue: 'Awake, thou Cook ... God yeve thee sorwe!' (H 15). In this prologue the Manciple adopts a different strategy, employing the more respectful title 'sire Cook' as part of an ironically courteous introduction in which he offers to relieve the cook of the burden of telling the next tale. The offer is couched in exceedingly polite language, in which he concedes to the wishes of the cook, the Host and all the pilgrims. However, it quickly becomes apparent that this is a ploy to appear sympathetic and polite, before proceeding to heap insults upon the drunken Cook who is unable to defend himself.

The form *thou* followed by a professional name is also employed by the Host when addressing the Nun's Priest, in a speech which is characteristically brusque and rude: 'Com neer, thou preest, com hyder, thou sir John!' (B2 4000). A further form of address adopted by the Host, and used with a variety of the more elevated pilgrims, is the term *maister*. This is used to address the Physician, Shipman, and the Friar. In the last case it is couched in particularly elevated terms of affection and respect, 'leeve maister deere' and 'myn owene maister deere', and functions as part of the Host's strategy to appeal to the Friar's noble nature in an attempt to defuse the quarrel between him and the Summoner.

Another possible, although much rarer, mode of address is the use of the first name, adopted by the Host when addressing the Miller and the Cook. These two pilgrims are at the bottom of the social hierarchy represented by the pilgrimage and it is therefore appropriate that the Host should avoid respectful forms of address. If we look at the uses of first name address more closely, we see that the Host's use of this form of address is strategic. In the Miller's Prologue the Host is trying to calm the Miller down and prevent him upsetting the social decorum that he has established by asking the Monk to follow the Knight. The use of the first name address is an attempt to establish solidarity between the Host and Miller, associating himself with the Miller while reminding him of their mutual lowly place in the social hierarchy:

Abyd, Robyn, my <u>leeve</u> brother;	dear
Som bettre man shal telle us first another.	
<u>Abyd</u>, and lat us <u>werken thriftily</u>.	wait; proceed properly
	(A 3129–31)

The use of the Cook's first name in the Cook's Prologue seems to have a different function, as here it is followed by a string of abuses about the poor quality of his merchandise. Here the first name may be intended to signal a lack of respect, adding strength to the insult, or it may be an attempt to couch the insult in such a way as to minimize the offence caused. This is what appears to be intended by the subsequent use of the form 'gentil Roger', when the Host appeals to his sense of humour and asks him not to take the joke seriously. Interestingly, the Cook responds by calling the Host by his full name 'Herry Bailly', telling him that he too must not be offended by the fact that he intends to tell a tale of an innkeeper. In all other instances the pilgrims address the Host as 'Hooste' or 'Sire Hooste'; this is the only example of a pilgrim addressing another using the full name. This form of address appears to imply a lack of respect similar to the use of the first name, as is suggested by the way the Cook threatens that he will tell a tale of an innkeeper to repay the Host for his insults. Another example of first name address occurs in the Miller's Prologue. Here the Reeve responds to the Miller's intention of telling a tale of a carpenter with outraged indignation, telling the Miller to 'stynt thy clappe!' The Miller attempts to calm the offended Reeve, and tries to establish a brotherly solidarity between them by referring to him by his first name: 'Leve brother Osewold'.

There are also various forms of address that are used to refer to the female pilgrims, such as *lady*, *dame* and *madame*. The Wife of Bath is referred to as 'Dame' or 'Dame Alys', which is evidently a respectful form of address, also used to refer to such elevated figures as Custance and Prudence. That this form of address was considered socially desirable is shown by the fact that Symkyn's wife wished to be given this title, and no one dared call her anything else: 'Ther dorste no wight clepen hire but "dame"' (A 3956). However, the form *madame* seems to be a more elevated form of address, as indicated by the Prioress's title 'Madame Eglentyne'. Other uses of this term are the sergeant addressing Griselda (E 526) and the messenger addressing Custance (B1 732), indicating that it is a term of address employed where the social distance is greater than that implied by the use of *dame*. It is also the form of address adopted by Aurelius when beseeching Dorigen to pity him and return his affection for her:

Madame, <u>reweth</u> upon my peynes <u>smerte</u>;   have pity; bitter
For with a word ye may me sleen or save.

(F 974–5)

The rank and respect associated with this title are further indicated by the socially aspirant wives of the guildsmen who view it as an index of social status: 'It is ful fair to been ycleped "madame"' (A 376).

Another respectful form of address is *lady* followed by a professional name, used by the Host in his polite request to the Prioress to tell the next tale: 'My lady Prioresse', and 'my lady deere Prioresse'. Female characters are very seldom referred to by their first name alone, especially those belonging to the courtly class. Where the first name is used, it tends to be softened by the use of other terms of endearment. For instance, Troilus rarely addresses Criseyde directly by name, and when he does it is generally accompanied by various other forms of address, such as 'O my Criseyde, O lady sovereigne' (4.316) or 'O lady bright, Criseyde' (5.1264). Other characters in the poem never address Criseyde using her first name. Diomede calls her *lady* and Pandarus always addresses her as *nece*.

The use of the unadorned first name as a form of address is generally reserved for use where the woman is of a lower social status than the man. This is best evidenced in the Clerk's Tale, where Walter addresses his subservient wife as 'Grisilde'. Where the first name is used in courtly speech, it is marked and suggests some important shift in the relationship between the man and woman. For instance, Arveragus addresses Dorigen using her first name just once, at a crucial point in the story. Dorigen has told him of her promise to Aurelius, and Arveragus responds with: 'Is ther oght elles, Dorigen, but this?' (F 1469). It is not clear exactly how we should interpret this use of the first name form of address here. Is Arveragus shunning the conventional terms of courtly address in order to express unity and solidarity with his wife, or is he adopting the language of a lord addressing a servant, similar to that used by Walter to Griselda? Whichever interpretation we favour, it is clear that this form of address is intended to be marked and signal some important shift in their relationship at this point in the tale (Pearsall 1995).

Politeness

The above discussion of forms of address has shown that ME had developed a number of pragmatic conventions with which to convey politeness. These conventions were particularly important in the Middle Ages, as speech was considered to be an outward reflection of inner personality. The correct observance of the codes of polite speech was therefore an important way of signalling a sound moral character, as is indicated by the narrator's statement about the purity of the Knight's speech in the General Prologue: 'He nevere yet no vileynye ne sayde' (A 70). This comment rests on the assumption that the purity of the knight's speech is a reflection of his moral purity. A similar assumption lies behind the identification of the dreamer in the *Romaunt of the Rose* as a member of the gentle class on the basis of the courtliness of his diction:

I love thee bothe and preise,	
<u>Sen</u> that thyn aunswar doth me ease,	since
For thou answerid so curteisly.	
For now I <u>wot</u> wel uttirly	know
That thou art gentyll by thi speche.	
For though a man fer wolde seche,	
He shulde not fynden, in certeyn,	
No <u>sich</u> answer of no <u>vileyn</u>;	such; peasant
For sich a word ne myghte nought	
<u>Isse</u> out of a vilayns thought.	issue

(RR 1983–92)

This quotation makes clear the assumption that it is impossible for a peasant to speak like a nobleman, a sentiment also expressed by the Parson, who claims that 'chidynge may nat come but out of a vileyns herte' (I 626).

In this section we will apply some of the techniques developed by linguists for the study of politeness strategies to Chaucer's works. A key concept in the analysis of politeness is that of 'face', a term that refers to a person's self-image or the way they perceive themselves. During an interaction we expect others to recognize this self-image and respect it, either by maintaining appropriate respect or by being friendly, depending on the nature of the relationship. Instead of respecting a person's face, a speaker may decide deliberately to

threaten their self-image by issuing a face-threatening act. This may
lead to a direct confrontation between the speakers, or confrontation
may be avoided by the use of a face-saving act. This may be exemplified by an exchange between the Host and the Miller in the Miller's
Prologue. The Knight has just finished his tale and the Host has
suggested that the Monk should follow, thereby observing the social
hierarchy that placed knights and monks above the other pilgrims,
especially the peasant classes. However, the Miller, who belongs to
the lowest class represented on the pilgrimage, decides to challenge
this hierarchy and issues a face-threatening act. The Host's response
to this is to try to deflect this threat by replying with a face-saving act,
appealing to the sense of social decorum and emphasizing the
communality between himself and the Miller. This attempt fails as the
Miller is determined to tell his tale next, and the Host immediately
gives up and resorts to insults. Here is the interaction:

The Millere, that <u>for dronken</u> was al pale,	because of being drunk
So that <u>unnethe</u> upon his hors he sat,	hardly
He <u>nolde</u> <u>avalen</u> neither hood ne hat,	would not; remove
Ne abyde no man for his curteisie,	
But in Pilates voys he gan to crie,	
And swoor, 'By armes, and by blood and bones,	
I <u>kan</u> a noble tale <u>for the nones</u>,	know; indeed
With which I wol now <u>quite</u> the Knyghtes tale.'	repay
Oure Hooste saugh that he was dronke of ale,	
And seyde, 'Abyd, Robyn, my <u>leeve</u> brother;	dear
Some bettre man shal telle us first another.	
Abyd, and lat us <u>werken thriftily</u>.'	proceed properly
'By Goddes soule,' quod he, 'that wol nat I;	
For I wol speke or elles go my wey.'	
Oure Hoost answerde, 'Tel on, <u>a devel wey</u>!	in the devil's name
Thou art a fool; thy wit is overcome.'	

(A 3120–35)

In the above example, the Host's attempt to save face is based upon
an appeal to solidarity within the peasant group represented on the
pilgrimage. He addresses the Miller by his first name and calls him
his brother, emphasizing a close kinship between them.

When making requests, such as 'Tell us a tale', or 'Read me a
story', it is common for speakers to use mitigating devices such as

'please' or 'would you mind?', which help to make the request less threatening. It is also common for speakers to use more elaborate politeness strategies in order to soften a request of this kind. The most common kind of strategy involves appealing to a person's need for independence and freedom in their actions, and their desire to have their wishes respected: this is known as a 'negative politeness strategy'. Examples of this are: 'Daddy, could you read me a story please?', or 'I'm sorry to trouble you Daddy as I can see that you're very busy, but would you mind reading me a story.' We see Harry Bailly employing a negative politeness strategy when requesting that the Prioress tell the next tale:

My lady Prioresse, by youre leve,	
So that I <u>wiste</u> I sholde yow nat greve,	knew
I wolde <u>demen</u> that ye tellen sholde	judge
A tale next, if so were that ye wolde.	
Now wol ye <u>vouche sauf</u>, my lady deere?	agree

(B2 1637–41)

Harry addresses the prioress as 'My lady Prioresse' and 'my lady deere' and couches his request in a series of conditional and subjunctive clauses so as not to offend her by making a demand that is against her will: 'by youre leve', 'if so were that ye wolde'. The actual request is postponed until the very end, and when it comes it is made in formal and elevated language: 'Now wol ye vouche sauf, my lady deere?' By showing considerable concern for the Prioress's wishes, Harry Bailly avoids any attempt to coerce her or place a demand upon her, despite the fact that she is bound by the terms of the contest to tell a total of four tales over the course of the journey. It is interesting to contrast this negative politeness strategy with the bald request for a tale made by the Host to the Nun's Priest:

Come neer, thou preest, com <u>hyder</u>, thou sir John!	here
Telle us swich thyng as may oure hertes <u>glade</u>.	please
Be blithe, though thou ryde upon a <u>jade</u>.	nag
What thogh thyn hors be bothe foul and lene?	
If he wol serve thee, <u>rekke</u> nat a <u>bene</u>.	care; bean
Looke that thyn herte be <u>murie</u> everemo."	merry

(B2 4000–5)

This request is not softened with any mitigating devices; it is a simple command with no attempt to save face. The request forms one of a sequence of direct commands made by Harry Bailly to the Nun's Priest: *Come neer*, *com hyder*, *telle us*, *Be blithe*, *looke that*, further emphasizing the contrast between this request and that addressed to the Prioress. The informal and disrespectful tone is further achieved through the use of the direct question, in which the Host criticizes the pilgrim's horse and then implies that it is nevertheless adequate for someone of his status. The word *jade*, meaning a 'nag' or 'hack', is a colloquial and disparaging term for a horse, used only here by Chaucer, while the phrase *rekke nat a bene*, is decidedly informal.

Contrasting with negative politeness is the concept of 'positive politeness', which seeks to emphasize friendship, solidarity and a person's desire to belong within a group and their shared values and goals. As an example, we might contrast the above requests for a story with the following: 'Daddy, shall we read a story', where the speaker is appealing to a shared enjoyment of the proposed activity. A positive politeness strategy is adopted by the Knight in his attempt to resolve the quarrel between the Host and the Pardoner following the exchange of insults and threats that is sparked off by the Pardoner's suggestion that the Host kiss his bogus relics. The argument culminates in the Pardoner's sullen silence and the Host's refusal to continue to participate in the spirit of the contest. At this point the Knight takes over and attempts to reconcile the two parties and reinstate the good humour that has characterized the contest:

This Pardoner answerde nat a word;	
So <u>wrooth</u> he was, no word ne wolde he seye.	angry
'Now,' quod oure Hoost, 'I wol no lenger pleye	
With thee, ne with noon oother angry man.'	
But right anon the worthy Knyght bigan,	
Whan that he saugh that al the peple <u>lough</u>,	laughed
'Namoore of this, for it is right <u>ynough</u>!	enough
Sire Pardoner, be glad and <u>myrie</u> of cheere;	merry
And ye, sire Hoost, that been to me so deere,	
I prey yow that ye kisse the Pardoner.	
And Pardoner, I prey thee, drawe thee neer,	
And, as we diden, lat us laughe and pleye.'	
Anon they <u>kiste</u>, and ryden forth hir weye.	kissed

(C 956–68)

This is an act of positive politeness as it emphasizes the importance of group solidarity, reinforcing the sense of camaraderie between the pilgrims that has been disrupted by the argument between the Host and the Pardoner. The Knight emphasizes the closeness of their relations, telling the Host that he is dear to him, while simultaneously maintaining a respectful tone by using the title 'sire Hoost' and the plural pronouns *ye* and *yow*. He also coaxes the Pardoner back into the group by asking him to come closer, so as to be physically identified with the group once more, and by emphasizing the former intimacy and good humour of the group.

Swearing

Having considered some of the politeness strategies adopted in Chaucer's works, we will now consider how speakers insult each other. To do this we will focus on the use of swearing in Chaucer, beginning with a consideration of the kinds of oaths employed by Chaucer, and then looking at the various functions that swearing has in his works.

Swearing in the Middle Ages was more concerned with blasphemy than with the kinds of sexual swear words that are considered shocking in today's society. The most serious kind of blasphemy was to swear by Christ's body, as this was held to be like crucifying Christ once more, as made clear by the Parson's condemnation of such swearing:

> For Cristes sake, ne swereth nat so synfully in dismembrynge of Crist by soule, herte, bones, and body. For certes, it semeth that ye thynke that the cursede Jewes ne dismembred nat ynough the preciouse persone of Crist, but ye dismembre hym moore. (I 591)

These kinds of oaths are particularly common in the mouths of the three rioters in the Pardoner's Tale, where the narrator explicitly comments upon the implications of such oaths:

> Hir othes been so grete and so dampnable
> That it is grisly for to <u>heere</u> hem swere.   hear
> Oure blissed Lordes body they <u>totere</u>-   tear apart
> <u>Hem</u> <u>thoughte</u> that Jewes <u>rente</u> hym noght ynough-   they thought;
>   tore

(C 472–5)

The rioters utter such oaths that they tear Christ's body to pieces, as if they did not consider his suffering at the hands of the Jews to have been sufficient. Another character fond of uttering such oaths is the Host, whose reactions to the various tales are often accompanied by a volley of swear words. For example, at the end of the Clerk's Tale, he responds to the tale of the patient wife Griselda as follows:

> Oure Hooste seyde, and swoor, 'By Goddes bones,
> Me were <u>levere</u> than a barel ale   rather
> My wyf at hoom had herd this legende ones!'
>
> (E 1212b–d)

At the end of the Physician's Tale, the Host launches into a tirade against false judges, swearing 'as he were wood': 'Harrow! ... by nayles and by blood' (C 288). As well as these conventional oaths by Christ's body, the Host also uses other related oaths, which may represent less blasphemous variants, such as 'cokkes bones', 'by corpus bones'. Perhaps the Latinate version 'corpus bones', along-side 'corpus dominus', is meant to suggest the Host's pretensions to sounding educated and learned in his swearing, while 'cokkes bones' is probably a euphemism for the taboo form 'Goddes bones'.

Given the attitudes to swearing by Christ's body in this period, it is interesting to note that the Miller's first words when he disrupts the hierarchy established by the Host in calling on the Monk to follow the Knight are a series of oaths on Christ's body: 'By armes, and by blood and bones,/I kan a noble tale for the nones' (A 3125–6), alerting us to his immorality before he has even begun. The church's opposition to swearing is indicated by the Parson's condemnation of swearing as sinful in his tale:

> What seye we eek of hem that deliten hem in sweryng, and holden it a
> gentrie or a manly dede to swere grete othes? ... Certes, this is horrible
> synne.   (I 601)

The Parson's dislike of swearing is also shown by his response to the Host's swearing in the Man of Law's Endlink, where the Parson confronts him, asking 'What eyleth the man, so synfully to swere?' (B1 1171). The Parson's offended response appears to have little effect on the Host, who takes his objection to swearing to be a sign of sympathy with the lollards and, just a few lines later, swears by 'Goddes digne passioun'.

In spite of the Parson's opposition, it is common for Chaucer's characters to swear by God in various ways, including 'so God yow save', 'by God', 'for Goddes love'. French versions of these oaths are less common, as, for example, the oaths 'mafay' used in *Troilus and Criseyde* only by Troilus, and 'pardieux and depardieux' reserved for just Troilus and Criseyde. These distinctions suggest that certain oaths were considered to be indicators of class, a suggestion that seems borne out by the evidence of the *Canterbury Tales*. Not all such oaths are associated solely with elevated usage. For instance the oath 'parfay' is used by Alla and Custance in the Man of Law's Tale and so would appear to have been appropriate in courtly speech. But it is also used by Absolon in the Miller's Tale and by Sir Thopas, suggesting that it could also be associated with the unfashionable language satirized in both these tales. The fact that it is also one of a small number of oaths used by the Parson in his tale perhaps indicates that it was considered to be rather mild. Another French oath, *depardieux*, is used just twice in the *Canterbury Tales,* with an interesting distribution. It is one of the first words uttered by the Man of Law: 'depardieux, Ich assente', and then is later used by the devil in the Friar's Tale. As well as these various oaths invoking the Christian deity, there are many instances of invocations and swearing to classical gods found in tales with classical settings, such as 'by myghty Mars' in the Knight's Tale and 'for Joves name in hevene' in *Troilus and Criseyde*.

It is important to draw a distinction between swearing in vain, as condemned by the Parson, and the various kinds of pious oaths where God is invoked to add moral weight to a particular statement. A good example is found in the Franklin's Tale, where Dorigen invokes God in her vehement denial that she has held anything back in her confession to her husband:

> 'Nay, nay,' quod she, 'God helpe me so as wys!
> This is to muche, and it were Goddes wille.'

> (F 1470–1)

Criseyde's insistence upon her own faithfulness is reinforced by an invocation of all classical deities, and every other kind of mythological creature:

> And this on every god celestial
> I swere it yow, and ek on ech goddesse,

On every nymphe and deite infernal,
On <u>satiry</u> and <u>fawny</u> more and lesse,   satyrs; fawns
That halve goddes ben of wildernesse;
And Attropos my thred of lif <u>tobreste</u>   break
If I be fals! now <u>trowe</u> me if yow leste!   believe

(4.1541–7)

Swearing by the Virgin Mary tends to be limited to the the morally dubious characters, such as the taverner in the Pardoner's Tale who utters the oath 'By Seinte Marie', or the similar oath uttered by the adulterous wife in the Shipman's Tale in her outraged denial that Daun John had repaid the loan to her: 'Marie, I deffie the false monk, daun John' (B2 1592). Another good example is found in the Friar's Tale where the old woman's shocked response to the Summoner's demand for twelve pence provokes an oath to Mary, while the Summoner's response is to issue a threat by her mother, St Anne:

'Pay me,' quod he, 'or by the sweete Seinte Anne,
As I wol bere awey thy newe panne'.   (D 1613–4)

We must also be careful to distinguish between swearing in vain and invoking a saint or deity in prayer or supplication. For instance, compare the above swearing by the Virgin Mary with the prayer uttered by Custance in the Man of Law's Tale, in which she calls upon Mary the mother of Christ in the following way: '"Mooder," quod she, "and mayde bright, Marie"' (B1 841), or with the pious invocation to Mary that prefaces the Second Nun's Tale of the life of St Cecilia.

Many characters swear by saints, often ones with specifically local connections. The northern student John in the Reeve's Tale swears by 'seint Cutberd'; St Cuthbert was the bishop of Lindisfarne and this oath is particularly appropriate in the mouth of a fellow northerner. A similar appropriateness is found in the Miller's Tale, where John the Oxford carpenter swears by 'seinte Frydeswyde', the patron saint of Oxford. The miller's wife in the Reeve's Tale swears by the 'hooly croys of Bromeholm', a Norfolk shrine not far from the tale's Cambridge setting and the Reeve's own native Bawdeswell. The *Canterbury Tales* also contains a number of oaths by St Thomas of Kent, particularly appropriate given that the pilgrims' ultimate destination was the shrine of St Thomas à Becket of Canterbury in Kent. There are numerous oaths to common saints such as St John, St Peter or St Augustine, while less well-known saints are frequently invoked in rhyming position, suggesting that they may represent a metrical convenience, such as St Joce and St Loy in the following:

> But he was <u>quit</u>, by God and by Seint Joce!   repayed
> I made hym of the same wode a <u>croce</u>;   cross
>
> (D 483–4)

> Ther was also a Nonne, a Prioresse,
> That of hir smylyng was ful symple and coy;
> Hire gretteste ooth was but by Seinte Loy;
>
> (A 118–20)

This last example is interesting for the suggestion that this oath was considered particularly mild, and thus a positive reflection of the Prioress's character. Swearing by the soul of a parent is also common among the low characters, but not found in the speech of more elevated persons. As we might expect, it is a feature of the language of the Host, as in the oath 'by my fader soule that is deed' (A 781).

As well as these kinds of oaths we also find examples where a character utters a curse. There are some particularly lively examples in the Wife of Bath's Prologue where they are directed at her husbands, such as 'Jhesu shorte thy lyf' or 'the devel go therwith'. Having cursed her previous husbands like this, it is striking that the Wife positively entreats God to protect the soul of her fifth husband, Jankyn: 'God lete his soule nevere come in helle!' (D 504). There is another example of a curse in the Reeve's angry response to the Miller's Tale, in which he promises to be revenged, and calls upon God to curse the Miller: 'I pray to God his nekke mote to-breke' (A 3918). The Wife of Bath's Prologue contains a range of various oaths, often used in particularly inappropriate ways. She often invokes God in her memories of her sexual exploits and in references to her sexual appetite, as in the following example:

> As help me God, I laughe whan I thynke
> How pitously a-nyght I made hem <u>swynke</u>!   work
>
> (D 201–2)

She appeals to God when recalling her lust: 'As help me God, I was a lusty oon' (D 605) and praises God for the five husbands that she has secured: 'Yblessed be God that I have wedded fyve!' (D 44). The inappropriate way she invokes God in these examples verges on blasphemy, while her elevation of the classical god Venus to the status of a Christian saint is overtly blasphemous: 'I hadde the prente of seinte Venus seel' (D 604).

Other kinds of oaths found in Chaucer's works include the very common 'so moot I thryve', as well as the less common 'by my thrift', and a range of expressions relating to the head, including 'by my hed', 'by my pan', 'by my croun', 'by myn hood' and the amusingly inappropriate 'by myn hat', spoken by the duck in the *Parliament of Fowls* (PF 589). Often oaths function as metrical fillers and this is especially true of the frequent appearance of *pardee, benedicitee, God woot.* Another form of swearing in Chaucer is name calling, such as when Alison calls Absolon 'Jakke fool', or when the rioters in the Pardoner's Tale address the old man disrespectfully as 'olde cherl' and 'thou false theef'.

It is noticeable from the above discussion that swearing in the Middle Ages made little use of the kinds of sexual or scatological oaths that are considered taboo in modern society. This is important to bear in mind when encountering words which are considered taboo in PDE, as it would be misleading to assume that they were also taboo in Middle English. An example of this is the word *shit,* which appears just once in Chaucer's works, in the description of the Parson in the General Prologue. Here it is used to mean 'dirty' or 'impure', contrasted with the *clene,* or 'pure' sheep: 'A shiten shepherde and a clene sheep' (A 504). It would be easy to view this example as carrying the same taboo connotations as it has today, yet the verb *shit* is found in many contemporary texts, including romances, scientific texts and even in the Wycliffite Bible translation, where the backside is described as 'the parte of the body by the whiche tordys been shetyn out'. These other examples indicate that the word *shit* was a perfectly acceptable way of describing this bodily function and had not yet come to be considered inappropriate in polite contexts.

Chaucer uses several other words for excrement: *donge,* which is generally used of animal excrement, *ordure* and *toord.* There is little evidence from the distribution of these words, and the contexts within which they occur, that one was considered more vulgar than another. However, French-derived *ordure* appears just once with the meaning excrement in the Parson's Tale and so may perhaps have been viewed as a more proper or acceptable term, while *toord* is used only by

Harry Bailly in his insulting responses to the performances of the Pardoner and Chaucer the pilgrim. At the end of the Pardoner's Tale, Harry threatens to enshrine the Pardoner's *coillons* 'testicles' in a 'hogges toord'. In his other use of the word he dismisses Chaucer's Tale of Sir Thopas as 'nat worth a toord'. So Chaucer's usage tends to suggest that *toord* was the vulgar term and *ordure* a polite alternative, although it is worth noting that *toord* also appears in contemporary saints' lives and the Wycliffite Bible. So it would seem from this distribution that the word *shit* was unmarked, while *ordure* was an elevated term, with *toord* appearing only in colloquial or insulting contexts. These examples also show that, while scatological and sexual references are less common in ME, they could be used in insults with a force that is easier for us to appreciate.

In contrast to the variety of curses and insults we find in the mouths of Chaucer's characters are a number of blessings and benedictions, such as the Knight's final blessing on the pilgrims at the end of his tale: 'And God save al this faire compaignye!' (A 3108). A similar kind of blessing is found at the end of the Reeve's Tale, although here the generosity of the sentiment is undermined by the closing reference to his vengeance upon the Miller:

> And God, that sitteth heighe in <u>magestee</u>,   majesty
> Save al this compaignye, grete and smale!
> Thus have I <u>quyt</u> the Millere in my tale.   repaid
>
> (A 4322–4)

Discourse markers

Discourse markers are elements which have little or no semantic meaning, but whose use is governed by pragmatic principles. They occur mostly in speech and can be single words or phrases, as in the following examples found commonly in PDE: *so*, *well*, *y'know*, *I mean*. ME employed discourse markers in similar ways to PDE and this section will investigate Chaucer's use of two such pragmatic features.

The first discourse marker we will consider is *well*, used in PDE in several different ways. In PDE *well* is used as a frame marker, to mark the beginning of a new topic or introduce a piece of reported direct speech. It is also used to mitigate a face-threatening act by reducing the force of a confrontation. It can also function as a qualifier, where a speaker fails to provide a complete or sufficient answer to a question. Finally, it also functions as a pause filler, helping to fill a silence or a gap in a conversation.

Most of these functions are attested in the ME uses of *wel*, and examples can be found in Chaucer's usage. For instance, *wel* may be used to introduce a new section or topic in a discourse, as in the following example from the *House of Fame*, where the eagle introduces a series of answers to Geoffrey's questions:

'Gladly,' quod I. 'Now wel,' quod he,
First, I, that in my <u>fet</u> have the ...'   feet

(HF 605–6)

A similar example occurs at the end of the Manciple's Prologue, where the Manciple draws attention to the beginning of his tale with the following call to attention: 'Wel, sire,' quod he, 'now herkneth what I seye' (H 104).

As well as functioning as a frame marker, *wel* may also be used to mitigate a face-threatening act, as in PDE. An example of this is also found in the Manciple's Prologue. Here the Host has subjected the Cook to a volley of insults and called upon him to tell the next tale. The Cook complains that he is too tired to tell his tale. The Manciple then joins in the discussion, attempting to defuse the confrontation by offering to tell a tale in the Cook's place. This interruption and offer is made with considerable politeness, as the Manciple works hard not to offend Cook, Host, or any of the pilgrims:

'Wel,' quod the Maunciple, 'if it may doon <u>ese</u>   ease
To thee, sire Cook, and to no <u>wight</u> displese,   person
Which that heere rideth in this compaignye,
And that oure Hoost wole, of his curteisye,
I wol as now excuse thee of thy tale.'

(H 25–9)

Here we see *wel* being used to play down any offence and avoid a direct confrontation, although this is only a temporary strategy soon replaced by direct rudeness. A similar kind of strategic use of *wel* is found in another confrontational scene, this time in the Merchant's Tale, although here *wel* is used to mark a direct and abrupt riposte by

January to Justinus's insulting suggestion that he will be unable to keep his wife happy. Instead of trying to deflect or downplay this insult, January prefers to confront it and reject it, marking his reply with the discourse marker *wel*:

> 'Wel,' quod this Januarie, 'and <u>hastow</u> ysayd?   have you
> Straw for thy Senek, and for thy proverbes!
> I counte nat a <u>panyer</u> ful of herbes   basket
> Of <u>scole</u>-termes. Wyser men than thow,   scholastic
> As thou hast herd, <u>assenteden</u> right now   agreed
> To my purpos. Placebo, what sey ye?'

(E 1566–71)

A similarly confrontational use of *wel* is apparent in the speech in which the enraged Thomas promises the friar a special donation in the Summoner's Tale:

> 'Now wel,' quod he, 'and somwhat shal I yive
> Unto youre hooly covent whil I lyve;'

(D 2129–30)

There is little evidence in ME of the use of *wel* as a qualifier, where it used by a speaker to avoid giving a direct response to a question. There is, however, one example in the *Canterbury Tales*, where it seems to function as a lead in to an attempt to gain more specific information, in the Host's desire to gain more information from the Canon's Yeoman regarding his master's occupation:

> 'Wel,' quod oure Hoost, 'I pray thee, tel me than,
> Is he a clerk, or noon? Telle what he is.'   (G 615–6)

A second example of a discourse marker that is used frequently by Chaucer is *lo*. This can be used to attract or direct an audience's attention, like 'behold', as in the following example taken from the Knight's Tale: 'Loo the ook, that hath so long a norisshynge' (A 3017), or the host's drawing the pilgrims' attention to places on their journey: 'Lo Depeford, and it is half-wey pryme!' (A 3906). But *lo* may also be used by the narrator to mark a rhetorical statement that conveys a truth that has a relevance beyond the immediate context of the story. An example of this is found in the Miller's Tale, where the narrator comments on the carpenter's credulity when accepting Nicholas's warning concerning the coming second flood:

> Lo, <u>which</u> a greet thyng is <u>affeccioun</u>!   what; emotion
> Men may dyen of ymaginacioun,
> So depe may impressioun be take.
>
>   (A 3611–13)

It is also used when a speaker cites a learned authority, as in the Wife of Bath's appeal to the example of Solomon: 'Lo, heere the wise kyng, daun Salomon' (D 35), the Summoner's reference to Moses: "Lo, Moyses fourty dayes and fourty nyght …" (D 1885), and the repeated references to Old Testament exemplars in January's discourse on marriage in the Merchant's Tale: 'Lo, how that Jacob … Lo Judith … Lo Abigayl …' (E 1362–9). Similarly it is also used to introduce a direct quotation from an authority, as in the following quotation from St Augustine in the Parson's Tale: 'Loo, what seith Seint Augustyn: "Ther is nothyng so lyk the develes child as he that ofte chideth"' (I 630). *Lo* can also be used as a framing device, to mark the beginning or end of a discrete piece of text, as in the Squire's introduction of his own tale with the line: 'My wyl is good, and lo, my tale is this' (F 8). The use of *lo* to mark the end of a piece of discourse or text is found at the conclusion of the reading of the bill in the Physician's Tale: 'Lo, this was al the sentence of his bille' (C 190). It is used by the Pardoner at the close of his account of his preaching methods, 'And lo, sires, thus I preche' (C 915), and also by Chaucer the pilgrim to announce the end of the second fit: 'Loo, lordes myne, heere is a fit!' (B2 2078).

Styles of speech

Colloquial style

Having considered various pragmatic features in isolation, the rest of this chapter will consider how Chaucer manipulated these various pragmatic conventions to represent different styles of speech, beginning with a study of colloquial speech.

One of the ways Chaucer represents colloquial speech is by using short interjections and phrases that are not typical of more formal written language. There are some good examples of this in the Miller's Tale, as in John's desperate attempt to rouse Nicholas from his trance: 'What! Nicholay! What, how! What, looke adoun!' (A 3477). Alison undercuts Absolon's attempt to woo her using high style romantic language with a series of abrupt monosyllables: '"Have do," quod she, "com of, and speed the faste"' (A 3728). A similar switch from high to low style is also seen in Absolon's speech after he receives his kiss, which reduces him to 'Fy! allas! what have I do?' (A 3739). Alison's phrase 'com of' is also used by John in the Reeve's Tale as he tries to spur Alayn into action: 'Step on thy feet! Com of, man, al atanes!' (A 4074). A similarly collo-quial phrase is 'go bet' meaning 'go quickly', which is used by one of the rioters in the Pardoner's Tale to his servant (C 667), as well as by Juno to her messenger in the *Book of the Duchess* (BD 136) and by the hunters in the Legend of Dido: 'Hay! Go bet! Pryke thow! Lat gon, lat gon!' (LGW 1213). The last example shows the use of repetition, another characteristic of colloquial language, which tends towards a greater redundancy than formal language.

The vehement exchange between the Friar and the Summoner at the end of the Wife of Bath's Prologue demonstrates similar charac-teristics in its representation of the colloquial idiom. Here the pilgrims address each other using direct statements, commands and questions without concern for politeness. The sentences rarely extend beyond the line and there is frequent use of short, idiomatic phrases, such as the Summoner's 'What! amble, or trotte, or pees, or go sit doun!' (D 838). Oaths and swearing are also a feature of this dialogue, as in the Summoner's curse 'I bishrewe thy face'. The Host's interjection displays similar colloquial features in his use of short, direct commands with a simple word order:

> Oure Hooste cride 'Pees! And that anon!'
> And seyde, 'Lat the womman telle hire tale.
> Ye <u>fare</u> as folk that dronken ben of ale.   behave
> Do, dame, telle forth youre tale, and that is best.'
>
> (D 850–3)

Colloquial language is also characterized by a variety of idioms, phrases and discourse markers, such as 'lat se now', 'so moot I gon', 'y trowe hyt', which suggest a speaker thinking out loud, or responding directly to an immediate audience. Examples of this technique are found in the Wife of Bath's Prologue, as in the following, where we witness her losing and then regaining her train of thought:

> But now, sire, lat me se what shal I seyn.
> A ha! By God, I have my tale ageyn.
>
> (D 585–6)

Alongside phrases and idioms of this kind are ones that are particularly common, such as *parde*, *ywis*, *certeyn*, although these are often found in more formal passages as well as in colloquial speech.

A helpful way of examining how Chaucer conveys colloquial style is to analyse some sample passages of spoken dialogue. The first example we will consider is the colloquial style adopted by Pandarus in his conversations with Troilus, as in the following:

> This Pandarus com lepyng in atones,
> And seyde thus: 'Who hath ben wel <u>ibete</u>   beaten
> To-day with swerdes and with slynge-stones,
> But Troilus, that hath caught hym an hete?'
> And gan to <u>jape</u>, and seyde, 'Lord, so ye <u>swete</u>!   joke; sweat
> But <u>ris</u> and lat us <u>soupe</u> and go to reste.'   rise; sup
> And he answerde hym, 'Do we as <u>the leste</u>.'   you please
>
> (2.939–45)

Here the informality is achieved through the use of direct questions and short, simple commands, exclamations and the comic observation of how sweaty Troilus appears after a day's heavy fighting.

This direct and conversational style may be contrasted with the high style of Troilus, found most prominently in his monologues, but also in his exchanges with Pandarus. For instance, in the dialogue in which Pandarus extracts the name of his love from Troilus, Troilus pleads for Pandarus' help in the following rhetorical set piece:

> Now, Pandare, I kan na more seye,
> But, thow <u>wis</u>, thow woost, thow maist, thow art al!   wise one
> My lif, my deth, <u>hol</u> in thyn hond I leye.   completely
> Help now!
>
> (1.1051–4)

This appeal employs various rhetorical devices, such as the patterned repetition of *wis* (wise one) and *woost* (know) and of the second person pronoun *thow*: *thow wis*, *thow woost*, *thou maist*, *thow art al* and the effective contrast of the following line: 'My lif, my deth'. The word order is reversed to bring the object to the beginning of the line, postponing the verb to the end of the line, while the plea for help is postponed until the fourth line. When it does come it is framed as a simple imperative, creating an effective shift from the high style to a simple unadorned and earnest cry for help.

Another good example of colloquial language is found in the speech of the eagle in the *House of Fame*.

And <u>thoo</u> gan he me to <u>disporte</u>,	then; cheer
And with wordes to comforte,	
And sayde twyes, 'Seynte Marye,	
Thou art <u>noyous</u> for to carye!	difficult
And nothyng nedeth it, <u>pardee</u>,	by God
For <u>also</u> wis God helpe me,	as
As thou noon harm shalt have of this;	
And this caas that betyd the is,	
Is for thy <u>lore</u> and for thy <u>prow</u>.	teaching; profit
Let see! Darst thou yet loke now?	
Be ful <u>assured</u>, boldely,	confident
I am thy frend.' And therwith I	
Gan for to wondren in my mynde.	

(HF 571–83)

The colloquial nature of the Eagle's speech is apparent from the use of oaths in which he swears by Mary and God, as well as the rude way he complains about Geoffrey's weight: 'Thou art noyous for to carye!' The use of the second person singular pronoun, *thou*, *the*, *thy*, marks an informal manner of address, and this is further established by the use of imperatives and direct questions: 'Be ful assured', 'Darst thou yet loke now?', where more formal speech would avoid such directness. The use of tag phrases, characteristic of spoken rather than written discourse, such as *pardee*, *let see*, also add to the colloquial nature of this speech.

The Eagle specifically describes himself as speaking 'symply, withoute any subtilite of speche', avoiding prolixity and specialized terms of philosophy, poetry or rhetoric, as this kind of speech can cause problems for the listener (HF 853–62). As we saw in the above extract, there is some truth in his assessment of his own style, although he does also employ specialized words like *cadence*, *covercle*, *palpable*, *renovelaunces*. In fact the eagle's speech provides an interesting mixture of complex and simple styles, particularly in the way long and complex sentences are broken up with the frequent use of interjections and tag expressions, such as 'dar I leye', 'Now herkene wel', 'Thou wost wel this', 'take hede now'. The use of direct and familiar forms of address, including the uncommon use of first name address, "Geffrey, thou wost ryght wel this ..." (729), and the familar 'brother' (795), adds to the colloquial and informal nature of the Eagle's style.

Courtly speech

Having looked at the features that characterize informal or colloquial speech, it will be useful to contrast this with the formal style associated with courtly or elevated discourse. There are several instances of the adverb *curteisly* being applied to a character's speech, although it seems significant that this adverb is never applied to the speech of genuinely noble characters. It is used to describe the Host's address to the Prioress in which he calls upon her to tell the next tale. The context for this address is also important, as it follows immediately from his brusque and highly colloquial reaction to the Shipman's Tale. The Host begins by swearing, by *corpus dominus* and by St Augustine, and then invokes a curse upon the monk in the Shipman's story. He also makes a rather crude appeal to the pilgrims to beware a trick of this kind, and to be cautious when offering monks hospitality. His language is colloquial, containing interjections such as 'A ha!' and idiomatic expressions such as 'a thousand last quade yeer' and 'putte in the mannes hood an ape'. However, when Harry Bailly turns to the Prioress to ask her to tell her tale next, he modifies his linguistic register accordingly, employing a style that is highly decorous and extremely polite, as we have already seen.

This example indicates that speaking *curteisly* is not intended to be a reflection of the courtly qualities of the speaker, but is rather a linguistic register employed for a specific occasion when addressing a particular person. As such it has the potential to be misused, enabling people with dubious motives to appear genuine. This potential is realized in two other uses of the adverb, where it describes the deceptive and manipulative speech of friars. The friar in the Summoner's Tale addresses Thomas 'curteisly and softe', and his speech is characterized by extreme politeness, blessings and flattery, as well as a smattering of Latin phrases for good measure:

> '*Deus hic!*' quod he, 'O Thomas, freend, good day!'   God be here
> Seyde this frere, curteisly and softe.
> 'Thomas,' quod he, 'God yelde yow! Ful ofte   reward
> Have I upon this bench faren ful weel;
> Heere have I eten many a myrie meel.'   merry
>
> (D 1770–4)

It is also interesting to note the friar's repeated use of the first name address, employed here as a way of establishing a relationship of intimacy and trust, further achieved by the familiar manner in which the friar brushes aside the cat and sits down on the bench without waiting for an invitation. The first name address is part of his strategy to establish a bond between himself and Thomas that will enable him to extract more money from him. It is used repeatedly throughout the tale, and is repeated three times in his familiar scolding of Thomas following the complaints made by his wife: 'O Thomas, *je vous dy*, Thomas! Thomas!' (D 1832). Similar features characterize the friar's greeting to Thomas' wife, although here he employs a more formal mode of address, using the respectful *Dame* and the pronouns *youre* and *yow*:

> 'Dame,' quod he, 'right weel,
> As he that is youre servant every deel,   completely
> Thanked be God, that yow yaf soule and lyf!   gave
> Yet saugh I nat this day so fair a wyf
> In al the chirche, God so save me!'
>
> (D 1805–9)

Here the flattery is directed at the wife's looks rather than hospitality and thus carries more suggestive and ambiguous connotations, which are further implied by his actions:

> The frere ariseth up ful curteisly,   rises
> And hire embraceth in his armes narwe,   tightly
> And kiste hire sweete, and chirketh as a sparwe   chirrups; sparrow
> With his lyppes.
>
> (D 1802–5)

Here the appeals to God become part of the flattery and thus are potentially blasphemous rather than blessings. That speaking *curteisly* was particularly associated with friars is further suggested by the reference to Daun John's devotions in the Shipman's Tale, which he said 'ful curteisly'. This image is directly contrasted and undermined by his subsequent innuendo to his host's wife, in which he suggests that her pale appearance is the result of her husband keeping her up all night.

Another interesting example of Chaucer's representation of courtly speech is found in an unlikely source: the *Parliament of Fowls*. Here we see how Chaucer's skilful handling of register and discourse conventions enables him to make social distinctions between the various categories of birds represented. Here is the speech made by the royal tercel, in which Chaucer employs the conventions of courtly speech to convey the bird's elevated status:

With hed enclyned and with humble cheere	
This royal <u>tersel</u> spak, and <u>tariede</u> noght:	male bird; delayed
'Unto my soverayn lady, and not my <u>fere</u>,	equal
I <u>chese</u>, and chese with wil, and herte, and thought,	choose
The <u>formel</u> on youre hond, so wel <u>iwrought</u>,	female bird; made
Whos I am al, and evere wol hire serve,	
Do what hire <u>lest</u>, to do me lyve or <u>sterve</u>;	please; die
'Besekynge hire of merci and of grace,	
As she that is my lady sovereyne;	
Or let me deye present in this place.	
For <u>certes</u>, longe may I nat lyve in payne,	certainly
For in myn herte is <u>korven</u> every veyne.	carved
Havynge reward only to my trouthe,	
My deere herte, have on my wo som <u>routhe</u>.	pity
'And if that I be founde to hyre untrewe,	
<u>Disobeysaunt</u>, or wilful necligent,	disobedient
<u>Avauntour</u>, or in proces love a newe,	boaster
I preye to yow this be my jugement:	
That with these foules I be al <u>torent</u>,	torn to pieces
That ilke day that evere she me fynde	
To hir untrewe, or in my gilt unkynde.	

'And <u>syn</u> that non loveth hire so wel as I,   since

Al be she nevere of love me <u>behette</u>,   promised

Thanne oughte she be myn thourgh hire mercy,

For other bond can I non on hire knette.

Ne nevere for no wo ne shal I <u>lette</u>   cease

To serven hire, how fer so that she <u>wende</u>;   travel

Say what yow <u>list</u>, my tale is at an ende.'   please

(PF 414–41)

This speech contains a number of features indicative of a high register. These include the forms of address, 'my soverayn lady', 'my lady sovereyne', 'my deere herte', and the use of the plural form of the second person pronoun: *yow*, *youre*. The high style is further achieved by the use of French vocabulary, such as *soverayn*, *merci*, *grace*, *disobeysaunt*, *necligent*, *avauntour*, *jugement*, *serve*. The complex syntax also serves to establish stylistic elevation, through the use of conditional and subjunctive clauses: 'And if that …', 'Al be she …', and verbs expressing wishes and desires rather than direct commands, for example 'I prey to yow this be my jugement'. It is also important to note that these stylistic features do not apply to the entire extract, and some of the effects derive from the use of simpler and plainer diction alongside these complex and marked stylistic devices. As well as using many French words, the tercel's speech draws a number of its key terms from the native word stock. Words such as *chese*, *wil*, *herte*, *thought*, *trouthe*, *routhe* are all ultimately of OE origin and show that high style did not always require a Romance vocabulary. Indeed, part of the strength of this appeal derives from the modulated style, which switches from the grandeur of the elevated Romance vocabulary to the heartfelt plea expressed in simple and plain terms.

We may contrast the above speech by the courtly tercel with those by the birds belonging to the lower social orders, such as the goose and the duck. Here are two speeches made by the goose:

The goos seyde, 'Al this nys not worth a flye!

But I can shape herof a remedie,

And I wol seye my <u>verdit</u> fayre and <u>swythe</u>   verdict; quickly

For water-foul, whoso be <u>wroth</u> or <u>blythe</u>!'   angry; happy

And for these water-foules <u>tho</u> began	then
The goos to speke, and in hire <u>kakelynge</u>	cackling
She seyde, '<u>Pes</u>! Now tak kep every man,	peace
And herkeneth which a resoun I shal forth brynge!	
My wit is sharp; I love no <u>taryinge</u>;	delay
I seye I <u>rede</u> hym, though he were my brother,	advise
<u>But</u> she wol love hym, lat hym love another!'	unless

(PF 501–4, 561–7)

The goose's speech is described as *kakelynge*, and it lacks many of the refinements associated with the high style seen in the previous example. Here the goose addresses his audience directly, issuing commands using the imperative: 'Pes, tak kep, herkeneth', and dismissing the complexities of the proceedings: 'al this nys not worth a flye.' The duck's intervention also serves to undermine the elevated discourse of the other birds, this time with the suggestion that the turtle-dove's profession of constancy is just a jest:

'Wel <u>bourded</u>,' quod the doke, 'by myn hat!	joked
That men shulde loven alwey causeles!	
Who can a resoun fynde or wit in that?	
Daunseth he <u>murye</u> that is myrtheles?	merry
Who shulde <u>recche</u> of that is <u>recheles</u>?'	care; careless
'<u>Ye queke</u>,' seyde the goos, 'ful wel and fayre!	you quack
There been mo <u>sterres</u>, God wot, than a payre!'	stars

(PF 589–95)

The duck's contribution consists of a series of direct questions, which are designed to ridicule and dismiss the loftier and more noble sentiments expressed by the turtle-dove. The low style speech of the goose and the duck consists of a larger proportion of native words than in the speech of the tercel, although these passages do include words of French origin as well. The goose uses the French words *remedie*, *verdit* and *resoun*, words that would all be acceptable within the speech of more refined characters. As well as being of French origin, these words also carry technical connotations that make them particularly appropriate in the present context. The word *resoun* is a term used to describe a formal statement of fact or opinion put forward as part of an argument, while *verdit* invokes a specifically legal context. But rather than adding dignity and learning to their opinions, such connotations serve to undermine and ridicule them further. There are other French words in these passages that are less clearly high style, such as the word *bourded* 'jested', which appears just once elsewhere in Chaucer, in the speech of one of the three rioters in the Pardoner's Tale:

> 'Bretheren,' quod he, 'taak kep what that I seye;
> My wit is greet, though that I <u>bourde</u> and pleye.'   joke
>
> (C 777–8)

These examples show how we need to pay attention to a range of factors when assessing the level of formality of a particular utterance. These factors include forms of address, politeness strategies, swearing and the use, or avoidance, of colloquial words and phrases. By being aware of a range of pragmatic conventions observed and manipulated by Chaucer we are able to gain deeper insights into his portrayal of individual characters through their speech, and the ways in which these characters interact with each other.

Further reading

Elliott (1974, Chapter 5) gives a useful overview of swearing in Chaucer, while polite usage is discussed in Burnley (1986b). Chaucer's use of address forms, and particularly first name address, is the subject of Pearsall (1995), while the relationship of Chaucer's forms of address to contemporary French usage is discussed in Burrow (1984).

Appendix: sample texts

From The Miller's Tale

This clerk was <u>cleped</u> *hende* Nicholas.		called
Of <u>deerne</u> love he *koude* and of *solas*;	3200	secret
And therto he was *sleigh* and ful <u>privee</u>,		private
And lyk a mayden meke *for to see*.		
A chambre hadde he in that hostelrye		
Allone, withouten any compaignye,		
Ful <u>fetisly</u> *ydight* with *herbes swoote*;	3205	elegantly
And he hymself as sweete as is the roote		
Of <u>lycorys</u>, or any *cetewale*.		licorice
His *Almageste*, and *bookes grete and smale*,		
His *astrelabie*, <u>longynge</u> for his art,		belonging to
His *augrym stones layen* faire apart,	3210	
On shelves couched at his beddes heed;		
His <u>presse</u> ycovered with a <u>faldyng</u> reed;		cupboard; cloth
And al above ther lay a gay *sautrie*,		
On which he made <u>a-nyghtes</u> melodie		at night
So swetely that all the chambre rong;	3215	
And *Angelus ad virginem* he song;		
And after that he song <u>the Kynges Noote</u>.		the King's Tune
Ful often blessed was his myrie throte.		
And thus this sweete clerk his tyme spente		
After his *freendes fyndyng* and his <u>rente</u>.	3220	income
This carpenter hadde wedded *newe* a wyf,		
Which that he lovede moore than his lyf;		
Of eighteteene yeer she was of age.		
<u>Jalous</u> he was, and heeld *hire* narwe in cage,		jealous
For she was wylde and *yong*, and he was *old*	3225	
And <u>demed</u> hymself been lik a <u>cokewold</u>.		considered; cuckold

3199   *hende* This word means 'noble' but its use by Chaucer is limited almost exclusively to Nicholas, a character of dubious morality.

3200   *koude* In ME the modal verb *kan/koude* retained its lexical meaning of 'know/knew how to'.

3200   *solas* This word has a broad semantic range and can refer simply to pleasure and entertainment, as well as more specifically to sexual pleasure. Here the context appears to imply a sexual meaning, suggested by the previous reference to 'deerne love', although there is a degree of ambiguity.

3201   *sleigh* This word is of ON derivation and, unlike its modern reflex *sly*, it can have positive as well as negative connotations. It can be used to mean 'wise', 'clever', 'skilful', although more commonly in Chaucer it describes someone who is 'cunning' or 'crafty'.

3202   *for to see* The use of the prepositions *for to* is a metrical expedient.

3205   *ydight* The southern form of the past participle, with the y-prefix, is required by the metre.

3205   *herbes swoote* In ME the adjective often followed the noun, a particularly useful option in rhyming verse.

3207   *cetewale* Zedoary, a type of spice similar to ginger.

3208   *Almageste* An astrological treatise by Ptolemy.

3208   *bookes grete and smale* The adjectives have <-e> endings to mark agreement with the plural noun *bookes*.

3209   *astrelabie* An astrolabe is an instrument used to determine the positions and movements of celestial bodies and calculate latitude and longitude. The ME form is derived from the Latin *astrolabium*.

3210   *augrym stones* Another technical term belonging to the field of astronomy. *Augrym* is derived from the OF *augorisme*, meaning 'arithmetic' and so *augrym stones* are 'counters'.

3210   *layen* The third person plural present indicative ending here is <-en>.

3213   *sautrie* A psaltery is a stringed instrument resembling a harp.

There is a deliberate contrast here with the description of the
clerk in the General Prologue, who would prefer to have books
containing philosophical works at the head of his bed than a
fiddle or a 'gay sautrie' (A 293–6). The instrument has religious
associations and derives ultimately from Latin *psalterium*, which
refers to the biblical Book of Psalms or 'psalter'. Nicholas uses
the instrument in the pursuit of secular rather than spiritual love,
strumming it energetically while flirting with Alison (A 3303–6).

3216   *Angelus ad virginem* Angel to the Virgin, a song on the
Annunciation.

3218   *Ful often blessed was* Following the adverbial 'ful often', the
subject and verb have been reversed.

3220   *freendes fyndyng* The <-es> ending on *freendes* is the genitive
plural ending, so that this should be translated 'friends' support'.

3221   *This* The demonstrative *this* is used here to introduce a new
subject, referring back to the carpenter introduced in the opening
lines of the tale.

3221   *newe* Adverbs in ME could end either <-ly> or <-e>. *Newe* is an
adverb and means 'recently'.

3222   *Which* In ME the relative pronoun *which* could be used to refer
to humans, where PDE would use 'who'.

3224   *hire* The third person feminine singular pronoun 'her'.

3225   *yong, old* These adjectives are 'strong' in that they are not
preceded by a determiner and therefore are endingless.

From The Wife of Bath's Prologue

Herkne eek, *lo*, which a sharp word for the nones,   listen; what
Biside a welle, Jhesus, God and man,   15
Spak in repreeve of the Samaritan: reproof
'*Thou* hast yhad fyve housbondes,' quod he,   had
'And that *ilke* man that now hath thee
Is noght thyn housbonde, thus seyde he certeyn.
What that he mente therby, I kan nat seyn;   20
But that I axe, why that the *fifthe* man   ask

Was noon housbonde to the Samaritan?
How manye myghte she have in mariage?
Yet herde I nevere tellen in myn age
Upon this nombre *diffinicioun*.   25
Men may *devyne* and *glosen*, up and doun,
But wel I woot, <u>expres</u>, *withoute lye*,   clearly
God <u>bad</u> us for to <u>wexe</u> and multiplye;   commanded;
                                                                                    increase

That gentil text kan I wel understonde.
<u>Eek</u> wel I woot, he seyde myn housbonde   30   also
Sholde <u>lete</u> fader and mooder, and take to me.   leave
But of no <u>nombre</u> mencion *made he*,   number
Of bigamye, or of octogamye;
Why sholde men thanne speke of it vileynye?

14   *lo Lo* is commonly used by Chaucer to mark a scriptural reference,
     as here.

17   *Thou* Christ addresses the Samaritan woman using the singular
     pronouns *thou*, *thee*, *thyn*, suggesting an intimacy and familiarity.

18   *ilke Ilke* can be used as a demonstrative to mean 'that', but here it
     means 'very'.

20   *What that* The conjunctions *what* and *but* (line 21) are often
     followed by *that* in ME.

21   *fifthe* As this adjective follows the determiner *the*, it has the weak
     inflexion <-e>.

25   *diffinicioun* This is a learned term used in academic contexts,
     derived from OF *definicion* and Latin *diffinitio*, here meaning
     'limitation or restriction'.

26   *devyne and glosen* These two verbs show how the variant forms of
     the infinitive could be used for metrical purposes. The <-e> of
     devyne would be elided with the following vowel, where the <-en>
     ending of *glosen* prevents elision with the following *up*.

27   *withoute lye* Repetition and redundancy are a feature of the Wife of
     Bath's lengthy monologue. Here the phrase *withoute lye* serves to
     strengthen her claim that the Bible is unequivocal in its command to
     procreation.

31   *sholde* The modal verb *shall/sholde* retained a lexical force in ME and should be translated as 'must'.

32   *made he* Here the object precedes the verb and the subject follows it, with the effect that the phrase 'of no nombre' is foregrounded. This more complex syntax reflects the Wife's command of rhetoric in structuring and conveying her argument. This is further conveyed by the rhetorical question with which the extract ends: 'Why sholde men thanne speke of it vileynye?'

From The Second Nun's Tale

Invocacio ad Mariam

And *thow* that <u>flour</u> of virgines art alle,		flower
Of whom that Bernard list so wel to write,	30	
To thee at my bigynnyng first I *calle*;		
Thou confort of us wrecches, <u>do</u> me <u>endite</u>		make; compose
Thy maydens deeth, that <u>wan</u> thurgh hire merite		won
The eterneel lyf, and of the feend *victorie*,		
As man may after reden in hire storie.	35	

Thow Mayde and Mooder, doghter of thy Sone,		
Thow welle of mercy, synful soules cure,		
In whom that God for *bountee* <u>chees</u> to wone,		chose
Thow humble, and heigh over every creature,		
Thow <u>nobledest</u> so ferforth oure nature,	40	ennobled
That no <u>desdeyn</u> the Makere hadde of <u>kynde</u>		scorn; nature
His Sone in blood and flessh to clothe and <u>wynde</u>.		wrap

Withinne the cloistre blisful of thy sydis		
Took mannes shap the eterneel love and pees,		
<u>That</u> of the <u>tryne</u> compas lord and gyde is,	45	He who; threefold
Whom erthe and see and hevene <u>out of relees</u>		endless
<u>Ay</u> *heryen*; and thou, Virgine <u>wemmelees</u>,		ever; spotless
Baar of thy body -and dweltest mayden pure-		
The *Creatour* of every *creature*.		

Assembled is in thee magnificence	50	
With mercy, goodnesse, and with swich *pitee*		
That thou, that art the sonne of excellence		
Nat oonly helpest *hem* that preyen thee,		

But often tyme, of thy <u>benygnytee</u>,   goodness
Ful frely, <u>er</u> that men thyn help biseche,   55   before
Thou goost biforn, and art *hir lyves leche*.

Now help, thow meeke and blisful faire mayde,
Me, <u>flemed</u> wrecche, in this desert of <u>galle</u>;   banished; bitterness
Thynk on the womman Cananee, that sayde
That <u>whelpes</u> eten somme of the <u>crommes</u> alle 60   dogs; crumbs
That from hir lordes table been <u>yfalle</u>;   fallen
And though that I, unworthy sone of Eve,
Be synful, yet accepte my <u>bileve</u>.   faith

And, for that feith is deed withouten *werkis*,
So for to werken <u>yif</u> me wit and space,   65   give
That I be quit fro <u>thennes</u> that most derk is!   thence
O thou, that art so fair and ful of grace,
Be myn *advocat* in that *heighe* place
Theras withouten ende is songe "Osanne,"
Thow Cristes mooder, doghter deere of Anne!   70

And of thy light my soule in prison lighte,
That troubled is by the contagioun
Of my body, and also by the <u>wighte</u>   weight
Of erthely *lust* and fals *affeccioun*;
O havene of <u>refut</u>, O salvacioun   75   refuge
Of hem that been in sorwe and in distresse,
Now help, for to my werk I wol me <u>dresse</u>.   address

Yet preye I *yow* that reden that I write,
<u>Foryeve</u> me that I do no diligence   forgive
This ilke storie *subtilly* to endite,   80
For bothe have I the wordes and <u>sentence</u>   sense
Of hym that at the seintes reverence
The storie wroot, and folwen hire legende,
And pray yow that ye wole my werk <u>amende</u>.   correct

29   *thow* It is common in religious writing for the singular pronoun
     thow to be used rather than the more distant and formal plural
     pronoun *ye*.

31   *calle* Calle is derived from ON and is less common in Chaucer's
     works than the OE equivalent *clepe*. Its use here is probably
     determined by its appearance in rhyme with *alle*.

34   *victorie* The direct object is postponed until after the indirect object, thus placing it in rhyme where it receives greater prominence.

38   *bountee* There are numerous words in this passage that are derived from French, which contribute to the high style of this invocation. These words include *bountee, humble, nobledest, desdeyn, benygnytee, pitee, magnificence.*

47   *heryen* In addition to the large number of French loanwords found in this passage, there are a number of key terms that are of Old English descent, which create an effective contrast with the French vocabulary. These include *heryen, biseche, leche, wemmelees.* Both *heryen* and *wemmelees* are uncommon and specialized religious terms, used infrequently by Chaucer, making their appearance here all the more striking.

49   *Creatour, creature* By placing these two related and similar sounding words together, Chaucer creates an effective parallel between the creator and the creature, using their superficial similarity to highlight the huge divide between the creator and the creation.

51   *pitee* In ME this word can refer to the quality of showing mercy as well as having the PDE sense of 'pity', or a feeling of sorrow at someone's distress. Here the word has its more spiritual sense of the quality of mercy or compassion.

53   *hem Hem* is the third person plural pronoun 'them', showing Chaucer's use of a form descended from OE rather than the ON derived form *them.*

56   *hir Hir* is the third person plural pronoun 'their', derived from OE rather than ON. This form differs from the third person feminine singular pronoun *hire* 'her' (lines 33, 35) in the lack of final -e.

56   *lyves leche* A further stylistic device employed by Chaucer in this passage is alliteration as in the phrases *lyves leche* and *synful soules* above.

64   *werkis* This noun shows the <-is> plural inflexion rather than the more common <-es>. Its use here is to allow the word to be rhymed with *is.* A similar explanation accounts for the appearance of *sydis* at line 43.

68   *advocat* This word was probably borrowed into ME from OF *avocat*, although the spelling used by Chaucer suggests that this form derives from Latin *advocatus.*

68   *heighe* The adjective *heigh* has an <-e> inflexion as it follows the demonstrative *that*.

74   *lust, affeccioun* The contrasting of OE and OF words is particularly effective, especially the use of a series of paired synonyms such as *lust* (OE) and *affeccioun* (OF), *havene* (OE) and *refut* (OF), *sorwe* (OE) and *distresse* (OF).

78   *yow* The switch to the plural pronouns *yow*, *ye* marks a shift from addressing the Virgin Mary to the reader of the work.

80   *subtilly* Here the Second Nun apologizes for her lack of skill in composition, claiming that she will not attempt to embellish her material but rather will follow her source closely.

From *Troilus and Criseyde* Book 5

Litera Troili

Right fresshe flour, whos I ben have and shal,		
Withouten parte of elleswhere servyse,		
With herte, body, lif, lust, thought, and al,		
I, woful <u>wyght</u>, in everich humble wise	1320	creature
That tonge telle or herte may devyse,		
As ofte as matere occupieth place,		
Me recomaunde vnto youre noble grace.		

Liketh yow to witen, swete herte,		
As ye wel knowe, how longe tyme agon	1325	
That ye me lefte in <u>aspre</u> peynes smerte,		bitter
Whan that ye wente, of which yet <u>boote</u> non		remedy
Have I non had, but evere wors <u>bigon</u>		beset
Fro day to day am I, and so <u>mot</u> <u>dwelle</u>,		must; remain
While it yow <u>list</u>, of <u>wele and wo my welle</u>.	1330	pleases; joy

For which to yow, with <u>dredful</u> herte trewe,   reverent
I write, as he that sorwe <u>drifth</u> to write,   drives
My wo, that everich houre encresseth newe,
Compleynyng, as I dar or kan endite.
And <u>that defaced is</u>, that may ye <u>wite</u> 1335 that which is defaced; blame
The teris which that fro myn eyen reyne,
That wolden speke, if that they koude, and pleyne.

Yow first biseche I, that youre eyen clere
To loke on this <u>defouled</u> ye nat <u>holde</u>;   defiled; consider
And <u>over al this</u>, that ye, my lady deere,   1340   moreover
Wol <u>vouchesauf</u> this lettre to byholde;   agree
And by the cause ek of my cares colde
That sleth my wit, if aught amys <u>m'asterte</u>,   escapes from me
Foryeve it me, myn owen swete herte!

If any servant dorste or oughte of right   1345
Upon his lady pitously compleyne,
Thanne <u>wene</u> I that ich oughte be that <u>wight</u>,   think; person
Considered this, that ye thise monthes tweyne
Han taried, ther ye seyden, soth to seyne,
But dayes ten ye <u>nolde</u> in <u>oost</u> sojourne –   1350   would not; army
But in two monthes yet ye nat retourne.

But for as muche as me moot nedes like
Al that yow liste, I dar nat pleyne moore,
But humblely, with sorwful <u>sikes</u> sike,   sighs
Yow write ich myn <u>unresty</u> sorwes soore   1355   restless
Fro day to day desiryng evere moore
To knowen fully, if youre wille it weere,
How ye han ferd and don whil ye be theere;   how you have been doing

The whos welfare and <u>hele</u> ek God encresse   health
In honour swich that upward in degree   1360
It growe alwey, so that it nevere cesse.
Right as youre herte <u>ay</u> kan, my lady <u>free</u>,   ever; beautiful
Devyse, I prey to God so moot it be,
And graunte it that ye soone upon me <u>rewe</u>,   pity
As wisly as in al I am yow trewe.   1365

And if yow liketh knowen of the <u>fare</u>   how I am doing
Of me, whos wo ther may no wit discryve,
I kan namore but, <u>chiste</u> of every care,   holder
At wrytyng of this lettre *I was on-lyve*,   alive
Al redy out my woful <u>gost</u> to dryve,   1370   spirit
Which I delaye, and <u>holde hym yet in honde</u>,   temporize with him
Upon the sighte of matere of youre <u>sonde</u>.   message

1317   *Right fresshe flour* This passage is an extract from Troilus' letter
         to Criseyde, which follows the conventions of letter writing as

they are manifested in contemporary letters in both English and French. Troilus' letter predates most of the extant English examples and was probably modelled on earlier French examples (Davis 1965). French influence is further indicated by the way Troilus signs off: 'Le vostre T.' Troilus' opening address to Criseyde is modelled on the standard formula in such letters, which frequently begin with a phrase such as 'Right worshipful husband' and so on.

1323   *Me recomaunde* Troilus recommends himself to his lady 'in everich humble wise' (1320), another standard feature of contemporary epistolary practice where writers recommend themselves humbly to their recipients.

1324   *Liketh yow to witen* This phrase echoes the way contemporary letter writers switch from the greeting to the message itself, found in phrases such as 'Please it you to wit that'.

1324   *swete herte* Troilus makes frequent use of elevated terms of address indicative of his great devotion. Other examples include: *my lady deere*, *myn owen swete herte* and *my lady free*.

1330   *wele and wo my welle* Here Troilus makes effective use of alliteration and the contrast between the similar sounding *wele* and *welle*. Compare also the similar-sounding pairs *sikes sike* and *sorwes soore*.

1358   *How ye han ferd* Here Troilus introduces a conventional request concerning the recipient's health and well-being: 'desiryng evere moore/To knowen fully … How ye han ferd and don whil ye be theere'.

1366   *And if yow liketh knowen* Troilus offers to tell Criseyde news of himself, although this is couched in suitably deferential terms so that he will only trouble her with details if she is willing to hear them.

1369   *I was on-lyve* Troilus follows the convention of giving an account of his own health, although rather than employing a standard formula expressing the writer's good health, Troilus is simply 'on-lyve' and nothing more.

From the Prologue of the Monk's Tale

Whan ended was my tale of Melibee,
And of Prudence and hire <u>benignytee</u>,   3080   graciousness
Oure Hooste seyde, 'As I am feithful man,
And by that precious corpus Madrian,
I hadde <u>levere</u> than a barel ale   rather
That Goodelief, my wyf, hadde herd this tale!
For she nys no thyng of swich pacience   3085
As was this Melibeus wyf Prudence.
By Goddes bones, whan I bete my <u>knaves</u>,   servants
She bryngeth me forth the grete *clobbed staves*,
And crieth, "Slee the *dogges* everichoon,
And brek hem, bothe bak and every boon!"   3090
And if that any neighebor of myne
Wol nat in chirche to my wyf enclyne,
Or be so <u>hardy</u> to hire to trespace,   bold
Whan she comth hoom she *rampeth* in my face,
And crieth, "False coward, <u>wrek</u> thy wyf!   3095   avenge
By *corpus bones*, I wol have thy knyf,
And thou shalt have my distaf and go spynne!"
Fro day to nyght right thus she wol bigynne.
"Allas!" she seith, "that evere I was <u>shape</u>   destined
To wedden a *milksop*, or a <u>coward</u> ape,   3100   cowardly
That wol been <u>overlad</u> with every wight!   dominated
Thou darst nat stonden by thy wyves right!"
This is my lif, but if that I wol fighte;
And out at dore anon I moot me <u>dighte</u>,   go
Or elles I am but lost, but if that I   3105
Be lik a wilde leoun, fool-hardy.
I woot wel she wol <u>do me slee</u> som day   cause me to kill
Som neighebor, and thanne go my way;
For I am <u>perilous</u> with knyf in honde,   dangerous
Al be it that I dar nat hire <u>withstonde</u>,   3110   resist
For she is *byg in armes*, by my feith:
That shal he fynde that hire mysdooth or seith-
But lat us passe awey fro this mateere.

3088   *clobbed staves* Club-shaped staffs, or cudgels, are a typically
          churlish weapon and help to situate this domestic scene within
          the world of the peasant. Elsewhere in ME *clobbed* is used to

mean 'crude', 'clumsy' or *boystows*, 'rough', all of which have connotations of low social status.

3089   *dogges* The use of this word as a term of abuse for a wretch is generally found in colloquial usage elsewhere in ME, such as in the representation of spoken dialogue found in ME drama.

3094   *rampeth* This verb is used elsewhere in ME to describe an animal, especially a lion, wolf or bear, rearing up on its hind legs in an attack (compare PDE *rampant* in its heraldic sense). Chaucer's use here is the first instance of it being applied to a human being, while subsequent uses are mostly descriptions of attacks by the devil.

3096   *corpus bones* This is a malapropism based on a misunderstanding of the Latin *corpus* 'body', revealing the speaker's ignorance and linguistic pretensions.

3100   *milksop* A milksop is literally 'a piece of bread soaked in milk' and this is the first instance of the word being used figuratively to refer to someone who is cowardly and effeminate. This is the only instance of this figurative use recorded by the *MED* and the next occurrence recorded by the *OED* is in 1569. The word was probably common as an insult in colloquial speech but generally avoided in the written register.

3111   *byg in armes* This phrase means 'sturdy' and is generally a masculine trait, particularly one associated with the peasant class, as suggested by the attribution of Arcite's ability to cut wood and carry water to his being 'big of bones' (A 1423–4).

From the Squire's Tale

This <u>strange</u> knyght, that cam thus sodeynly,		foreign
Al armed, <u>save</u> his heed, ful richely,	90	except
<u>Saleweth</u> kyng and queene and lordes alle,		greets
By ordre, as they <u>seten</u> in the halle,		sat
With so heigh reverence and obeisaunce,		
As wel in speche as in <u>contenaunce</u>,		manner
That *Gawayn*, with his olde curteisye,	95	
Though he were comen ayeyn out of Fairye,		
Ne koude hym nat amende with a word.		

And after this, biforn the heighe <u>bord</u>,   table
He with a manly voys seide his message,
After the forme used in his langage,   100
Withouten <u>vice</u> of silable or of lettre;   defect
And for his tale sholde seme the bettre,
Accordant to his wordes was his <u>cheere</u>,   expression
As techeth *art of speche* hem that it <u>leere</u>.   learn
Al be that I kan nat <u>sowne</u> his stile,   105   imitate
Ne kan nat clymben over so heigh a style,
Yet seye I this, as to commune entente:
Thus muche amounteth al that evere he mente,
If it so be that I have it in mynde.
He seyde, 'The kyng of <u>Arabe</u> and of <u>Inde</u>,   110   Arabia; India
My lige lord, on this solempne day
Saleweth yow, as he best <u>*kan*</u> and <u>*may*</u>,   knows how to; is able
And sendeth yow, in honour of youre feeste,
By me, that am al redy at youre <u>heeste</u>,   command
This steede of <u>bras</u>, that esily and weel   115   brass
Kan in the space of *o day natureel* –
This is to seyn, in foure and twenty houres –
Wher-so yow lyst, in droghte or elles shoures,
<u>Beren</u> youre body into every place   carry
To which youre herte wilneth for to <u>pace</u>,   120   go
Withouten <u>wem</u> of yow, thurgh foul or fair;   hurt
Or, if yow lyst to <u>fleen</u> as <u>hye</u> in the air   fly; high
As dooth an egle whan hym list to soore,
This same steede shal bere yow evere moore,
Withouten harm, til ye be ther yow leste,   125
Though that ye slepen on his bak or reste,
And turne ayeyn with <u>writhyng</u> of a *pyn*.   turning
He that it wroghte <u>koude</u> ful many a <u>gyn</u>.   knew; contrivance
He wayted many a constellacion
Er he had doon this operacion,   130
And knew ful many a <u>seel</u> and many a <u>bond</u>.'   seal; controlling force

91-3   *Saleweth* Before speaking, this knight greets the assembled lords
         and ladies courteously and in sequence. The salutation or greeting
         was an important component of courtly speech, as is apparent
         from the advice given by the God of Love in the *Romance of the
         Rose*, see *Romaunt*, lines 2216–22.

95   *Gawayn*   Gawain was renowned for his courtly manners, as is seen in *Sir Gawain and the Green Knight*. The passage in the *Romaunt* mentioned above also refers to Gawain as a paragon of courtesy: 'As fer as Gaweyn, the worthy,/Was preised for his curtesy' (2209–10).

104   *art of speche*   Medieval rhetorical theory taught that the manner of delivery, which included pronunciation and facial expression, was an important aspect of courtly speech. Here the knight adopts a faultless pronunciation and an expression that is in accord with the content of his speech.

111   *My lige lord*   The knight uses an elevated term of respect to refer to his king, as is typical of courtly speech.

112   *Saleweth yow*   The message from the king also includes a formal salutation.

112   <u>*kan*</u> *and* <u>*may*</u>   Another feature of high style is the use of doublets, or pairs of words with similar or contrary meanings, and this is found in several places in this passage. Other instances of doublets include *esily* and *weel*, *in droghte or elles shoures*, *thurgh foul or fair*.

116   *o day natureel*   This speech includes a number of technical terms that are a further characteristic of high style. The phrase *day natureel* is explained in the *Treatise on the Astrolabe* (II.7) as 'the revolucioun of the equinoxial with as muche partie of the zodiak as the sonne of his propre moeving passith in the mene while'. In both cases the use of this technical term is accompanied by an explanation: 'This is to seyn, in foure and twenty houres'. Other technical astronomical terms in this passage include *constellacion* and *operacion*, which are both foregrounded by their appearance in rhyme.

125   *Withouten harm*   This phrase parallels the earlier *Withouten wem*, with variation in the use of the synonym *harm* for *wem*.

127   *pyn*   This marks the end of the opening sentence of the knight's message, showing how high style employs a complex syntactic structure, which includes numerous subordinate clauses such as 'as he best kan and may', 'that am al redy at youre heeste'.

Glossary of linguistic terms

affixation	The formation of new words by adding prefixes or suffixes to existing words.
aureate diction	An elevated rhetorical style of writing characterized by a large number of Latinate loanwords.
borrowing	The process by which words are adopted into one language from another.
compounding	The formation of new words by joining two existing words.
diphthong	A vowel cluster with a glide from one vowel to another.
impersonal verb	A verb without a subject.
inflexion	A grammatical ending added to a word to mark case, number, tense and so on.
intransitive verb	A verb that cannot take a direct object, such as *arrive* or *come*.
lexicon	The collection of words, or lexemes, that make up the vocabulary of a language.
loanword	A word borrowed from another language.
macaronic	The use of two or more languages in a single text.
monophthong	A pure vowel with no change in quality.
monosyllabic	A word consisting of a single syllable.
polysyllabic	A word consisting of more than one syllable.
prefix	A morpheme that is added to the beginning of a word
register	A variety of language determined by use rather than by user, such as colloquial and formal registers.

schwa

A centralized vowel that frequently appears in unstressed syllables, like the final syllable in *china*; transcribed phonetically as [ə].

standard

A fixed variety of a language that does not tolerate variation, and whose use is not restricted to a specific region.

strong verb

A verb that forms its preterite tense by changing its stem vowel rather than by adding an inflexion, such as *ride*, *rode*.

suffix

A morpheme that is added to the end of a word.

transitive verb

A verb capable of taking a direct object, such as *take* or *eat*.

weak verb

A verb that forms its preterite tense by adding an inflexion, such as *play*, *played*.

Bibliography

Aston, Margaret, 'Wyclif and the Vernacular', in *From Ockham to Wyclif* (eds) Anne Hudson and Michael Wilks (Oxford: Blackwell, 1987) pp. 281–330.

Barber, Charles, *The English Language: A Historical Introduction* (Cambridge: Cambridge University Press, 1993).

Baugh, A.C. and T. Cable, *A History of the English Language* (London: Routledge, 2002).

Benskin, Michael and Margaret Laing, 'Translations and *Mischsprachen* in Middle English Manuscripts,' in M. Benskin and M.L. Samuels (eds), *So Meny People Longages and Tonges: Philological Essays in Scots and Mediaeval English presented to Angus McIntosh* (Edinburgh: MEDP, 1981) pp. 55–106.

Benson, Larry D. (gen. ed.) *The Riverside Chaucer* (Oxford: Oxford University Press, 1988).

Bergen, Henry (ed.) *Lydgate's Troy Book Part I*. EETS ES 97 (London: Kegan Paul, 1906).

Blake, N.F., *The Textual Tradition of the Canterbury Tales* (London: Arnold, 1985).

Blake, N.F., (ed.) *The Cambridge History of the English Language* Volume II 1066–1476 (Cambridge: Cambridge University Press, 1992).

Blake, N.F., *A History of the English Language* (Basingstoke: Macmillan – now Palgrave Macmillan, 1996).

Bornstein, Diane, 'Chaucer's *Tale of Melibee* as an example of the Style Clergial', *Chaucer Review*, 12 (1978) 236–54.

Botterill, Steven (ed. and trans.) *Dante: De vulgari eloquentia* (Cambridge: Cambridge University Press, 1996).

Bragg, Melvyn, *The Adventure of English* (London: Hodder & Stoughton, 2003).

Burnley, J.D., *Chaucer's Language and the Philosophers' Tradition* (Cambridge: D.S. Brewer, 1979).

Burnley, J.D., *A Guide to Chaucer's Language* (Basingstoke: Macmillan – now Palgrave Macmillan, 1983).

Burnley, J.D., 'Curial Prose in England', *Speculum*, 61 (1986a) 593–614.

Burnley, J.D., 'Courtly Speech in Chaucer', *Poetica*, 24 (1986b) 16–38.

Burrow, John, 'Four Notes on Chaucer's *Sir Thopas*', in *Essays on Medieval Literature* (Oxford: Clarendon Press, 1984) pp. 60–78.

Burrow, J.A. and Thorlac Turville-Petre, *A Book of Middle English* (Oxford: Blackwell, 2004).

Cannon, Christopher, *The Making of Chaucer's English: A Study of Words* (Cambridge, Cambridge University Press, 1998).

Chambers, R.W. and M. Daunt (eds) *A Book of London English 1384–1425* (Oxford: Clarendon Press, 1931).

Coghill, Nevill (trans.) *The Canterbury Tales* (London: Penguin, 1958).

Davis, Norman,'The *Litera Troili* and English Letters', *Review of English Studies*, n.s. 16 (1965), 233–44.

Davis, Norman, 'Chaucer and Fourteenth-Century English', in Derek Brewer (ed.) *Geoffrey Chaucer* (Cambridge: D.S. Brewer, 1974), pp. 58–84.

Davis, Norman et al., *A Chaucer Glossary* (Oxford: Oxford University Press, 1979).

Donaldson, E. Talbot, 'Idiom of Popular Poetry in the Miller's Tale', in *Speaking of Chaucer* (London: Athlone, 1970) pp. 13–29.

Eisner, Sigmund, 'Chaucer as a Technical Writer', *Chaucer Review*, 19 (1985) 179–204.

Elliott, Ralph W.V., *Chaucer's English* (London: André Deutsch, 1974).

Fisher, John H., 'A Language Policy for Lancastrian England', *PMLA*, 107 (1992), 1168–80; repr. in *The Emergence of Standard English* (Kentucky: University Press, 1996), pp. 16–35.

Horobin, Simon, '*Phislophye* in *The Reeve's Tale* (Hg 4050) in Answer to *Astromye in The Miller's Tale* (3451)', *Notes and Queries*, n.s. 48 (2001) 109–10.

Horobin, Simon, *The Language of the Chaucer Tradition* (Cambridge: D.S. Brewer, 2003).

Horobin, Simon, '*The Manciple's Tale* (line 256)' (forthcoming).

Horobin, Simon and Jeremy Smith, *An Introduction to Middle English* (Edinburgh: Edinburgh University Press, 2002).

Jones, Terry, *Who Murdered Chaucer?: A Medieval Mystery* (London: Methuen, 2003).

Kökeritz, Helga, *A Guide to Chaucer's Pronunciation* (Toronto: Toronto University Press, 1978).

Machan, Tim William, *English in the Middle Ages* (Oxford: Oxford University Press, 2003).

McCarren, V.P. and D. Moffat (eds) *A Guide to Editing Middle English* (Ann Arbor: University of Michigan Press, 1998).

Mersand, Joseph, *Chaucer's Romance Vocabulary* (New York: Comet, 1937).

Middle English Dictionary (Ann Arbor: University of Michigan Press, 1952–2001).

Mooney, Linne R., 'Chaucer's Scribe', *Speculum*, 81 (2006) 97–138.

Mustanoja, T., *A Middle English Syntax*, Vol. 1 (Helsinki: Société Néophilologique, 1959).

Owen, Charles, A. Jr., *The Manuscripts of the Canterbury Tales* (Cambridge: D.S. Brewer, 1991).

Oxford English Dictionary, 2nd edn (Oxford: Oxford University Press, 1989).

Pearsall, Derek, '*The Franklin's Tale*, Line 1469: Forms of Address in Chaucer', *Studies in the Age of Chaucer*, 17 (1995) 69–78.

Pearsall, Derek, 'Chaucer and Englishness', *Proceedings of the British Academy*, 101 (1999) 77–99.

Rothwell, William, 'The Trilingual England of Geoffrey Chaucer' *Studies in the Age of Chaucer*, 16 (1994) 45–67.

Ruggiers, Paul G. (ed.) *A Facsimile and Transcription of the Hengwrt Manuscript, with Variants from the Ellesmere Manuscript* (Oklahoma: Pilgrim Books, 1979).

Salter, Elizabeth, 'Chaucer and Internationalism', *Studies in the Age of Chaucer*, 2 (1980) 71–9.

Samuels, M.L., *Linguistic Evolution with Special Reference to English* (Cambridge: Cambridge University Press, 1972).

Samuels, M.L., 'Some Applications of Middle English Dialectology', *English Studies*, 44 (1963) 81–94, repr. in Margaret Laing (ed.) *Middle English Dialectology: Essays on Some Principles and Problems* (Aberdeen: Aberdeen University Press, 1989), pp. 64–80.

Sandved, Arthur O., *Introduction to Chaucerian English* (Cambridge: D.S. Brewer, 1985).

Schlauch, Margaret, 'The Art of Chaucer's Prose', in D.S. Brewer (ed.) *Chaucer and Chaucerians* (London: Nelson, 1966) pp. 140–63.

Smith, Jeremy J., *An Historical Study of English: Function, Form and Change* (London: Routledge, 1996).

Smith, Jeremy J., 'John Gower and London English', in Siân Echard (ed.) *A Companion to Gower* (Cambridge: D.S. Brewer, 2004) pp. 61–72.

Stubbs, Estelle (ed.) *The Hengwrt Chaucer Digital Facsimile* (Leicester: Scholarly Digital Editions, 2000).

Sutherland, Ronald (ed.) *The Romaunt of the Rose and Le Roman de la Rose: A Parallel-Text Edition* (Oxford: Blackwell, 1967).

Tolkien, J.R.R. and E.V. Gordon (eds) *Sir Gawain and the Green Knight* (Oxford: Clarendon Press, 1967).

Trotter, D.A. (ed.) *Multilingualism in Later Medieval Britain* (Cambridge: D.S. Brewer, 2000).

Turville-Petre, Thorlac, *England the Nation: Language, Literature, and National Identity, 1290–1340* (Oxford: Clarendon Press, 1996).

Wimsatt, James I., *Chaucer and the Poems of 'Ch' in University of Pennsylvania MS French 15* (Cambridge: D.S. Brewer, 1982).

Windeatt, B.A. (ed.) *Geoffrey Chaucer, Troilus and Criseyde* (London: Longman, 1984).

Index